SHARING THE *SACRA*

SHARING THE *SACRA*

The Politics and Pragmatics of Intercommunal Relations around Holy Places

Edited by

Glenn Bowman

berghahn
NEW YORK • OXFORD
www.berghahnbooks.com

Published in 2012 by

Berghahn Books

www.berghahnbooks.com

©2012, 2015 Glenn Bowman
First paperback edition published in 2015

Library of Congress Cataloging-in-Publication Data

Sharing the *sacra* : the politics and pragmatics of intercommunal relations around
  holy places / edited by Glenn Bowman.
     p. cm. Includes bibliographical references and index.
   ISBN 978-0-85745-486-7 (hardback : alk. paper) -- ISBN 978-1-78238-744-2
(paperback : alk. paper) -- ISBN 978-0-85745-487-4 (ebook)
   1. Religions--Relations. 2. Sacred spaces. 3. Pilgrims and pilgrimages.
  I. Bowman, Glenn.
  BL410.S45 2012
  203'.5--dc23   2011048446

British Library Cataloguing in Publication Data

A catalogue record for this book is available from
the British Library.

ISBN 978-0-85745-486-7 (hardback)
ISBN 978-1-78238-744-2 (paperback)
ISBN 978-0-85745-487-4 (ebook)

*My thanks to Elizabeth Cowie for her generous support
and intellectual engagement*

CONTENTS

LIST OF FIGURES AND TABLES

Figures

Table

Introduction: Sharing the *Sacra*

Glenn Bowman

In his recent *War on Sacred Grounds*, political scientist Ron E. Hassner cites examples ranging from Ayodhya to Jerusalem to contend that sacred places "cannot be shared" (Hassner 2009: 3). Hassner's analysis resonates with a wide range of popular and academic identitarian discourses contending that, for various reasons, cultural identities are essential, exclusivist, and therefore inherently antagonistic to those of others. Although Hassner concentrates on intercommunal violence around holy sites, his argument is consonant with those of Bernard Lewis (1990), Samuel Huntington (1993, 1996), and others who see the world as an arena made up of cultural "blocs" contending with each other for hegemony along what Huntington, instantiating the "clash" between Islam and the West, terms "bloody borders" (Huntington 1993: 35). Whereas, for Huntington and Lewis, conflict erupts when incommensurate civilizational identifications are brought into contact, for Hassner the problem—likewise territorial—is the "indivisibility" of sacred sites:[1]

> Sacred places are integrated monolithic spaces that cannot be subdivided; they have clearly defined and inflexible boundaries.... [T]he religious prerequisites for safeguarding these sites from desecration require believers to have complete and exclusive control over them. Thus, competing groups may resort to violence in order to gain control over such a site. (Hassner 2009: 43 and 3)

Religious sites are here the repositories of core identities, and just as those identities must remain inviolate so too the sites must be protected from the presence of corrupting others by all means possible.

The following chapters seek to complicate the issue of conflict over holy places and, by extension, of the "clash of civilizations", by attentive readings of intercommunal relations around sites or practices that are deemed holy by the persons or groups involved. The authors do not seek, in so doing, simply to counter the conflict-centered perspectives of Hassner, Lewis, Huntington, et al. with bourgeois cosmopolitan pleas for pluralism. Instead they inadvertently seem to have followed the advice Fredrik Barth gave to anthropologists in a post-9/11 interview where he suggested that we should "speak to historians and political scientists who say things about the clash of civilizations … [so as to] disturb and subvert their frames of reference by undermining one or more of the premises on which they base their arguments, showing how it does not make sense from a broader perspective" (Borofsky 2001). The chapters that follow, for the most part written by anthropologists (the two exceptions, one by a scholar of religion and the other by a linguist, are each products of empirical field research), "disturb and subvert" these identitarian frames of reference by refusing to take "identity" for granted.

Identity-based models, particularly those working with paradigms such as "indivisibility," must presume that difference necessitates conflict when parties with different identities are invested in the same "property."[2] The texts in this book treat identity as an emergent, situational, and ofttimes contingent property, and thus, rather than assuming the priority of conflict, investigate the complex processes through which social interactions, ritual performances, and historical transformations are worked out as two or more "communal" groups circulate through and around "shared" holy places. Rather than presuming the necessity of conflict, as approaches which foreground incompatible core identities necessarily do, the chapters which follow ask "why, in many cases, does conflict not arise?", "how, when conflict does occur, is it disarmed or circumvented?" and "what, when intercommunal relations become difficult or cease, has brought about that change?" The collection is able, in this manner, not only to show that intercommunal conflict is not inevitable but also that the field of interaction around groups with different sectarian identities is far richer, busier, and more intriguing than any conflict-based model could suggest or show.

* * *

Although all the essays in this volume have very different genealogies, the collection has a history which goes back to the publication, in April 2002, of Robert Hayden's "Antagonistic Tolerance: Competitive Sharing of Religious Sites in South Asia and the Balkans" (Hayden 2002). In that article Hayden, very aware from his research in [now Former] Yugoslavia of the way intercommunal relations can collapse into extreme internecine violence when populist ethnocracy replaces state-supported ethnic diversity, extended that insight to research on sacred sites in India (which he compared with those of Yugoslavia), arguing that apparent situations of syncretism around holy places were, despite appearance, no more than temporary manifestations of a "tolerance" of the other brought about either because the other was too weak to threaten the dominant group's control of the shrine or because the balance of power between the two groups was too close to allow one to expel the other. Thus "processes of competition between groups that distinguish themselves from each other may be manifested as syncretism yet still result, ultimately, in the exclusion of the symbols of one group or another from a religious shrine" (Hayden 2002: 228; see also Hayden 2005). Hayden's argument is explicitly addressed in the contribution by Albera.

Because of work I had published on Muslim-Christian co-usage of shrines in Palestine in *Man* (Bowman 1993, see also Bowman 2012a), I was asked to comment on Hayden's *Current Anthropology* article. That, and the issues it foregrounded, pushed me into further field and analytical work on Palestinian "mixed" shrines as well as on examples in Macedonia (F.Y.R.O.M.) (Bowman 2007, 2009, 2010, 2012b and Bowman forthcoming). Subsequently a group in France, including Maria Couroucli and Dionigi Albera, organized a seminar entitled *Les Lieux partages du religieux et les pelerinage interconfessionnels en Mediterranee: Approches anthropologiques* under the aegis of Ramses II which took place in late March 2006 at the Laboratoire d'Ethnologie et de Sociologie Comparative, Université Paris Ouest Nanterre, and drew on diverse work being done on shrine sharing around the Mediterranean Basin.[3] A month after that I convened a triple session—"Syncretism: Sharing or Tolerance? The Politics and Pragmatics of Mixed Holy Places"—at the ASA Diamond Jubilee Conference at Keele University in the U.K. that engaged a number of scholars published in the current volume (Albera, Bastin, Carpenter-Latiri, Chau, Couroucli, Kwon, and Tuladhar-Douglas), and included a late-night debate with Robert Hayden who had flown in from Pittsburg for the event. In February 2008, Elazar Barkan and Yitzhak Reiter organized a conference entitled "Sharing Sacred Space: Religion and Conflict Resolution" which took place at Columbia University and led to Anna Bigelow and Aomar Boum contributing to this volume.[4]

I chronicle this history as it indicates the degree to which the issue of "shared" or "mixed" shrines[5] remains alive and salient—perhaps because of its pertinence to the "clash of civilizations" discourse. Certainly through the past decade what I have termed the "identitarian" approach has remained strong, as indicated not only by the publication of texts such as *War on Sacred Grounds* by prestigious presses such as Cornell but also by the support given in 2007 by the National Science Foundation and the Wenner Gren Foundation for Anthropological Research to Robert Hayden's *Antagonistic Tolerance: A Comparative Analysis of Competitive Sharing of Religious Sites* project. Hayden's project engages a number of researchers in gathering data in Turkey, Bulgaria, India, and Portugal to prove that, despite long histories of apparent sharing of holy places, the antagonism that underlies all mixing will inevitably, when the balance of power is disrupted by political change, lead to the violent expulsion of one of the sharing groups and, in most cases, the extirpation of all signs of its previous presence (Hayden et al. 2011).

The "non-identitarian" cadre has simultaneously been engaged in elaborating an increasingly sophisticated "choreography" of intercommunal relations around holy places, which this text makes manifest. At the core of that "choreography" is a partial shift of focus from temporal developments—the historical trajectory of holy places, often involving, as Hayden elaborates, a displacement of sharing by exclusivity—to the spatial interaction of communities in and around sites. This shift certainly does not indicate a simple synchronicity, much less, as Hayden has claimed, the presumption of "stasis in social structures, an error generally thought to have passed with structural functionalism" (Hayden et al. 2011: 15); what it entails is attention to the minutiae of engagements, avoidances, mimickings, avowals, and disavowals through which members of interacting communities manage the presence of the others. Historical changes in those interactions are central to analysis, but such changes are seen not only to bring about shifts in communal relations around the sites but also transformations in the identities, practices, and self and other representations of those involved in such relations.

Antagonistic polarization and subsequent displacement—the tropes of identitarian representations of culture contact—are, to misquote Lévi-Strauss, "easy to think with" in that they organize narratives of clearly defined entities involved in clearly comprehensible acts of self-defense and expropriation. What is less easy to conceptualize, and far richer to think with, is the complexity of interrelations and self-conceptualizations in "border zones" where identities are local products rather than extensions of the hegemonic orthodox discourses of state and sect. Recent work by authors in this collection, most notably Bastin's *The Domain of Constant Excess: Plural Worship at the Munnesvaram Temples in Sri Lanka* (2002) and Bigelow's *Sharing the Sacred: Practicing Pluralism in Muslim North India* (2010), evidence this work of invention and reinvention, and throw back from the margins of more homogeneous practices troubling questions about the character of religion, the nature of community, and the identity of identity.

* * *

One of the questions that emerges very strongly from this collection is "how do social fields surrounding sacred spaces relate to, and impact upon, those spaces?" Hayden is firmly cognisant of the way changes in power relations between communities encompassing holy places affect relations within what are in effect the "arenas" of those places. For him the balance of power between groups sharing a site is rarely if ever changed by what happens within its boundaries; although the contest between groups occupying a holy place is for control of the site and its resources, it is shifts of power in the wider field of politics and the state that trigger the shift from muted struggle to fierce bouts of expulsive violence. Thus, while relations in and around the holy places are substantively affected by intercommunal interactions in the surrounding political world, those relations are only allowed close scrutiny (often retrospectively) after the "stasis" of seeming sharing is transformed into open antagonism.

In contradistinction, the following chapters attend closely to the details of intercommunal interactions at holy places and events, and link these to the relations between the communities that share or mix at shrines. One consequence of this is the realization that there are multiple ways in which individuals and groups approach and relate to sacred objects and rituals. Diverse interpretations of the significance of the same objects and actions are means of enabling groups, whose religious conceptions and practices would seem incommensurate, to gather reverentially around the same site, while mimicry, imitation, disavowal, and avoidance are core strategies of mixing the nominally incommensurate in and around the same place. Conceptions and practices of contact with the divine vary widely, encompassing everything from ecstatic communion with a saint or divinity to achieving healing through making contact with an object that one has heard, from others of other religious affiliations, has power. In Dionigi Albera's examination of Muslim usage of Marian shrines in the Mediterranean Basin we can see how variant interpretations of the same signifiers—sometimes interpretations only distinguished from the nominally "correct" meanings by the most subtle of diacritics—can enable the coming together of representatives of "civilizations" that Huntington, Lewis and others would tell us can only meet in battle.

The role of religious authorities, and those who claim to be religious authorities in various sites, differs widely and can—sometimes depending on the respect accorded them, or not, by local populations—either open sites to diversity or purge them of all but those they deem orthodox (as in Rohan Bastin's description of the role, and subsequent expulsion, of the liberation theology priests in a Sinhalese shrine). For the most part, the essays in this volume treat religious sites and practices maintained by and closely articulated with local populations, rather than those administered and "owned" by central authorities that legislate their practices for the use of pilgrims, priesthoods and others. These local sites can thus be seen to reflect and amplify images of the consociality of the communities that surround, or had surrounded, them. Relations in and around the sites are rarely simply harmonious; they reflect and replay the complex, and occasionally conflictual, choreographies that mark the everyday social lives that take place between variously affiliated communities in the adjoining territory. Strict harmony comes with disciplining—with the exclusion of difference—and emerges when sacred sites are brought under the control of monolithic authorities which purify the sites, restrict the flow of people from outside their borders into their domains, regiment their symbologies and rituals, and organize their activities to ensure the glorification of particular identities before divinities associated with those authorities. That imposed harmony is, however, the product of a violence inflicted upon those who "enjoy" it, and is frequently manifest in the violence they turn on those who are different. The harmony we see in this volume, fragile as at times it may seem, is instead grounded in the commitment of neighbors to neighbors, or of persons to an image of self and community they feel is important to maintain; as the essays of Bigelow, Couroucli, and Tuladhar-Douglas demonstrate, it may be less imposing, but it is also more flexible and more organically connected with the communities for which, and to which, it speaks.

* * *

Perhaps more central, however, is that the following chapters bring to the fore the degree to which the social fields encompassing the holy places constitute those places and the rituals which take place within them. Throughout the chapters, which investigate sites ranging from the northern and southern Mediterranean, through India, Nepal and Sri Lanka to Vietnam and China, we see a close relation between peoples' conceptions of the place they inhabit (and those they cohabit within it) and the sorts of interactions they engage in around the holy places within that territory. In nearly all the chapters presented in this volume, the religious sites and their rituals body forth images of imagined communities—past, present, and future—with which participants (or, in the Moroccan and Tunisian cases, organizers) feel a connection.

In some cases, most notably Anna Bigelow's chapter on Muslim shrines in post-partition Punjab and Maria Couroucli's study of the ceremonies at St. George's Monastery on Princes' Island off Istanbul, ceremonies bring together members of different confessional communities in an echo of an intensive earlier intercommunality which, while having largely disappeared from quotidian life, still resonates in practices of sharing holy space. Both chapters demonstrate how sacred sites gather members of different confessional communities who, deeply informed by what I would term a "practical nostalgia" for the cultural mixing which preceded the 1929 population transfer between Greece and Turkey (Clark 2006) and the 1948 partition of India and Pakistan, seek out holy spaces—whether deliberately or not—that evoke intercommunal encounters that have, under the pressure of demographic disparities, largely disappeared from everyday life. Here, in effect, an image of a remembered community is reconstituted and embodied in practices around the shrines.

The idea of a "practical nostalgia" implies that the impulse towards sharing sites and practices around sites is often neither conscious nor ideological, but instead is resident as a sort of *habitus* within images of efficacious activities appropriate to the sites. While the concept of an efficacy transcending confessional difference is developed later in Rohan Bastin's study of Sinhalese *haskam*, it is spectacularly displayed in Adam Chau's historical investigation of the "ritual polytropy" of elite funerals in Late Imperial China and Republican China. Chau examines the 1939 Beijing funeral of General Wu Peifu as an exemplary, and inflated, instance of gathering a multitude of religious specialists in a single space to ensure that, in effect, all bases were covered to guarantee the deceased general the most auspicious afterlife. By focusing on a gathering of the *sacra* of a multitude of religions in a single space rather than on the coming together of persons of different confessions in the place (or places) of single sects, Chau highlights the practical, as opposed to confessional, aims of the sorts of ritual events which allow mixing and sharing.

In Will Tuladhar-Douglas's study of the annual procession of the Buddhist deity Vajrayoginī through the Nepalese town of Pharping we observe the strategies by which a community with plural (largely nominal) sectarian identities is able collaboratively to celebrate a "Pharping identity" without exclusion or conflict. The only problem with this ritual assertion of a public united in its diversity is the refusal by resident Tibetan Buddhists to engage in what they term a "Hindu" procession. Tuladhar-Douglas's nuanced study of the Pharping population's "hard work" of disavowing this refusal is a fascinating testimonial to the commitment of some mixed communities to assert local, territorial identities over and against exclusive sectarian identities.

Rohan Bastin's study of Hindu-Buddhist-Catholic "sharing" in Sri Lanka investigates the Sinhalese conception of an overarching religious potentiality known as *haskam* to demonstrate the way in which, in the Sinhalese context, Śaivite Hindu, Catholic, Buddhist, and to some degree Muslim theologies could be worked to bring about syncretic practices around shared shrines such as St Anthony's Church in Kochikade, Colombo. He also shows how, in response to a local priesthood working to embrace alterity and develop wider conceptions of community and sacral efficacy, the Catholic Church under Pope John Paul II responded by imposing orthodoxy, expelling "heretical" priests, and "sanctifying" the sites by cleansing them of non-Catholic practices.

Aomar Boum and Dora Carpenter-Latiri, working in Morocco and Tunisia respectively, look at another level of institutional interference whereby state officials, developing tourism agendas, "reinstate" sharing around sites where mixing may have previously occurred by redefining the sites and the sorts of activities that take place around them. In the Morrocan instance examined by Boum, the "revitalization" of Essaouira, historically a city dense with Jewish and Muslim shrines, into the site of the annual Gnawa and World Music Festival is intended to subsume potentially exclusivist sectarian identities within the framework of a multiculturalism, and is motivated both by a will to celebrate tolerance and a drive to profit from international tourism. Its eventual impact on local identities and relations remains to be seen. In Jerba the programme by the Tunisian government to promote the ancient Ghriba synagogue as a celebrated example of Jewish-Muslim shrine sharing has, in effect, halted whatever sharing may have previously existed due to the constraints of the rigorous security required to protect European and Israeli Jewish visitors, especially in the wake of a 2002 al-Qaeda attack on the shrine. In these cases, as with the Catholic Church's purging of shrine sharing and its advocates in Sri Lanka, we witness the imposition of identity practices onto local communities rather than the growth of such practices out of local solidarities. These impositions are clearly future-oriented and intended to transform existing conceptions of community into new configurations of imagined community—configurations which may or may not be accepted and embraced by the populations affected.

Finally, Heonik Kwon investigates the way the "inhabiting" of family ancestral altars in postwar Vietnam is changing in the wake of ideological liberalization that now allows ideological "enemies", who are nonetheless kin, to reconvene after death on the commemorative altars. In contemporary Vietnam, families that had been divided by the ideological polarization effected by the "American War" are now installing images on ancestral altars of those who died "bad deaths" (i.e., were killed fighting on the side of the South Vietnamese and American armies) alongside those with "good deaths." This retrospective reconstitution of kin and community ties by modifying shrine practices affirms a motif that runs through all of the chapters. Throughout, intercommunal interactions around shared shrines are variously revealed not simply as the effects of spatial choreographies but also as moments in temporal sequences linking the realities of everyday life with images of community drawn from past, present, and future *desiderata*. At times, as with the cases of "antagonistic tolerance" presented by Hayden, these moments of sharing may be shadowed by an active anticipation of a future time when mixing can be expunged, but in the cases set out in the following pages mixing and sharing express various degrees of commitment—conscious and at times unconscious—to imagined communities which bring together persons, groups and localities that history and sectarianism seek to divide.

Notes

1. The Latin word *sacra* refers to all transactions related to worshipping the gods, in particular prayers and sacrifices. In the context of this volume it relates to a range of sites and activities, including ancestral altars, holy places (shrines, synagogues, churches, and mosques), funerals, religious processions, and festivals (even those which "secularize" the sacred). "Sharing" is a more problematically multivalent term (see note 5 below) ranging in significance from syncretism to simple temporal and spatial coexistence (see Stewart and Shaw 1994); it is the task of this volume to explore the contexts in which it may, or may not prove apposite.
2. "[I]ndivisible disputes are indivisible in two distinct ways. First, parties in these disputes view the issue as indivisible in and of itself, meaning that it cannot be taken apart, and second, they consider the issue indivisible from themselves, signifying that they will not tolerate parting with it" (Hassner 2009, see Bowman 2011). By "issue," Hassner refers to that of the control of holy places.
3. This seminar generated a recent publication—*Religions traversées; Lieux saints partagés entre chrétiens, musulmans et juifs en Mediterranée* (Albera and Couroucli 2009)—which has since been translated into Spanish (Albera and Couroucli 2010) and English (Albera and Couroucli 2011).
4. A follow-up to the Columbia conference took place in Istanbul in May 2010; it was co-organised by Elazar Barkan and Karen Barkey under the title "Choreography of Sacred Spaces: State, Religion, and Conflict Resolution."
5. I have tended, in my own usage, to term these shrines "mixed" rather than "shared," as "shared" connotes an amity I feel one cannot presuppose. Categorizing Muslim-Christian co-usage of an Orthodox church which may, in the past, have been the *turbe* (tomb room) of a Sufi *tekke* (monastery) as "mixing," for instance, neither presupposes antagonism nor syncretism but simply indicates a simultaneous usage of the same site (Bowman 2010: 200–206).

References

Albera, Dionigi and Maria Couroucli, eds. 2009. *Religions traversées; Lieux saints partagés entre chrétiens, musulmans et juifs en Mediterranée*. Arles: Actes Sud.
———. 2010. *Religiones entrecruzadas: Lugares santos compartidos entre cristianos, musulmanes y judios en el Mediterraneo* (trans. Josep Tarragona Castells). Lleida: Editorial Milenio, 7–36.
———. 2012. *Sharing Sacred Spaces in the Mediterranean: Christians, Muslims, and Jews at Shrines and Sanctuaries*. Bloomington: Indiana University Press.
Bastin, Rohan. 2002. *The Domain of Constant Excess: Plural Worship at the Munnesvaram Temples in Sri Lanka*. New York and Oxford: Berghahn Books.
Bigelow, Anna. 2010. *Sharing the Sacred: Practicing Pluralism in Muslim North India*. New York: Oxford University Press.

Borofsky, Robert. 2001. "Envisioning a More Public Anthropology: An Interview with Fredrik Barth, April 18th, 2001." *Public Anthropology: Engaging Ideas. http://www. publicanthropology.org/Journals/Engaging-Ideas/barth.htm.* Accessed 12 May 2010.

Bowman, Glenn. 1993. "Nationalizing the Sacred: Shrines and Shifting Identities in the Israeli-Occupied Territories." *Man: The Journal of the Royal Anthropological Institute* XXVIII (3): 431–60.

———. 2007. "Nationalising and Denationalising the Sacred: Shrines and Shifting Identities in the Israeli-Occupied Territories" (in Arabic). *Chronos: Revue d'histoire de l'Université de Balamand* XVI: 151–210.

———. 2009. "Processus identitaires autour de quelques sanctuaires partagés en Palestine et en Macédoine," in *Religions traversées: Lieux saints partagés entre chrétiens, musulmans et juifs en Méditerranée*, eds. D. Albera and M. Couroucli. Arles: Actes Sud, 27–52.

———. 2010. "Orthodox-Muslim Interactions at 'Mixed Shrines' in Macedonia," in *Eastern Christians in Anthropological Perspective*, eds. C. Hann and H. Goltz. Berkeley: University of California Press, 163–83.

———. 2011. "'In Dubious Battle on the Plains of Heav'n': the Politics of Possession in Jerusalem's Holy Sepulchre." *History and Anthropology* XXII: 3. 371–399.

———. 2012a. "Nationalizing and Denationalizing the Sacred: Shrines and Shifting Identities in the Israeli-Occupied Territories," in *Sacred Space in Israel and Palestine: Religion and Politics*, eds. Y. Reiter, M. Breger and L. Hammer. London: Routledge. 195–227.

———. 2012b. "Identification and Identity Formations around Shared Shrines in West Bank Palestine and Western Macedonia," in *Sharing Sacred Spaces in the Mediterranean: Christians, Muslims, and Jews at Shrines and Sanctuaries, New Anthropologies of Europe*, eds. D. Albera and M. Couroucli. Bloomington: Indiana University Press, 11–30.

Clark, Bruce. 2006. *Twice a Stranger: How Mass Expulsion Forged Modern Greece and Turkey.* London: Granta.

Hassner, Ron. 2009. *War on Sacred Grounds.* Ithaca: Cornell University Press.

Hayden, Robert. 2002. "Antagonistic Tolerance: Competitive Sharing of Religious Sites in South Asia and the Balkans." *Current Anthropology* 43(2): 205–31.

———. 2005. "Religious Structures and Political Dominance in Belgrade." *Ethnologia Balkanica* IX: 213–24.

———, Hande Sözer, Tuğba Tanyeri-Erdemir and Aykan Erdemir. 2011. "The Byzantine Mosque at Trilye: A Processual Analysis of Dominance, Sharing, Transformation and Tolerance." *History and Anthropology* 22(1): 1–18.

Huntington, Samuel. 1993. "The Clash of Civilizations?" *Foreign Affairs* LXXII(3): 22–49.

———. 1996. *The Clash of Civilizations and the Remaking of World Order.* New York: Simon and Schuster.

Lewis, Bernard. 1990. "The Roots of Muslim Rage." *The Atlantic Monthly* CCLXVI(3): 47–60.

Stewart, Charles and Rosalind Shaw, eds. 1994. "Introduction: Problematizing Syncretism," in *Syncretism/Anti-Syncretism: The Politics of Religious Synthesis*, eds. C. Stewart and R. Shaw. London: Routledge, 1–26.

Chapter 1

COMBINING PRACTICES AND BELIEFS: MUSLIM PILGRIMS AT MARIAN SHRINES

Dionigi Albera

In an influential article, Robert Hayden (2002) reinvigorated debate on shrines shared by different religions. Focusing on South Asia and the Balkans, he suggested that syncretism does not imply a tolerant attitude, in the sense of a positive posture of mutual respect, but at best corresponds to a moment of non-interference in the course of a process of expulsive competition. Rather than representing a static condition of synthesis between religious communities, sharing is a manifestation of a temporary balance of power between them. To describe situations of syncretism, Hayden insisted we view them from a processual perspective, and proposed the notions of "competitive sharing" and "antagonistic tolerance" to characterize situations in which different religious communities appear to share sacred sites and combine practice and beliefs. These phrases, strikingly oxymoronic, link up with the term "ambiguous sanctuaries" used by Frederick Hasluck many years earlier (1929) in describing the ambivalent nature of sacred places claimed and frequented by two or more religions. Like Hayden, he contended that moments of apparent sharing are simply way stations along the route to the consolidation of control over the shrine by one of the contending groups. In the following pages I will argue for the necessity of reformulating notions of "competitive sharing," "antagonistic tolerance," and, indeed, "ambiguous sanctuaries" so as to embrace aspects of, and contexts for, intercommunal interaction overlooked in these somewhat unidirectional characterizations.

A central feature of Hayden's approach is his insistence on bringing time into analysis and thus on viewing syncretism as a temporal manifestation. Although this temporalization is without doubt an important move, in his work the mobilization of history goes invariably in only one direction. In the processual perspective he proposes, syncretism represents a contingent phase in the confrontation between groups which continue to compete and differentiate (Hayden 2002: 207). The examples he examines seem to all emanate from the same script; after a period of sharing the sequence goes towards conflict, separation, and sometimes even the destruction of the sanctuary. This is the end of the story (ibid., 218).

In this chapter I will adopt the comparative and processual approach recommended by Hayden. I will look at examples of shared shrines in several countries around the Mediterranean, following a *longue durée* perspective. More particularly, I will concentrate on attendance at several Marian sanctuaries by Muslim believers. This will show that sharing of worship is not always a contingent and frail phenomenon connected to the transfer of a sanctuary from one religion to another, and that it can be relatively independent of the issue of the control of shrines. A discussion of the interplay between attendance at the same shrines, circumstances of violent confrontation, and different idioms of nationalism will confirm that a more balanced approach to mixed worship and shared sanctuary is needed.

Muslim Attendance at Marian Sanctuaries

In order to grasp the phenomenon of sharing sacred sites we should go beyond a simple dichotomy between local practices on the one hand and the action of religious or political leaders on the other, or—in other words—between little and great traditions. Examining forms of sharing in sacred sites dedicated to the Virgin Mary implies a wider detour, taking into account some cross-cultural symbolic elements, as well as the legacy of connected histories. Devotion for the Virgin Mary is indeed well implanted in the Islamic tradition; sacred texts sanction it. Mary has a very significant place in the Qur'an. She is the only female figure designated by name, while all the other women are simply indicated as daughter, wife, mother, or sister of a man whose name is given. Moreover, the name of Mary recurs more times in the Qur'an than in the whole of the New Testament: 34 occurrences against 19 (Dousse 2005: 14). In addition to evocations scattered in the text, Mary is a central figure in two suras. One, the nineteenth, bears her name; the other, the third, is entitled "The family of Imran [the father of Mary]." According to tradition, these two suras were among the five held to be most dear to the prophet. The Qur'an mentions the nativity of Mary, her presentation to the Temple, the Annunciation, the virginal conception and the birth of Jesus. Mary appears as a sign for humanity and an example for believers; she is a model of confidence in God, of abandonment to divine will, of modesty and piety. A verse summarizes the pre-eminent position of Mary: 'so the angels said, "Mary God has selected you and purified you. He has selected you over all the women in the Universe"' Qur'an 3:42 (Irving 1985: 29).

The vision of Mary in the Qur'an presents some peculiarities. The most disconcerting aspect for a Christian reader is probably the fusion which operates there between the Old Testament Mary, sister of Moses and Aaron, and that of the Gospel, mother of Jesus. With a telescoping which defies any chronological order, the Qur'an carries out, under the sign of Mary, a junction between the Old and

New Testaments (Dousse 2005). The references to Mary, in the allusive, fragmentary and atemporal style which is specific to the Qur'an, have been widened in a much more prolix way by Muslim traditions in the *hadith*, the comments of the Qur'an, the mystical literatures, and elsewhere.

This textual dimension was constantly accompanied by important demonstrations of devotion. Mary has been and still is venerated by Muslims, who often frequent Christian sanctuaries for this reason. Many sources attest to the tenacity of this worship through the centuries, showing forms of sharing in the *longue durée* (Cuffel 2003). In the following pages I will briefly refer to some examples of longstanding Muslim attendance at Marian sanctuaries.

In the Holy Land the sites connected to the presence of the Virgin constituted points of encounter between Christians and Muslims. Bethlehem can be considered the epicenter of the Islamic topography of the Virgin Mary. According to some of the traditions of Mohammed's night journey to Jerusalem, the prophet Muhammad, the first Muslim pilgrim, was transported from Mecca to Jerusalem and stopped at Bethlehem where he was instructed by the angel Gabriel, his guide, to pray at the place where "his brother Jesus" had been born (see Bencheik1988: 17).

In the tenth century, Eutychius, a Melchite Patriarch of Alexandria, reported that Muslims gathered for prayer in the Church of the Nativity in Bethlehem (Bashear 1991: 268). Until the time of the Crusades, this church, although controlled by the Christians, contained a section reserved for the Muslims, with a *mihrab* (Grabar (1984) 1998: 68–69). Accounts of Christian pilgrims constantly report, through the centuries, the presence of Muslims who came to Bethlehem to worship the Virgin. It was possible to meet them in the Church of the Nativity, but also in other places where the Marian epic had left its print: for instance, around the tree under which the Virgin had rested on the way to Jerusalem and in the place where the angel announced the Holy Nativity to the shepherds. In the cave where Mary took refuge with her child, before fleeing to Egypt, some drops of her milk fell, conferring a miraculous power to its walls. Century after century, until the present day, women of different religions have crushed fragments of the rock walls into powder which, mixed with water, they drank to ensure the abundance of their own milk. Such piety is not confined to women, or to the lower classes. When the pilgrim Jacques de Villamont came to Bethlehem in the second half of sixteenth century, he met the Cadi of Jerusalem, who had come with his wife and children to pay a visit to the sanctuary. The group stayed initially in the gardens of the convent and then crossed the threshold into the Church of the Nativity (de Villamont 1600: 192).

The virtues of Myriam pervade other places. Let us go in the steps of another pilgrim, Laurent d'Arvieux (who was the collaborator of Molière for the "turqueries" of the "Bourgeois gentilhomme"). In Nazareth, in the chapel of the Annunciation, two marble columns mark, according to tradition, the places where the Virgin and the angel sat at the time of the Annunciation. Muslims, like Christians, hold them in great veneration. They pass between them and rub the sick parts of their bodies there. D'Arvieux, who visited the church in 1660, describes these practices. In Jerusalem, Muslims visit the well of Mary with reverence, drink water and make ablutions. In the Virgin's Tomb there are altars belonging to various Christian confessions, but also a *mihrab*. D'Arvieux reports that "the Turks dug a sort of niche in the wall, which is used by them as a mosque, where they make their prayers." At Mount Carmel, the Muslims admire a painting of the Virgin on the altar of a chapel and make their acts of devotion (d'Arvieux 1735, II: 270–71, 174, 280, 315, 462).

In all these cases, we are confronted with a sharing spanning the *longue durée* of several centuries, without becoming the Trojan horse of the occupation of these Christian sites by Muslims. The same phenomenon is present in Syria at sanctuaries consecrated to the Virgin Mary. The most important is the monastery of Saidnaya, approximately 25 kilometers from Damascus. The monastery sits on a peak overlooking the Damascene plain. It belongs to the orthodox Patriarchy of Antioch and is inhabited by a community of nuns. Its origins are very ancient. According to tradition, it was founded by the emperor Justinian in the sixth century. During a hunt in Syria, the emperor witnessed an apparition of the Virgin Mary and gave the order to build a sanctuary in this place (Gharib 1988: 28).

Saidnaya was immensely popular during the Middle Ages and attracted a great number of pilgrims. Particularly reputed was an icon of the Virgin attributed to St. Luke to which many miracles were credited. A perfumed liquid, with miraculous properties, was collected under the icon and distributed to pilgrims. The veneration of the Madonna of Saidnaya was common to Greek Orthodox, Catholics, and Ethiopians. Several Christian communities asked to have an altar in the church of Saidnaya, exactly as was the case in the church of the Holy Sepulchre in Jerusalem (see Nasrallah 1971: 15). Moreover, some medieval accounts affirm that Muslims frequented this sanctuary in order to pray to the Virgin Mary and mention miracles concerning Muslim faithful (see Devos 1947). According to tradition, even Malek al-Adel (a brother of Saladin, who ruled over both Egypt and Syria for nearly two decades at the beginning of the thirteenth century) miraculously recovered from a disease thanks to a pilgrimage to the Madonna of Saidnaya (Nasrallah 1971: 16–17; Gharib 1988: 30). In the seventeenth century, d'Arvieux remarked that the sanctuary was frequented by Muslims, who entered "after being purified, as when they enterin their Mosques" (d'Arvieux 1735, II: 462). Up to this day, streams of Christian and Muslim pilgrims go to Saidnaya. In 1994, the British writer William Dalrymple visited the monastery. He was impressed by a mixed ceremony he observed in the church:

> the congregation seemed to consist not of Christians but almost entirely of heavily bearded Muslim men. As the priest circled the altar with his thurible, filling the sanctuary with great clouds of incense, the men bobbed up and down on their prayer mats as if in the middle of Friday prayers in a great mosque. Their women, some dressed in full black *chador*, mouthed prayers from the shadows of the exo-narthex. A few, closely watching the Christian women, went up to the icons hanging from the pillars of the church; kissed them, then lit candles and placed them in the candelabra in front of

the images. As I watched from the rear of the church I could see the faces of the women reflected in the illuminated gilt of the icons. Towards the end of the service, the priest reappeared with a golden stole over his cassock and circled the length of the church with his thurible, gently and almost apologetically stepping over the prostrate Muslims blocking his way, treading as carefully as if they were precious Iznik vases. (Dalrymple [1997 2005: 187)

Our Lady of Saidnaya is particularly reputed for fertility. The most important site of devotion is a small chapel, near to the main church, where the icon supposedly painted by Saint Luke is hidden under a profusion of silver, gold, and gems. The pilgrim or other visitor who today enters the chapel is invited to remove his shoes. The place is literally filled with icons, ex-votos, and precious gifts. Candles and oil lamps burn day and night. Christian and Muslim pilgrims, coming principally from Syria or Lebanon, carry out identical rites, mainly related to the oil collected under the image. During a visit in 2003, I was told by a nun of sacrifices of lamb accomplished by Muslims. Again this *longue durée* sharing has not produced a shift of religious affiliation.

In Egypt several sacred sites linked to the tradition of the Holy Family's passage have been jointly worshipped by Christians and Muslims. Matariyeh (near Cairo) has been mentioned by Coptic, Muslim, and Catholic authors since the Middle Ages as a place where the Holy Family stayed in Egypt (Zanetti 1993). Throughout these several centuries, features of the landscape have been remarked upon by chroniclers: a garden of fruit trees; the sycamore where the Virgin hid her child; balsamic trees with therapeutic virtues; a miraculous source. In 1384, an Italian traveler noted therapeutic practices common to Christians and Muslims relating to the sycamore. People entered its hollow trunk hoping to be cured (Valensi 2002: 136). The healing virtues of the spring, which appeared miraculously in response to the needs of the Holy Family, also attracted a mixed attendance, as is attested by the accounts of European travelers and Muslim sources (Cuffel 2005: 410). Already by the twelfth century, a European traveler had affirmed that the Saracens venerated this spring and came to bathe (Zanetti 1993: 52). Symon Semeonis—an Irish pilgrim who was there in 1323—was told by the Muslim guards of the place that they had witnessed several appearances of the Virgin Mary close to the source (Régnier-Bohler 1997: 987). At the end of sixteenth century, the Venetian Prospero Alpino gave several examples of Muslim devotion at this Christian holy place (Zanetti 1993: 57–59), while in the mid-seventeenth century, another Western pilgrim observed that "the Mohammedans have great veneration for this place and they will bathe with devotion and tell that many miraculously recovered health by this means" (Brémond 1974: 89–90).

During the long history of Matariyeh, religious buildings have been built and subsequently appropriated by different denominations (Copts, Muslims, and Latin Christians). While these claims and counter claims generated tensions and confrontations, they did not put an end to mixed access to the place. During the twelfth century a church was built by the Copts in the neighboring village, but some years later it was taken by Muslims. Matariyeh was also a strategic place, firmly controlled by Ayyubid and Mamluk regimes. The production of balsam—an extremely precious item—was organized by the state. The government had a monopoly on this product, which was given as a present to ambassadors or other political authorities (Valensi 2002: 130). Matariyeh was also a thermal resort for wealthy Mamluks. In the fifteenth century an emir built a domed house, which was also frequented by the sultan Qait Bey (Meinardus 1986: 38).

Despite these appropriations and exploitations, the heart of this site—and the center of its symbolic power—continues to be the space of the garden and the spring. Ordinary people (both Coptic and Muslim) as well as Western pilgrims have had access to this religious space throughout the changes. Since the twelfth century, Coptic priests have celebrated mass here using a stone near the source as an altar (Zanetti 1993: 32–39). Around 1480, Felix Fabri and Joos van Ghistele saw a rudimentary building, without a roof, enclosing the pool of miraculous water and the stone where the Virgin would have put the Infant (Fabri 1975: 385; van Ghistele 1976: 70–72). Some years later a more solid structure made of brick was erected. According to Francesco Suriano (1949: 145), who visited this place towards the end of the fifteenth century or the beginning of the sixteenth century, this small edifice was sponsored by the same sultan Qait Bey. In the following centuries this structure (referred to by Western pilgrims as a chapel, a mosque, or the house of the Holy Family) was used by both Christians and Muslims for prayer and for bathing. It contained an altar on which Christian priests could say mass. At the beginning of seventeenth century, one of them, Father Boucher, stated that when he was celebrating mass there, Muslims came in to make their devotions and perform ablutions (Fedden 1944: 41). Although the cultivation of the balsam trees declined in the sixteenth century and had vanished by the seventeenth century, the garden did not disappear. It remained a place of promenade for both ordinary people and the elite during the Ottoman period. When at the beginning of the eighteenth century the religious building collapsed (Meinardus 2002: 92) the devotional interest of Christians and Muslims focused on the sycamore. That medieval tree died in the seventeenth century, but was replaced by another tree, planted in 1672 and attributed with the same virtues. This reached an imposing size but itself fell down in 1906 (Meinardus 1986: 39–40). The remains of that tree, surmounted by yet another replacement, are still the focus of the garden (see http://members.virtualtourist.com/m/p/m/296798/, accessed 13 July 2009).

On the whole, the examples I have considered show that the sharing of worship is not necessarily connected to the transfer of a sanctuary from one religion to another, and can be relatively independent from the issue of the control of the shrine. In several cases, moreover, shared sites of worship are located in natural settings—in the vicinity of trees or wells—which often escape the control of religious hierarchies. Many Christian travelers describe places of this type, where people of different religions share the search for well-being and often practice the same rites. In the fifteenth century, the Dominican Felix Fabri mentions a very old tree in Cairo, venerated jointly by the Christians and the Muslims, which according to tradition had offered its shade to the Virgin and the child (Fabri 1975: 446–47 and 921). The relative dissociation between worship and control appears even more clearly when the shared places of devotion are situated at the margins of inhabited lands, without a clerical power being clearly in command of them. Certain pilgrimages in honor of the Virgin move towards mountain tops dedicated to her. For example, we find in the seventeenth century a chronicle describing a pilgrimage to Pashtrik Mount, at the border between Albania and Kosovo, where in 1681 an ecumenical crowd gathered. The pilgrims spent the night there, playing musical instruments, singing, and dancing. After midnight, they started a three-hour mixed procession around the top of the mountain with both Christians and Muslims carrying candles proportional in length to the age of the faithful (Elsie 2001: 173).

Another significant case is that of Lampedusa. The island was a significant stopover for Mediterranean navigation. Ottoman or European sailors, who frequently stopped there to supply themselves with water, visited its small sanctuary and left offerings. This was described by the 4th Earl of Sandwich, John Montagu:

> The whole of its inhabitants consists in one single hermit who leads a solitary life in an artificial grotto cut out of the rock, far from the intercourse of mankind, whom he seems desirous to shun. His chief pleasure is in the cultivation of a small garden and vineyard which he maintains with great care and nicety. … Joining to the cavern serving for his habitation is the chapel of the same nature, in which he celebrates mass according to the Roman Catholic rite. Opposite to this chapel is another grotto, in which is the tomb of a Turkish saint, who died and was buried here at a time when the Grand Signor's fleet was at anchor before the island. The hermit keeps a lamp always burning at the head of this tomb, upon which account he remains unmolested by the Mahometans who frequently come to Lampedusa to water their ships and gallies. (Montagu 1799: 988)

Several voyagers' accounts confirm this situation for the eighteenth century. In the seventeenth century, travelers mentioned only the chapel, without referring to the hermit. Nonetheless even then there was a strong sense of a powerful presence at the holy place. Every vessel would leave goods at the shrine: biscuits, oil, gunpowder, clothes, and cordages. When sailors stood in need of any of these things, they would take them, but they had to be sure to leave something of equivalent worth if they did not want to be punished by the winds. This remote shrine, quite independent from institutional control, allowed for a sharing of vital resources between enemies in the violent Mediterranean seaways of those centuries.

Sharing of Shrines and Interfaith Violence

I will now concentrate on periods in which shared sanctuaries were severely affected by conflict. The first example is the Maronite sanctuary of Saïdet-el-Tallé, which means "Our Lady of the Hill," situated in the historical heartland of Mount

Lebanon, the Shouf, where the majority of the population are Druze. The church is located in the small town of Deir-el-Qamar, which was the capital of Mount Lebanon between the sixteenth and early nineteenth centuries. In the town there are also mosques and a synagogue.

For several centuries, Saïdet-el-Tallé was frequented by various religious groups who used it as a site for making oaths. People came to swear in front of the image of the Virgin. The Druze used the site as a pilgrimage center. A Christian inhabitant of the city, questioned by father Pierre-Marie Martin in 1870, asserted that "[b]efore 1845, Saïdet-el-Tallé was more venerated by the Druze than by us. They came from far to pray to her in their fashion and obtained a host of miracles. We said laughing: It is the Virgin of the Druze!" (Goudard [1955] 1993: 61). In the first part of the nineteenth century, Druze leaders came to Saïdet-el-Tallé to implore the Virgin before battle. Before going off to war they would touch the image of the Virgin with their flags and put dust taken from under the altar in their turbans.

In 1860 the region experienced an outbreak of hostilities between Muslims and Christians. The violence started in Damascus, and then infected Mount Lebanon, opposing principally Druze and Maronites. It was a period of death, destruction, and atrocities (Fawaz 1994). When the Druze attacked Deir-el-Qamar at the time of the bloody confrontations of 1860, many Christians sought refuge in the church. They counted on the respect that the Druze had always manifested for the place. Nevertheless, scores of men and male children were killed there and the miraculous image was shot up and destroyed. The church was plundered.

This would seem brutal confirmation of the thesis of competitive sharing argued by Hayden. Yet this terrible manifestation of antagonism did not mark the end of sharing of worship between Druze and Maronites in Saïdet-el-Tallé. In the decades following the massacre the Druze started again to worship at this shrine:

> The pilgrimage began again. A new painting replaced the old one; a great enthusiasm reappeared; in the restored and expanded church the chaplet, the month of Mary, the visits to the Madonna flowered again … One noticed a recrudescence of miraculous favours. At the beginning, the Druze did not dare to show themselves in the district, and sent their wishes to Saïdet-el-Tallé by means of Christian peasants: oil, incense, candles, money. Then, with time, forgiveness came, and the adversaries of the day before started again meeting familiarly in the lane that goes down towards the church. (Goudard (1955) 1993: 62)

This case is far from being exceptional. The long civil war (1975–1990) which opposed the various Lebanese religious groups did not put an end to devotional porosity. In spite of the ferocity of the battles and the massacres, even today there are numerous shrines attended by different religious communities (Farra-Haddad 2005). Among the Christian shrines which are also frequented by Lebanese Muslims of different denominations (Sunnis, Shiites, and Druze) there are several Marian sites, such as the monastery of Saïdet-en-Nourié in the region of Tripoli, the sanctuary of Saïdet-el-Mantara near Sidon, and that of Our Lady of Lebanon in Harissa. Moreover, Muslim visitors to the latter shrine come from Iran and the Gulf countries. There one can see Muslim women, wrapped in their long black clothes, lighting candles or climbing on the base of the immense statue of the Virgin overhanging the sea.

These examples suggest that overt conflict between religious groups does not necessarily put an end to religious sharing or to syncretistic practices. On the contrary, these practices seem to be important in rebuilding a *modus vivendi* after civil war. More generally, these Lebanese examples show a complex interplay between communalism and porosity of practices, which cannot be reduced to a lineal sequence.

Let us examine another case of interrelation between conflict and sharing in Algeria. There, during the nineteenth century, the construction of the French colonial state was punctuated by religious symbols (churches, chapels, statues) meant to bring together a population of disparate European origins. Within this framework, several places of worship devoted to the Virgin Mary are frequented by Muslims (and in some cases also by Jews). Certain urban sanctuaries, such as Our Lady of Africa in Algiers and Our Lady of Santa-Cruz in Oran, and some rural chapels (for example in Misserghin) attract a disparate "clientele" belonging to the three religions. This phenomenon is already attested to in 1880 in Algiers, where Muslim and Jewish women used to visit the basilica and light candles in front of the statue of the Virgin of Our Lady of Africa (Albera 2005a).

Muslim presence at Marian shrines in Algeria has become quite usual since the early twentieth century. Especially on Sundays, mingled among the Christians, one can see Muslim women entering the sanctuaries, approaching the statues, leaving candles, making their devotions, and offering ex-votos. Many of these practices resisted the war of independence, the rise of Islamism and the civil war of the 1990s. In this violent context, in which the populations of European origin almost entirely abandoned the country, several Christian buildings were damaged or transformed in mosques. Yet, even in the most dangerous moments of the 1990s, Muslims continued their devotions to Our Lady of Africa. Overhanging Bâb el-Oued, a "sensitive" district, Our Lady of Africa is still among the most important places of pilgrimage in the Algerian capital. According to information that I collected during a visit in 2003, it can be estimated that forty thousand people visit it annually, and more than 95 percent of these are Muslims. Gifts of different nature (money, flowers, small cakes, carpets) are brought to the sanctuary for wishes to be fulfilled, and it is possible to see, inside the church, ex-votos and prayer slips left by Muslims. Some forms of devotion, more sporadic, were also preserved at Our Lady of Santa Cruz in Oran, a sanctuary outside the city at the top of Murdjajo Mount, which was the site of several attacks in the 1990s. Other cases remain even more secret, such an old people's home managed by Christian nuns in Oran, which I visited in 2002, where a statue of the Virgin receives pious visits by Muslim inhabitants of the district.

Even in Algeria we see that, contrary to the hypotheses formulated by Hayden, after (and also during) periods of violence, syncretistic practices continue.

Furthermore, the phenomenon of sharing does not seem linked to the control of sacred sites. Even in a situation in which the Christian presence is extremely reduced—no more than a few small scattered groups of friars and nuns remain in Algeria—the appeal of Christian sites is still alive for Muslims. In spite of the violent hostility and the growth of fundamentalism, there is continuity of symbols and of syncretic practices.

Nationalism, Syncretism and Marian Apparitions

A testimony to the complex imbrications between conflict and sharing, between monolithic religious identities and the hybridity of practices, is given by the huge impact of recent apparitions and miracles of the Virgin Mary in some Arab countries. Not only have Muslims been major constituents of the crowds gathered at these sites, but Muslims have also played important roles in validating these miraculous phenomena.

In a church located in Zaytûn, a district at the periphery of Cairo, the Virgin appeared repeatedly at the end of the 1960s. Hundreds of thousands of people claimed to have seen her. The first to distinguish the luminous image of the Virgin on the roof of the church were some Muslims of the vicinity. Immense crowds of Christians and Muslims were mixed in the immense crowds that gathered in subsequent months around the church, hoping to see the Virgin. Several Muslims claimed to have benefited from the Virgin's miracle. Between 1968 and 1970 the Coptic weekly newspaper *Watani* published some seven hundred accounts of miraculous healing linked to the Virgin: more than 10 percent of these were recounted by Muslims (Keriakos 2009: 269).

The apparitions gave form to a vast "social drama" (Turner 1974) that had a strong impact on Egyptian society for at least two years. Starting in April 1968, the apparitions continued until April 1970. From the beginning, the miraculous phenomena of Zaytûn were legitimated by the Coptic hierarchy and approved by the Egyptian political authorities. They were widely interpreted as a symbol of the resurrection of the Egyptians after the humiliation of their 1967 defeat by Israel in the Six-Day War, which entailed the loss of the Sinai and the Israeli occupation of the Gaza Strip. The Egyptian press covered the apparitions enthusiastically, devoting whole pages to the miraculous events, describing the crowds that gathered to experience the vision, and interviewing Christian and Muslim witnesses. The media promoted the declarations of Coptic bishops who spelled out the political connotations of the apparitions while proposing themselves as spokesmen for the unity of the Egyptians. They claimed that the apparition of Zaytûn showed that the Virgin was saddened by the Israeli invasion of Palestine. They interpreted the phenomena in terms of the escape of the Holy Family to Egypt, arguing that the mother of Jesus chose to flee to Egypt to get away from the brutality of the Israeli occupation and that that choice was a sign of the future victory of the Arabs (Voile 2004: 234; Keriakos 2009: 283–84). The political authorities approved of the Church's nationalist discourse, and even Nasser went to the site, spending a night there awaiting the apparition of the Virgin. Accounts circulated affirming that he saw her at five o'clock in the morning. Moreover the appearances at Zaytûn had international repercussions, attracting thousands of pilgrims from Europe and America, and thereby not only generating tourism income for a country recently shunned by tourists but as well providing a positive image of Egypt to the world. The management of the apparitions was entrusted to the Ministry for Tourism which published several booklets, a book and a commemorative stamp of the apparitions (Voile 2004: 215–43; Keriakos 2008: 171–339).

In this climate of religious effervescence, other apparitions occurred. In Tanta, in the Nile Delta, a miraculous image of Saint George seen above a church during two weeks in April 1969 had a strongly nationalist tone. Crowds of Christians and Muslims met to attend the miraculous manifestation of this martial saint, with Muslims greeting him with the cry of *Allâhu Akbar*. Saint George was seen as having come to give victory to the Arab nation, and was referred as a "Palestinian saint" (Voile 2004: 238–39). Several other Marian apparitions were recorded in Egypt during the following decades. Muslim attendance has been documented at these sites, as well as Muslims' role as witnesses to manifestations. For instance, in 2000, the person who first perceived supernatural phenomena at a church in Assiout was a local Muslim. However in the current climate, with the growing strength of communalist tendencies among both Copts and Muslims, the interpretation of such apparitions as symbols of national unity and resurrection seems to have been muted (Keriakos 2008: 451–542).

A Marian apparition with a markedly syncretistic dimension took place in 1983 in the small town of Beit Sahour, in the Palestinian West Bank. An image of the Virgin appeared there, on the interior wall of a cistern within a small shrine that had, in 1974, been erected after earlier sightings of the Virgin. That shrine had been built by the Beit Sahour Municipality (instead of by any of the religious communities represented in the town) for the use of Muslims and Christians of all denominations, and the 1983 appearance revitalized visits to the site. The structure of this small sanctuary evoked that of a Muslim *maqâm*, although surmounted by a cross. A quantity of objects offered by the faithful of several religious affiliations (Catholic, Greek Orthodox, Muslim) were piled up inside. Visitors of different religions gathered water from the cistern to which they attributed therapeutic qualities. The control of the sanctuary remained in the hands of the municipality, with the aim of preventing its appropriation by only one religious group. This sharing, and the political machinations which accompanied it, seems to have been consolidated by a context in which all of the local Palestinians shared the common experience of conflict with Israeli soldiers and settlers (Bowman 1993).

A more massive display of mixed devotion occurred more recently, on 21 August 2004, in a village in the Bekaa Valley (Lebanon) around a miraculous manifestation of the Virgin Mary (Aubin-Boltanski 2008; Noun 2010). A Jordanian Muslim child who, with his parents, was visiting a church (attended by

Muslim worshippers over the past several centuries) in Bechouate, saw a statue of the Virgin become animated while a prayer came spontaneously from his mouth. Other people saw the statue exuding odorous oil. The church was immediately submerged under a wave of devotion, and according to local clergy nearly a million pilgrims (Catholic and Orthodox Christians as well as Shiites, Sunnis, and Druze) had visited it by the end of 2004. A series of miraculous cures occurred, several of which concerned Muslims (including the father of the Jordanian child). One could see Muslims making their prostrations on carpets inside the church. When I visited this site in October 2005, the priest told me that he had seen the faithful from all of the Lebanon's eighteen officially recognized denominations praying in this shrine (he excepted the Jews, whose number is in any case extremely low in the country). The pilgrimage rapidly became a symbol of national unity in a context marked by shared opposition to the Syrian occupation of parts of Lebanon, including the Bekaa valley (Aubin-Boltanski 2008).

In all these examples, religious syncretism seems to convey something of the original meaning attributed to this term by Plutarch when he described how quarrelling Cretans could reconcile their differences when confronted by a common enemy (*synckretizein*) (Stewart 1999; Lambropoulos 2001). It is worth noting that in Egypt, Palestine, and Lebanon these manifestations of shared worship occurred in a context characterized by an "Islamization" of society and the growing influence of fundamentalism. This suggests the complexity of the elements at stake and the mobility of the alignments. Monolithic religious nationalism does not represent the only option, and in some circumstances nationalism may be articulated by common attendance at the same sacred sites.

Conclusion

The cult of the Virgin Mary is an important bridge between Christian and Muslim faithful. This devotion has some theological ground in the founding texts of Islam, and shows a protracted presence in history. The examples given reveal that even now Marian sanctuaries are currently visited every year by many thousands of Muslims. These Islamic refractions of Marian worship are only one chapter of a wider set of religious exchanges. One could multiply the paths by concentrating on other symbolic mediators. Thus it would be possible to show other ramifications in the inventory of devotional aggregations and fusions (see Albera 2005 b; 2008).

On the basis of a comparative scrutiny of several Marian shrines in the Mediterranean, I have tried to re-examine some implications of Hayden's pessimistic philosophy of the history of religious cohabitation. The vicissitudes of these shrines show a surprising continuity of sharing and syncretism. These phenomena do not represent a temporary stage in a process of transfer of sacred sites from one religion to another. Religious sharing and syncretistic practices seem able to survive the most difficult moments and reappear. They may even continue to exist after violent manifestations of conflict between groups, and in some instances seem to contribute to reshaping a living together after civil war. Moreover, some contemporary examples suggest that mixed frequentation of the same shrines is not ontologically contradictory to the idiom of nationalism, and can foster an interfaith coalition against a common enemy.

The long-lasting Muslim attendance at Marian sanctuaries does not imply that we should conceive syncretism as a static situation of synthesis between religious communities which indefinitely perpetuates itself. On the contrary, the overall permanence of cross-faith participation in pilgrimages and rituals at Marian sites is the result of a number of temporal manifestations of relations between individuals and groups, in which continuity of shared worship, crisis, rupture, and return to mixed attendance depend on the historical context. In order to grasp these multifarious phenomena, the label of "syncretism" is probably too general. We should refine our analytical vocabulary to take into account the broad spectrum of instances in which people combine practices and beliefs at the same shrine.

References

Albera, Dionigi. 2005a. "La Vierge et l'islam. Mélange de civilisations en Méditerranée." *Le Débat* 137: 134–44.

———. 2005b. "Pèlerinages mixtes et sanctuaires 'ambigus' en Méditerranée," in *Les pèlerinages au Moyen-Orient: espaces public, espaces du public*, eds. S. Chiffoleau and A. Madoeuf. Beyrouth: Institut Français du Proche-Orient, 347–78.

———. 2008. "'Why are you mixing what cannot be mixed?' Shared Devotions in the Monotheisms." *History and Anthropology* 19(1): 37–59.

Arvieux, Laurent d'. 1735. *Mémoires du chevalier d'Arvieux...* Paris: C.-J.-B. Delespine.

Aubin-Boltanski, Emma. 2008. "La Vierge et la nation (Liban, 2004–2007)." *Terrain* 50: 82–99.

Bashear, Suliman. 1991. "Qibla Musharriqa and Early Muslim Prayer in Churches." *The Muslim World* 81(3–4): 267–82.

Bencheikh, Jamel-Eddine. 1988. *Le voyage nocturne de Mahomet*. Paris: Imprimerie Nationale.

Bowman, Glenn. 1993. "Nationalizing the Sacred: Shrines and Shifting Identities in the Israeli-Occupied Territories." *Man* (New Series) 28(3): 431–60.

Brémond, Gabriel. 1974. *Voyage en Égypte de Gabriel Brémond, 1643–1645*, présenté et annoté par Georges Sanguin. Cairo: IFAO.

Cuffel, Alexandra. 2003. "'Henceforward All Generations Will Call Me Blessed': Medieval Christian Tales of Non-Christian Marian Veneration." *Mediterranean Studies* 12: 37–60.

———. 2005. "From Practice to Polemic: Shared Saints and Festivals as 'Women's Religion' in the Medieval Mediterranean." *Bulletin of SOAS* 68(3): 401–19.

Devos, Paul. 1947. "Les premières versions occidentales de la légende de Saïdnaia." *Analecta Bollandiana* 65: 212–78.

Dalrymple, William. (1997) 2005. *From the Holy Mountain*. London: Harper.

Dousse, Michel. 2005. *Marie la musulmane*. Paris: Albin Michel.

Elsie, Robert. 2001. *A Dictionary of Albanian Religion, Mythology and Folk Culture.* London: Hurst & Company.

Fabri, Félix. 1975. *Voyage en Égypte de Félix Fabri, 1483*, 3 vols, édité et traduit par Jacques Masson. Cairo: IFAO.

Farra-Haddad, Nour. 2005. "Les pèlerinages votifs au Liban: chemins de rencontres des communautés religieuses," in S. Chiffoleau and A. Madoeuf (dir.), *Les pèlerinages au Moyen-Orient: espaces public, espaces du public.* Beyrouth: Institut Français du Proche-Orient, 379–95.

Fawaz, Leila. 1994. *An Occasion for War: Civil Conflict in Lebanon and Damascus in 1860.* Berkeley: University of California Press.

Fedden, Robin. 1944. "Two Notes on Christian Cairo in the Turkish Period." *Bulletin de la Société d'Archéologie Copte* 10: 33–42.

Gharib, Georges. 1988. *Le icône mariane. Storia e culto.* Rome: Citta Nuova Editrice.

Goudard, Joseph. (1955) 1993. *La Sainte Vierge au Liban* (troisième édition entièrement refondue par le p. H. Jalabert). Beyrouth: Dar El-Machreq.

Grabar, André. (1984) 1998. *L'iconoclasme byzantin. Le dossier archéologique.* Paris: Flammarion.

Hasluck, Frederick. (1929) 2000. *Christianity and Islam Under the Sultans* (edited by Margaret M. Hasluck). Istanbul: The Isis Press.

Hayden, Robert. 2002. "Antagonistic Tolerance: Competitive Sharing of Religions Sites in South Asia and Balkans." *Current Anthropology* 43(2): 205–31.

Irving, Thomas (ed. and trans.). 1985. *The Qur'an: The First American Translation.* Brattleboro, VT: Amana Books.

Keriakos, Sandrine. 2008. *Saintetés en partage. Mythes et enjeux du rapprochement entre chrétiens et musulmans autour des reliques et des apparitions de saints dans l'Egypte contemporaine (1968–2006).* Thèse de doctorat. Université de Genève/Université d'Aix-en-Provence.

———. 2009. "Les apparitions de la Vierge en Egypte: un lieu privilégié de la rencontre entre coptes et musulmans?" in *Religions traversées. Lieux saints partagés entre chrétiens, musulmans et juifs en Méditerranée*, eds. D. Albera and M. Couroucli. Arles: Actes Sud, 255–94.

Lambropoulos, Vassilis. 2001. "Syncretism as Mixture and as Method." *Journal of Modern Greek Studies* 19(2): 221–35.

Meinardus, Otto. 1986. *The Holy Family in Egypt.* Cairo: The American University in Cairo Press.

———. 2002. *Coptic Saints and Pilgrimages.* Cairo/New York: The American University in Cairo Press.

Montagu, John. 1799. *A Voyage Round the Mediterranean in the Years 1738 and 1739.* London: Cadell and Davies.

Nasrallah, Joseph. 1971. *Le culte de Marie en Orient. Conférence prononcée au centre des Intellectuels Catholiques Français, à Paris, en 1954.* Paris.

Noun, Fady. 2010. "Béchouate, un sanctuaire marial partagé," in *Figures et lieux de la sainteté en christianisme et en islam*, eds. L. Boisset and G. Homsy-Gottwalles. Beyrouth: Presses de l'Université Saint-Joseph, 205–12.

Régnier-Bohler, Danielle (ed.). 1997. *Croisades et pèlerinages. Récits, chroniques et voyages en Terre Sainte, XIIe-XVIe siècle.* Paris: Robert Laffont.

Stewart, Charles. 1999. "Syncretism and Its Synonyms: Reflections on Cultural Mixture," *Diacritics* 29(3): 40–62.

Suriano, Francesco. 1949. *Treatise on the Holy Land.* Translated from the Italian by Fr. Theophilus Bellorini O.F.M. and Fr. Eugene Hoade O.F.M., with a Preface and Notes by Fr. Bellarmino Bagatti O.F.M. Jerusalem: Franciscan Press.

Turner, Victor. 1974. *Dramas, Fields, and Metaphors: Symbolic Action in Human Society.* Ithaca and London: Cornell University Press.

Valensi, Lucette. 2002. *La fuite en Égypte. Histoires d'Orient et d'Occident. Essai d'histoire comparée.* Paris: Éditions du Seuil.

Van Ghistele, Joos. 1976. *Voyage en Egypte de Joos Van Ghistele, 1482–1483.* Traduction, introduction et notes de Renée Bauwens-Préaux, Le Caire, IFAO.

Villamont, Jacques de. 1600. *Les voyages du seigneur de Villamont...* Paris: C. de Montreuil et J. Richer.

Voile, Brigitte. 2004. *Les coptes d'Egypte sous Nasser. Sainteté, miracles, apparitions.* Paris: CNRS Editions.

Zanetti, Ugo. 1993. "Matarieh, la sainte famille et les baumiers." *Analecta Bollandiana* 111: 21–68.

Chapter 2

EVERYBODY'S BABA: MAKING SPACE FOR THE OTHER

Anna Bigelow

Shared sacred sites are often treated in both the media and scholarship as flashpoints for conflict, ticking time bombs, and places of antagonistic contestation between religions. Although such cases certainly exist and have a profound effect on interreligious relations, it is important to recognize that many, many shared sites allow and even promote prosocial encounters. The conflicts that do occur at places like Ayodhya in India, or Dome of the Rock on the Temple Mount in Jerusalem, serve to remind us of the symbolic power of shared sites—but the reality of conflict is not the whole story. At sacred sites humans communicate most directly with their sense of ultimate reality, and at these sites the transcendent power of the ultimate becomes manifest and accessible. Controlling these sites demonstrates and validates both worldly and spiritual authority. Thus, as Roger Friedland and Richard Hecht have argued, disputes over sacred space are also necessarily struggles over the choreography of daily life (Friedland and Hecht 1998: 101). In this chapter an examination of effective interactive choreography at three shared sites will illuminate modes, systems, and strategies of exchange that substantively contribute to, or detract from, the production and perpetuation of peace. In particular, attention will be paid to the ritual, narrative, and administrative arenas of exchange that are produced and grounded in shared sacred sites. The quality of these interactions is a key indicator of the degree of conflict or cooperation at such places, and the ways in which these places affect the communities in which each shrine is situated. All of the sites in this study are located in Punjab, North India, and each is identified to some extent as Muslim, although the clientele and custodians are from various religious backgrounds: one is a *dargah* (tomb shrine of a Sufi saint), another is a shrine memorializing a Sufi saint's presence in the region, and the last is a *maseet* (mosque).

Punjab is an interesting region to explore because it is the region most violently divided during the partition of India and Pakistan in 1947. Hundreds of thousands died and millions were displaced during the migration that accompanied the independence of these two countries from the British Empire. Religious politics have remained volatile in the region, as exemplified by the Sikh nationalist movement which reached a peak in the 1980s and 1990s, accompanied by militant activities that resulted in the deaths of tens of thousands. Although in the 1951 census the Muslim population in Indian Punjab could be seen to have dropped from about 55 percent to below 1 percent, Islamic shrines continue to activate the religious landscape.[1] At these sites Sikh, Hindu, and Muslim pilgrims engage together in a variety of encounters that demonstrate how shared sacred places in many instances express and facilitate the convergence of complex and contradictory beliefs and actions, rather than provide points for disputation and the articulation of oppositional identities.[2] After discussing the challenges of sharing such places, I will examine the three shared shrines, highlighting points of manifest variation between religions, such as disparate modes and methods of worship, and pointing out the potential for ritual conflicts around the timing of events or actual practices. Then I will elucidate how the constituent communities of caretakers, ritual specialists, and devotees choreograph their interactions and express their variant conceptions and claims in order to mitigate possible tension. In each case, the physical spaces, narrative traditions, and administrative regimes are differently configured, but all the sites are engaged by plural communities in such a way as to facilitate the simultaneous presence of multiple and even conflicting beliefs and behaviors.

In South Asia the lines drawn between religions can be lethal. One of the most devastating recent examples took place in the western state of Gujarat in 2002, when a conflagration on a train loaded with Hindu pilgrims ignited a systematic anti-Muslim pogrom resulting in hundreds of deaths and over 125,000 refugees. Indeed, in 2003 and 2004 the US Commission on International Religious Freedom (USCIRF), an agency of the US State Department, listed India as a "Country of Particular Concern" (*Annual Report* 2003). In 2004 the USCIRF wrote, "despite India's democratic traditions, religious minorities in India have periodically been subject to severe violence, including mass killings," and further noted, "those responsible for the violence are rarely ever held to account" (*Annual Report* 2004). The report implicates the Hindu nationalist BJP (Bharatiya Janata Party) government, which has ruled in Gujarat from 1999 to the present. The BJP also ruled at the national level from 1999 to 2004, but lost power after the promised economic development did not reach most people. However, in Gujarat, in spite of the riots in 2002, the BJP has been re-elected twice, most recently in December 2007. The USCIRF report noted that in India, "an increase in such violence has coincided with the rise in political influence of groups associated with the Sangh Parivar."[3] The empowerment of the Hindu nationalist BJP and its affiliated organizations (called the Sangh Parivar) has resulted in a growing "climate of immunity for the perpetrators of attacks on minorities" (USCIRF 2004). In this climate of fear, amid clear evidence that pogroms against Muslims will not only go unpunished but also provide substantial electoral gains, the nature of daily interactions between Hindus, Muslims, Sikhs and others throughout India becomes a matter of urgent concern. The foot soldiers of Hindu nationalism frequently target sacred sites of Muslims and Christians, regarding these communities as fundamentally alien to Indian culture.[4] The Hindu nationalist ideology of *hindutva* (Hinduness), to which the BJP and its allies adhere, equates "being Indian" with "being Hindu." As put by V.D. Savarkar, one of the chief ideologues of *hindutva*,

> These are the essentials of Hindutva—a common nation (*rashtra*), a common race (*jati*), and a common civilization (*sanskriti*). All these essentials could best be summed up by stating in brief that he is a Hindu to whom Sindhusthan [India] is not only a [Fatherland] but also a [Holy Land]. For the first two essentials of Hindutva—nation and *jati*—are clearly denoted and connoted by the word *pitrabhumi* [Fatherland] while the third essential of civilization is pre-eminently implied by the word *punyabhumi* [Holy Land]. (Savarkar [1923] 1969: 116)

In this sense, *hindutva* indicates a profoundly Indian cultural and territorial identity that excludes from national membership those whose holy lands are outside the borders of India. Since Muslims and Christians identify with religions that are not only associated with former imperial powers but also have their roots and holiest places in the Middle East, they are seen as suspect and only partially loyal to the fatherland of India.

However, there are countless Muslim holy places in India that sacralize the landscape and integrate Islam into the fabric of Indian social life. Mosques, tomb shrines, and other places associated with Sufi saints are all evidence that India is also a Muslim holy land. Indeed some shrines are so significant that some Muslims declare that a pilgrimage to them can substitute for the hajj to Mecca if one cannot afford the longer journey. Significantly, these profoundly Islamic sites are often revered by non-Muslim Indians as well. The uneventful daily reality of coexistence and interaction at shared sites belies religious chauvinism within all the traditions whose adherents collectively acknowledge the sacred power of the places. Given India and Punjab's experiences of religious tension and conflict, it is all the more important to understand how such sites function within communities to establish positive community relations and stable civil societies.

In addition to the transactions between the mundane and the divine occurring at shared sacred sites, such places also mediate transactions between multiple actors and divine agencies through a diverse repertoire of rituals, narratives, and authoritative schemes. In some cases this multiplicity and simultaneity occurs uneventfully. Other situations require highly elaborate systems, such as the time-share arrangement at the Holy Sepulcher and the Church of the Nativity (Hecht 1994)—or even regulatory personnel, such as police or military. However, as the phenomenologist of space, Edward Casey, asserts, one of the unique qualities of place is its ability to incorporate without conflict the most diverse elements constituting its being. He writes: "there is a peculiar power to place and its ability to contain multiple meanings, diverse intentions, contradictory interactions. Surpassing the capacity of humans to sustain such a gathering, place permits a simultaneity and a filtering of experience, history, imagination, action" (Casey 1996: 26). The multiplicity itself, the suspended tensions of contradictory beliefs and practices, and the gathering power of spatial and narrative symbols constitute, in part, the significance of shared sacred sites. In other words, by physically and discursively connecting people and their practices at a single site, by gathering and then maintaining that gathering, place is animated, enlivened and made meaningful.

This view is not without its critics. In a provocative article entitled "Antagonistic Tolerance," Robert Hayden disavows the possibility of non-contentious sharing of sacred space. In his view, sites that scholars portray as uncontested are in fact exemplary of a "negative definition of tolerance as passive noninterference" (Hayden 2002: 206). For Hayden, depictions of "uncontested" or peaceful shrines require a false erasure of time from the theoretical analysis that obscures a socially enforced political stasis. Synthesis of traditions, he writes, is a "temporal manifestation of relations between social groups, which continue to differentiate themselves from each other" (Hayden 2002: 207). It is, indeed, inaccurate to claim that shared sites are perpetually devoid of competition or the possibility of antagonism. However, given the situation on the ground at many shared sites, Hayden overstates his case by asserting that the competitive sharing of sacred space is inherently antagonistic.[5] Competition at shared sites may be episodic and contextual. For example, the ownership of a site may be clear, but ritual authority less so, as in the case of the tomb of Haider Shaykh in Punjab that will be discussed below. There the hereditary caretakers, *khalifah*s, are descended from the saint and oversee an entirely different complex of rituals than those mediated by the *chelas*— individuals possessed by the saint's spirit. This example is one of many in which even a site with multiple owners and ritual authorities is neither inevitably antagonistic nor harmonious. Clearly, we must examine specific situations of sharing to determine patterns of conflict and cooperation. Conditions facilitating non-conflictual sharing may be unusual, as Ron Hassner argues, but such sharing is not impossible and depends in no small part upon the active roles of religious leaders, constituent communities, and political authorities in facilitating the process (Hassner 2002: 11).

In India, shared sacred sites frequently thwart spatial and iconographic categorization. Indeed in some cases, attendees of these shrines indicate how misguided notions of fixed religious identity may be, by not identifying themselves with an institutional religion, that is "Hinduism" or "Islam." While Joyce Flueckiger, in her study of a Muslim healer in Hyderabad India, points out that "differences between Hindus and Muslims matter very much" in relation to some issues or concerns (marriage, employment, admissions, elections), in certain situations, such as in the healing room she describes, "these differences are overridden by what is shared" (Flueckiger 2006: 168–69). Flueckiger's study further demonstrates that it is not merely the need for healing that is shared, but also the "ritual grammar" that bespeaks efficacy.

The rejection of sectarian religious identity within the confines or environs of a shared sanctuary does not mean that religious identity has no significance. Religious identities *do* matter to people and understanding how, when, and why is essential to our understanding of the broader phenomenon of interreligious relations

(Gilmartin and Lawrence 2000; Brass 2000; Hasan 1994 and 1998; Robinson 2000). This is particularly important in relation to minority religious groups who must situate themselves between national- and local-level identity discourses. The national requires minority populations to project a defensive image emphasizing their non-threatening, pacific identity, while the local demands that interreligious friction be suppressed and denied to maintain the dominant ethic of harmony. The shared space of *dargahs* and other Muslim shrines provides an ideal stage upon which to perform this ethic of harmony and promote a collective identity rejecting communalism. This enables minority Muslims to demonstrate their integration into the secular Indian polity and proactively counter the criticism that they are somehow less Indian than others. Shared sites provide *loci* for actors to publicly reject sectarianism, communalism, and the religious orthodoxies that criticize shared practices. India was founded as a secular country, and its constitution guarantees significant rights of religious autonomy and self-determination without establishing any one faith as the religion of the state. Hindu politicians from secular national or regionally based parties court the minority vote, whether Muslim, Sikh, Christian, or other, and are often dependent upon these constituencies to secure election against the communally based parties like the BJP. Politically speaking, therefore, secularism is an ideology of enlightened self-interest in some circumstances. Socially speaking, in mixed communities there is social capital to be gained by being known as a secular person who can be trusted to arbitrate disputes fairly, give equal treatment to customers, clients, and employees, and associate openly and universally with people of all religions. Shared sacred sites are ideal stages upon which to demonstrate one's secular credentials.

The public performance of secular sentiment and shared pietistic practice is observable at the three shared sacred sites under examination. First, located in Malerkotla, is the *dargah*, or tomb shrine, of Haider Shaykh, a fifteenth-century Sufi saint.[6] The cult of Haider Shaykh draws devotees from all over Punjab and its diaspora. Since the Partition of India and Pakistan in 1947 and the exodus of most Muslims from the region, these pilgrims are mostly Sikhs and Hindus; but the popularity of the site has only grown in recent years. The second site is a complex of shrines sacred to Baba Farid Shakarganj in and around the town of Faridkot near the Pakistani border. Baba Farid is one of the most famous South Asian Sufi saints and is said to have passed through this area carrying out a *chilla* or forty-day retreat, and performing several miracles. There are very few Punjabi Muslims in Faridkot, but local Sikhs and Hindus maintain their connection to the saint through several narrative strategies, as does the growing population of non-Punjabi Muslims. The third shrine is a mosque in Sri Hargobindpur, widely believed to have been built by the sixth Sikh Guru, Hargobind, for his Muslim followers.[7] In the post-Partition absence of any Muslim population the mosque has been cared for by a group of Nihang Sikhs. As we shall see, their custodial role was challenged recently by some Muslim activists from outside, but efforts to establish an exclusive identity have thus far failed to take root. These are three different types of sacred spaces located in different regions of Indian Punjab, thus making a comparison of their dynamics of sharing particularly illuminating for the purposes of this volume.

Malerkotla: Ritual Integration

The shrine of Shaykh Sadruddin Sadri Jahan, popularly known as Haider Shaykh, is in Malerkotla, the only town in post-Partition Punjab with a Muslim majority. Prior to 1947, Punjab's population had a slight Muslim majority. After Partition, the percentage of Muslims dropped below 1 percent and remains under 2 percent today. However, in Malerkotla the Muslim population actually increased as Muslims in the region fled during the crisis to this former princely state for protection (Copland 2002: 682). In 1948 the princely state was dissolved and became a town, developing into an industrial center in district Sangrur. Today the Muslim population is approximately 70 percent of Malerkotla's 106,000 people, with the remainder mostly Sikhs and Hindus. Malerkotla is famous throughout Punjab, not only for its Muslim population, but also because no one there was killed in interreligious violence during the traumas of Partition. Many locals and visitors believe that it is through the blessings of Haider Shaykh, who is credited with founding the town, that the town remained unscathed. Furthermore, and perhaps unsurprising given the demographics, Sikhs and Hindus in far greater numbers than Muslims attend the festivals for Haider Shaykh, although the Muslim descendants of the saint continue to own and manage the site; and local Muslims attend the shrine, but mostly just on non-festival occasions. However, the non-Muslim clientele is not a new phenomenon at all. For example, the *Maler Kotla State Gazetteer* of 1904 puzzles over the saint's festivals, saying, "it is strange that these fairs are mostly attended by Hindus, though Sadr-ud-Din was a Muhammadan Saint" (*Maler Kotla State Gazetteer* 1904: 44). The multireligious appeal of such places draws from their perceived efficacy, their ecumenical identity, and the non-sectarian ethos that inheres in these shrines.

Haider Shaykh's tomb is a primary marker of local identity and is an important site for religiously based strategies of community building. Local and regional politicians visit the *dargah* as a crucial gesture of respect for the state's only Muslim constituency. Both the descendants of the town's former princes and the caretakers of the tomb shrine are descended from the saint, and they remained influential even after the dissolution of the princely state of Malerkotla in 1948, often serving as elected representatives to local and state office. Pilgrims from all over the world come to the tomb to make and fulfill vows, pay homage, honor family traditions, and experience the multicultural *communitas* that characterizes saints' shrines throughout the subcontinent. In this way, the shrine sustains and is sustained by other local centers of power—the government, the home, the neighborhood. Temporal authorities must attend the saint and devotees must enter a public sphere of exchange where interreligious interaction is likely, if not inevitable. Although the possibility of interreligious encounters could be minimized through careful timing,

Figure 2.1. Sikh visitors to the Sufi saint's tomb. Photo A. Bigelow.

the shrine is universally celebrated for its plural appeal. The saint *is* the past of the town, and one's presence there acknowledges that debt and entails encounter between self and other through the mediating presence of the saint, the space, and the multivocal interlocutors of the saint's spirit and traditions. Exchanges occur at the *dargah* not only between visitors and the dead saint, but also between the pilgrims and the caretakers who may belong to other religious traditions.

In order to sustain multiple practices and perceptions, the ritual life of the shrine exceeds a single religious idiom. Indeed, many rituals enacted at the shrine—such as prostration, circumambulation, distribution of *tabarruk* or *prasad* (items or food blessed by contact with the tomb), occasional *qawwals* (devotional music), possession, and offerings—are not exclusive to one religion or another.[8] Rather, these ritual performances defy communal limitations and involve a range of localizing practices that situate Haider Shaykh and his devotees within a self-identifying community of faith and practice.[9]

These site-based ritual performances give rise to potential conflict over the appropriate form of ritual action at the shrine. One of several possible points of contestation is the fact that the status of the saintly dead is understood quite differently within each religion. Many Hindu and Sikh devotees express their understandings by asserting that the saint is, in fact, God. Time and again Sikhs and Hindus at the tomb of Haider Shaykh informed me *"voh hamare bhagwan hai"* (he is our god). Such declarations are antithetical to the Muslim perspective in which the unity and singularity of Allah is unassailable. Muslim constituents are aware of these different beliefs, and the Muslim *khalifahs*, who are the caretakers of the *dargah* and descendents of the saint, facilitate the ritual devotions of Hindus and Sikhs in full consciousness of these conflicting ideas about the nature of the saint. For example, the ritual life of the tomb includes many *chelas*, people who profess to be possessed by the spirit of Haider Shaykh, who come with large retinues of followers who believe the *chelas* will transmit to them the blessings and the advice of the saint. Rather than monopolizing the devotional energies of their entourages, the *chelas* often refer their disciples to the tomb itself and direct them to seek the mediating power of the *khalifahs* to secure their blessings, an encounter that may also include financial offerings. In a less materialistic example of making space for the other, a *khalifah* and *chela* discussed their theological differences and concluded that their contrasting notions were in fact part of God's plan. Agreeing upon the divine origin of humanity, the variety of humans is likewise seen as God's will and therefore the variant perspectives and practices must also be sanctioned.

Another potential source of conflict is the presence of two categories of ritual specialists mentioned above. First there are the *khalifahs*, descendants of Haider Shaykh who sit at the tomb, collect offerings, return *tabarruk*, and provide blessings to the faithful. Occasionally they provide spiritual guidance, but largely their role is to facilitate temporally limited devotions at the shrine. Although some pilgrims have long-standing relations with the *khalifahs*, by far the majority only encounter them long enough to touch their feet or knees, or simply to bow in their direction. However, as descendants of the saint they bear his blood, and therefore also his *baraka*. Thus physical contact with a *khalifah* is regarded as an essential element of ritual efficacy by many of those in attendance, especially non-Muslims. In addition to the saint's descendants, the saint's *baraka* is made present through the bodies of certain devotees who are possessed by his spirit. These individuals, often called *chela* (a sanskritic term for disciple), are overwhelmingly Sikh and Hindu.[10] The Sikh and Hindu *chelas* come to the shrine for festivals, and occasionally on Thursday nights, along with groups of followers ranging from a few to a few hundred. In addition to paying respects at the *dargah* and receiving blessings from the *khalifahs*, the *chelas* and their entourages set up satellite ritual spaces, called *chaunki*, in which the spirit of Haider Shaykh is invoked into the body of the *chela* through whom his spiritual, personal, medical, and psychological healing powers are made available to the gathering. Although these supplementary spaces could potentially provoke clashes between the Muslim owner/caretaker *khalifahs* and the Sikh and Hindu itinerant *chelas*, this does not occur. One might expect the *khalifahs* to ban or exile the *chelas* from the *dargah*'s environs in that they are the undisputed owners of the site. That they do not do this is significant, as Ron Hassner claims that it is the 'lack' of an absolute monopoly on hierocratic religious authority that is a key factor in producing conflict over sacred space by opening space for competition (Hassner 2002: 21–22). In this instance, however, the lack does not give rise to competition or antagonistic contestation. Rather, the two ritual systems exist side by side, with many devotees transacting without inhibitions between them. Indeed, the fact that *khalifahs* and *chelas* perceive an economic symbiosis in their cooperation is an important factor in their continued coexistence. But these relations go beyond mutual self-interest as both parties often seek ways to validate each other, even though they may not participate in, support, or agree with one another's perspectives or ritual practices.

This validation is vividly illustrated by a conversation between a *khalifah* (who does not sit at the tomb) and a Hindu *chela*, during which the subject of apparent contradictions between Hindu and Muslim rituals and beliefs arose. The *khalifah* described a spiritual encounter in which Haider Shaykh manifested himself to him and his teacher, summoning them to a conversation in an empty building. During this vision of Haider Shaykh, the *khalifah* took the opportunity to pose the question of difference and how it should be managed and understood. He asked the saint,

> "Hazrat, people come here, they come for a wish. They come for a boy child, some say our business is not going well. But it is written in our book that whatever you ask, ask it from God. But thousands of people come and ask from you. So what is the order for us, and what are the orders for them?" And so he [i.e. Haider Shaykh] responded, "This is the secret of God," he said. "Let them do their work and you do yours." He didn't say you are right or they are right, he said these are the secrets of God. I asked what are those secrets and he said that only God knows.

By leaving judgment over these contradictory practices and conceptions up to God, the *khalifah* is able to establish his own authority and simultaneously legitimate the beliefs and practices of the Hindu devotee. Furthermore, the *khalifah* asserted his credentials as an orthodox Muslim by prefacing his account saying that the interview occurred when he had just returned from the hajj. Finally, he concludes his narrative with Haider Shaykh's declamation "Let them do their work and you do yours." This assertion evokes the 109th Surat al-Kafirun of the Qur'an, which ends "to you be your religion, and to me, mine." Thus, by directly addressing the difference between Muslim, Hindu, and Sikh ritual practices, the *khalifah* receives a carefully worded reply reminding the audience that Allah alone knows best why he created people to believe and act in a variety of ways.

For his part, the Hindu *chela* acknowledged that the *khalifah*, as a descendant of the saint, was able to meet the saint personally, while he and those with him had to negotiate a different sort of relationship with Haider Shaykh. This relationship includes rules for behavior that do not apply to Muslims. For example, Hindu and Sikh devotees are often instructed by Haider Shaykh during *chaunkis* to abjure the consumption of meat. Yet the Muslim descendants do eat meat, which is regarded by these non-Muslim followers as a special dispensation for them. Such encounters demonstrate that interactions at the *dargah* are capable of actually facilitating ritual and theological variance rather than contesting or prohibiting it. This demonstrates also that given conditions of support from both groups of religious authorities, the potentially divisive factor of a multivocal religious tradition is neutralized by the leaders and validated by the constituency.

Baba Farid Shakarganj: Narrative Exchange

Shared sacred sites are engaged narratively as well as ritually. Owners, patrons, caretakers, and pilgrims imagine and articulate a site's identity through the body of oral and written lore about a shrine. Multiconfessional sites require a degree of multivocality, enabling fluid interactions and thwarting the aggressive articulation of oppositional identities. In Faridkot, near the Pakistan border, there are two shrines sacred to the thirteenth century Sufi saint Baba Farid Shakarganj (d.1265). He is not only one of the most influential saints of the powerful South Asian Chishti lineage, but is also beloved by Sikhs who include poetic compositions attributed to him in the holy book of the Sikhs, the Guru Granth Sahib. In Faridkot, Baba Farid is narratively appropriated and incorporated into the landscape, personal lives, and oral traditions of the largely Sikh population through stories of the origins of the shrines, accounts of miracles past and present, and the strategic performance of poetic works attributed to the saint.

Every resident and devotee I encountered at the shrines dedicated to Baba Farid knew the story of the saint's connection with the area. After performing a solitary *chilla*, or forty-day meditative retreat, Baba Farid was pressed into labor there by soldiers of the local Hindu ruler to help build a new fort. But rather than struggling under the burden of bearing bricks, Farid made his basket float in the air above his head, apparently weightless. The ruler, recognizing him as a holy man, begged forgiveness for showing the saint disrespect, and renamed his domain Faridkot. Today there are two shrines in the area. First is a shrine called Tilla Baba Farid, consisting of three structures—a relic shrine, a *gurdwara* (house of the guru), and a mosque—providing ritual spaces for all Baba Farid's devotees. These sites memorialize the saint's encounter with a Hindu king who became his devotee but did not convert. This encounter set a local precedent for non-Muslims who can now participate in the worship of a Muslim holy man without abandoning their own religious identities.[11] The other site is a Sikh temple, *gurdwara*, called Godhri Sahib Gurdwara just outside of town at a site believed to be the place where Baba Farid performed his meditational *chilla*.

The small Muslim community in Faridkot is mostly non-Punjabi, but they also take great pride in their connection to the famous saint. The current imam of the Baba Farid mosque next door to Tilla Baba Farid is from Uttar Pradesh and does not frequent the neighboring shrine, nor does he encourage Muslims to do so. In fact, he actively discourages Muslims from making offerings at the shrine, pointing out that it is not a tomb and therefore not, in his view, appropriate to worship Baba Farid in that place. Still, the imam does revere Baba Farid and invokes blessings upon him, "*rehmat Allah alayhi*" (mercy of God be upon him), whenever he mentions his name. He does not oppose Sikh or Hindu patronage of Tilla Baba Farid and has congenial relations with the Tilla management. The brother of the mosque's imam expresses the special bond between the Muslim community and Baba Farid saying, we also fully love Baba Farid's place [the Tilla], we respect it, but in our religion, to prostrate before any photo or idol is banned. This is because you can prostrate only before God who made this world. That is why we believe in Baba Farid completely with a full heart. He was our *wali* [saint], a *buzurg* [pious elder], he has shown us good ways.

Here Baba Farid's Muslim identity is emphasized—he is 'our *wali*'—and the distinctions between Muslim and non-Muslim worship are clearly drawn. The imam himself also highlights the reality of difference between these communities, and asserts the importance of holding fast to one's own faith, no matter what that faith might be. He says "any religion, Hindu, Muslim, Sikh, Christian, in whichever religion one is, one should hold it properly. Hold the rope of one religion tightly; do not try to hold the ropes of other religions. You should sail in one boat, if you sail in two boats you will sink." However, although the imam advocates singular religious affiliation, he also frequently provides counsel and produces healing amulets called *tawiz* for a largely non-Muslim clientele. So even if difference is articulated, potential conflict is obviated, at least in part, through ritual exchange. Thus his symbolic authority as the local Muslim leader, with perhaps a natural affinity for or even a privileged relationship with Baba Farid, is established and the site is validated as a Muslim space with a multiconfessional clientele.[12]

However, the tacit, though peaceful competition over the significance of Baba Farid is evident in the non-Punjabi Muslim population's efforts to celebrate the Punjabi saint's legacy in spite of their small number and status as outsiders to the region. For example, the local Muslims contribute their energies to the annual festival marking Baba Farid's arrival in the area, which is mostly organized and sponsored by the non-Muslim majority in Faridkot. In addition, a local group called the Muslim Welfare Society, composed of Muslims, Sikhs, and Hindus, sponsored a Vishal Dharmik Samaroh (religious gathering) at which several well-known Muslim preachers gave speeches on the importance of true religion as something internally realized and universal, rather than dependent on a particular faith. This gathering was comparatively small, with perhaps one hundred in attendance, while thousands swarmed the Tilla and attended the *kirtan darbar* (musical gathering). Nonetheless the activities geared towards the Muslim population not only gave the Muslim minority an opportunity to take center stage, but also gave the whole proceedings additional legitimacy as an event celebrated by Baba Farid's co-religionists as well as non-Muslim devotees. For similar reasons the main organizers of the festival take care to invite a group of Muslim *qawwals* (singers of Sufi devotional music) from Delhi to perform Baba Farid's *kalam* (spiritual compositions) at a *kirtan darbar*.

The *baraka* of Baba Farid's presence is also associated with the Godri Sahib Gurdwara, about five kilometers from the Tilla Baba Farid. At this site, almost exclusively visited by Sikhs, Baba Farid's retreat is rendered into a Sikh religious idiom narratively, ritually, and practically. This is evidenced by the words of an elderly male Sikh devotee who explained the power of the site thus:

> This is a place where Baba did *bhagati* [worship] and this place gathered powers. This place has special importance, so whenever somebody comes here and bows and touches their forehead here, some power comes in us, if we are ill we get well, if we are unhappy we will get happiness, that is one becomes healthy. When for the first time someone comes here with *sharda* [faith] he gets blessed.

Hindus and Sikhs employ non-Islamic terms of reference for the Muslim saint's activities (i.e., *bhagati* instead of *chilla*, *khalwa*, or *murakaba*; and *sharda* instead of *iman*). In other interviews, Baba Farid's *murshid* (spiritual guide), Khwaja Qutb ud-Din Bakhtiyar Kaki, is referred to as his *guru*. At this site there is now a *gurdwara* and a shrine with a tree to which devotees attach *godris*, or small cushions for sitting such as the one on which the saint would have meditated. Here there is an interesting ritual acknowledgment of Baba Farid's piety, in that rather than performing meditative retreats, the Sikh and Hindu devotees offer forty days of *seva*, or service, at the *gurdwara*. This is an example of non-Muslims reworking a Muslim practice in their own religious terms, replacing *murakaba* with *seva*, but still making a ritual link with the seven-hundred-year-old saint. The Sikh religion advocates discipline, but not asceticism, and fasting is generally rejected as being disrespectful to the body. These features demonstrate a narrative as well as ritual appropriation of Baba Farid, effectively incorporating him into a non-Muslim idiom.

Baba Farid's continuing presence in Indian Punjab is most deeply and pervasively manifest through the frequent deployment of verses attributed to him from the Guru Granth Sahib. Although there have been debates among scholars concerning the authorship of these Punjabi verses, recent work by Christopher Shackle argues that Farid was the author, and they are popularly seen as unquestionably Farid's. (Shackle 2009)[13] Furthermore, many people believe them to be the very first compositions in the Punjabi language. Most Sikhs know portions of the Guru Granth Sahib by heart, and many of those in attendance were able to recite upon request. The verses of Baba Farid most often volunteered by Sikh devotees are several that emphasize the importance of forgiving those who strike you, resisting anger, and avoiding provocative and insulting speech. Among these, two of the most commonly cited compositions are the following:

> Farid, if you are wise, then do not write evil against others
> Look into your own heart instead

> Farid, do not turn and strike those who strike you
> Kiss their feet, and return to your own home.

Many times these two passages, and others, were recited to me unsolicited, merely as conversational examples of the essence of Baba Farid's teachings and his philosophy of life. The popularity of such verses is generally ascribed to their sentiment as they express a conciliatory, forbearing, and magnanimous ideal of behavior. The recitation and repetition of poetic compositions attributed to Baba Farid ground the saint's sentiments of forbearance, tolerance, and forgiveness in the earth at his shrines in Faridkot. By narratively establishing a privileged relationship with the holy man, the Sikh and Muslim community in Faridkot creates space for specificity of belief, while maintaining the multivocality of the traditions associated with the saint and his shrines.

Historical studies of shared narrative traditions, such as Tony Stewart's examination of the rich body of literature on the Hindu-Muslim traditions of Satya Pir in Bengal (Stewart 2001), suggest that these stories may provide indices of the quality and depth of interreligious exchange. Furthermore, studying change in such traditions over time may provide crucial early warning signals of heightened communal tension in the gradual or abrupt erasure of Muslim, Sikh and/or Hindu elements from an active repertoire. These ritual and narrative arenas of exchange are almost entirely neglected by social scientists and policy analysts seeking to understand religious conflict. However, it is clear that these cases demonstrate the possibility of deep conceptual links between religious groups, observable in integrated spiritual and ritual vocabularies. The interactive choreography facilitating the simultaneous presence of difference may also enable the trust building conducive to peaceful communities.

Sri Hargobindpur: Administrative Cooperation

In the final case, the administration of a mosque shrine is shared by multiple religions. In Sri Hargobindpur, District Gurdaspur, Punjab there is a seventeenth-century mosque known as the Guru ki Maseet, or Guru's mosque, which is cared for by a group of Sikhs. According to popular tradition, the sixth Sikh Guru, Hargobind, after defeating a Mughal army in battle, insisted on building not only a *gurdwara* but also temples and a mosque so that all the residents of the region would have places to worship.[14] This firmly established the Sikh leader as a patron and benefactor of the Muslim minority community. Sikh proprietary claims remain in force even today as, since Partition, there has been no Muslim population in this small town of just under four thousand; no Muslim worship has taken place in the mosque for over fifty years.[15] Although Muslim religious sites and endowments abandoned in 1947 nominally became property of the Waqf Board, in reality many Muslim properties became temples, houses, shops, and even barns. In Sri Hargobindpur the Guru ki Maseet was not wholly neglected, even though it was inactive as a mosque and declining in condition. A local band of Nihang Sikhs, the antinomian sect who style themselves the Guru's army, took over the site in the 1980s.[16] A Nihang caretaker erected a small building at the side of the mosque and resided there, doing his *seva*, or service to the Guru, caring for the mosque, placing the Guru Granth Sahib in the mosque, and erecting a Sikh flag outside. As these are standard markers of Sikh sacred space, the building's identity as a *maseet* (mosque) became questionable.

In 1997, a survey team with an non-sectarian architectural restoration group called Cultural Resource Conservation Initiative (CRCI) came to Sri Hargobindpur, saw the *maseet*, heard the story of its construction, and undertook its restoration.

In conjunction with the conservation of the mosque, the CRCI worked to re-establish links between the site, the idealized event it represents, and the citizens of the town by hiring and training locals in the work, running programs in the schools, and initiating other development projects. Through this process the ostensibly Muslim space, in a majority Sikh and Hindu town, appropriated by antinomian Nihang Sikhs, began to embody meanings both old and new for the residents of Sri Hargobindpur. Local residents organized a *seva* with a *langar* (communal kitchen) that brought people from the entire region to work on the *maseet*. These activities served to incorporate the site into local religious life, as *seva* and *langar* are two of the principal expressions of devotion and affirmation of community in the Sikh tradition.

However the process was not wholly smooth. Publicity about the site brought a challenge to the process of restoration and to the Nihangs' role as caretakers. A leading Muslim activist and former MP, Syed Shihabuddin, who has been instrumental in the Babri Masjid Action Committee and legal efforts to restore the mosque at Ayodhya, heard about the Guru ki Maseet from newspaper accounts and raised objections. Dismayed by what appeared to be yet another case of non-Muslims usurping Muslim property in a place where few Muslims lived and could defend their legal ownership, Shihabuddin lodged a complaint with the United Nations Committee on Human Rights (UNCHR) and alerted the Waqf Council. Waqf representatives visited the site and the police were called to take statements from CRCI and locals about the mosque's history and status. The situation became tense, and the site that had begun to be heralded in the press as evidence of India's rich, plural culture was in danger of becoming another example of politicized religion and contestation, not unlike Ayodhya. Yet this did not happen.

Instead, measures were taken to preserve the identity of the site and maintain its cohesive nature over and against efforts to manipulate, appropriate, or politicize its public meaning. A new space was built and the Guru Granth Sahib was moved out of the *maseet*. Various officials visited the *maseet* to observe the status of the site. In February 2001 the Secretary of the Central Waqf Council and the head of the Nihang group met in order to determine the future management of the Guru ki Maseet. At one point during the meeting the octogenarian Nihang leader declared, "Nobody can damage this *maseet*. We will protect it like it was a *gurdwara*. This *maseet* was established by our Guru. If anyone tries to damage it, we will kill him." These efforts to find common ground resulted in a Memorandum of Understanding, establishing terms of joint management of the mosque. Under the agreement, the Nihangs continue the daily upkeep of the shrine and the Waqf reserves all proprietary rights. The multiple identities and plural appeal of the site are acknowledged in the memorandum itself, which opens by declaring that Guru Hargobind "conceptualized this Maseet as a symbol of peace and unity between the Sikhs, Muslims and the Hindus." Finally, on 23 April of this year, *namaz* (prayer) was performed in the mosque for the first time since 1947. This event was widely reported in India's Muslim press as a much-needed gesture of goodwill and harmony during the dark days following anti-Muslim pogroms, which took place in Gujarat two months earlier. In the *Islamic Voice* Andalib Akhtar wrote, "at a time when the nation is at the crossroads of communal hatred and disbelief, the Sikhs of this small village … have set a unique example of love, brotherhood and communal harmony. They quietly handed over 'Guru ki Maseet', a historical Masjid built by the sixth Sikh Guru Hargovind in the early 17th century, to the Muslims" (Akhtar 2002).

Due to the history of the site and the process of its restoration, the Guru ki Maseet is sacred to multiple religions. Interestingly, in this case, it was possible for the mosque to be integrated into the community and to take on multiple meanings for the various constituents only after all parties acknowledged the single identity of the site as a mosque. Successful negotiation was possible in part because, although the interests and intentions of the parties involved were divergent in some areas, the overall will of the decision makers and the community was to promote understanding and effect a resolution. This challenges Hayden's assertion that representations of shared religious sites as non-conflictual is a function of the analyst's failure to historicize the shrine. Here we see a historical process in which competition is managed and conflict averted. Through the struggles over the Guru ki Maseet's administration, the place was 'made' a kind of secular monument, the very existence of which contests religious divisions and represents an ideal of peaceful exchange, both in the past and the present. Significantly this did not occur through an uncontested, spontaneous, or unconscious acknowledgment of the site's identity. Rather this came about through dialogue and a series of compromises and strategic efforts by the interested parties, giving everyone a stake in the success of the restoration, maintenance, and ongoing significance of the Guru ki Maseet.[17]

Conclusion

Having surveyed three different dimensions of interreligious relations at three different shared sacred sites in Punjab, India, it is important to recall that situations of peaceful exchange are not exclusive to Punjab or to India. In his study of sites shared by Muslims and Christians in Palestine, Glenn Bowman described those shrines as "semantically multivocal" (Bowman 1993: 431). Semantic multivocality allows multiple users to maintain relations with a site that is central to their local and/or religious identity without over-determining the site and rendering it fixed and unavailable to contradictory uses and interpretations. In Bowman's study in Palestine, as in my study in Punjab, the openness of a shrine is deliberately maintained through actions and interactions among the constituents that are intended to allow for a lack of uniformity of belief and practice. Indeed, the communities in which such places are situated often value shared sites precisely for their quality of openness. As Bowman put it, "while the miraculous power seen to be resident there served as a general pretext for the gathering of local persons of Muslim and various Christian persuasions, the specific reasons people gave for attending ranged from the need for cures through the demands of religion, to the pleasures of conviviality" (Bowman 2002: 220). Thus a common primary motivator for allegiance to the shrine, its miraculous power, facilitates and perhaps even draws from another powerful factor in the site's appeal: its multireligious constituency. Furthermore, part of the appeal for the Muslim and Christian groups under Israeli rule was the opportunity to experience and demonstrate solidarity against the Israeli regime (Bowman 1993: 442–48). At least within the confines of the shrines, normally disempowered minorities exercise a degree of autonomy. United in their resistance to Israeli authority, the symbolic value of public exchange at the shrines demonstrates an unforeseen power of the usually divisive religious politics in Israel-Palestine to intensify the bonds between the disempowered.

Ritual, narrative, and administrative dimensions of these three sacred sites in Punjab demonstrate how shared shrines are able to promote, and even generate, a dynamic of interreligious engagement deliberately designed to support cooperation and discourage discord. In particular, these shared shrines illuminate the ways in which the relations between Hindus, Sikhs, and Muslims are negotiated on a daily basis through symbolic zones of exchange. At these sites, non-Muslims and Muslims alike engage Islamic space ritually and discursively, deriving spiritual and political benefit from the interreligious experience. In the case of Haider Shaykh, ritual conflicts are circumvented through dialogue and mutual validation. At Faridkot, stories and poetic performances ground the Muslim saint in a Sikh community. And finally, at the Guru ki Maseet, proprietary competition is managed and the claims of each party ultimately affirmed. In each case there is a twofold dynamic, one which particularizes, specifies, and personalizes the saint and the site, and the other which simultaneously generalizes, incorporates, and includes. Contrary to the assumption that shared shrines are inherently conflicted, these places show that, although distinctions between religions are often made, discrepancies are rarely seen as antagonistic or threatening. On the contrary, the multivocality of the shared ritual, narrative, and administrative life of the shrines is not only part of the appeal but is also a source of their effective power. Thus, these shared sacred places serve as powerful resources for community building and the promotion of harmonious civil society. As interactive nodes between individuals, religions, genders, classes, age groups, and so on, the bodily and discursive practices and experiences at the site are opportunities for the public performance of community and individual identities characterized by openness and inclusiveness rather than exclusivity and hostility.

Notes

1. The Muslim population of Punjab remains below 2 percent, according to the 2001 Census of India. Data available for registered users at: http://www.censusindia.gov.in/Census_Data_2001/Census_Data_Online/Social_and_cultural/Religion.aspx?cki=feCEiLeZOMU (accessed 24 October 2009).
2. There are Christians, Jains, and Buddhists in Punjab, but the majority of shrine attendees are Muslim, Hindu, and Sikh.

3. The Sangh Parivar or "Family of the Sangh" refers to the group of Hindu nationalist organizations affiliated with the Rashtriya Swayamsevak Sangh (National Volunteer Corps), which was founded in 1925 to mobilize Hindus to defend and uphold their religion. The political wing is the BJP (Bharatiya Janata Party) and the religious wing is known as the Vishwa Hindu Parishad (VHP). There are numerous other affiliated groups such as the militant outfit of the Bajrang Dal.

4. As recently as Christmas 2007, a number of Christian villages in Orissa were attacked, their churches burned, and their residents terrorized into fleeing.

5. This view is typical of conflict studies scholars, such as Sissela Bok (1990), who view the activation of conflicts as the strategic action of rationally motivated actors taking advantage of perceived opportunities to advance their interests.

6. Shaykh Sadruddin Sadri Jahan is the saint's full name, but he is popularly known as Haider Shaykh.

7. In the period of Guru Hargobind (1595–1644), the Sikh community was still taking shape as a religious entity, and many of the Guru's followers were Muslims and Hindus who did not abandon their religious identities even as they were loyal to the Guru.

8. *Tabarruk* and *prasad* are respectively the Islamic and Hindu terms for the items returned to devotees after being offered at a shrine. Having come into contact with the shrine's sacred precincts the items are regarded as possessing residual power. In the case of Islam, this is *barakat* (spiritual power) that clings to the place of interment of a holy person in the case of saints' tombs, or a point of access to the divine such as the Ka'ba. In the Hindu traditions, *prasad* is understood as the leftovers of the divine being who has gathered the pure and rarefied essence of whatever has been offered. The portion returned to the devotee is seen as *jutha*, or polluted by prior consumption, but is still far purer than something consumed by a human, and thus by receiving *prasad*, the devotee is purified. In both cases, a portion of the items offered are retained at the shrine and a portion returned to the offerer.

9. A term often adopted by devotees is the *pirpanth*, or party of the saint, a designation that draws on the Muslim honorific *pir* and the Hindu word *panth*, meaning group. Thus those in the *pirpanth* do not see their primary religious identity as Hindu, Muslim or Sikh, but as particular to the traditions of the saint's worship.

10. In fact in a year and a half I never witnessed or heard of a Muslim who was "played" by the spirit of the saint at this shrine. A common term for being possessed by the saint is *khelna*, or playing.

11. In addition, the town and shrine have gained a heightened status in post-Partition Punjab, as the actual *dargah*, or tomb shrine, of Baba Farid is in Pakpattan in Pakistan and is therefore inaccessible to most Indian devotees.

12. Another mode of exchange at the shrines to Baba Farid occurs as non-Muslims rework Muslim practices into their own religious terms, such as performing forty days of *seva* (service) instead of a forty-day meditative retreat.

13. Some scholars have argued that the verses are likely the work of Baba Farid's descendant, Shaykh Ibrahim. However, Christopher Shackle points out in a recent paper that a number of contemporary researchers do claim that Shaykh Farid Ganj-e Shakar was in fact the true author, even if some alterations occurred during the various stages of recording and compiling the Granth. See Christopher Shackle, "Punjabi Sufi Poetry from Farid to Farid', paper given at *New Directions in Sikh Studies* conference, UC Santa Barbara, November 14–15, 2009.

14. This is described in Macauliffe's section on Guru Hargobind in *History of the Sikhs*: "He projected the construction of a Sikh temple, but it occurred to him that his Muhammadan troops and laborers would also require a temple for their worship. He therefore constructed with thoughtful impartiality both a temple and a mosque" (Macauliffe [1909] 2000: 119).

15. The population was 3,993 according to the 2001 Census of India.

16. "Nihangs or Nihang Singhs, originally known as Akalis or Akali Nihangs, are endearingly designated the Guru's knights or the Guru's beloved for the military air they bear and the heroic style they continue to cultivate. They constitute a distinct order among the Sikhs and are readily recognized by their dark blue loose apparel and their ample, peaked turbans festooned with quoits, insignia of the Khalsa (define), and rosaries, all made of steel. They are always armed, and

are usually seen mounted heavily laden with weapons such as swords, daggers, spears, rifles, shotguns and pistols" (Nihangs in *The Encyclopaedia of Sikhism*, ed. H. Singh. Retrieved 27 August 2003 from http://thesikhencyclopedia.com).

17. The joint oversight of the Guru ki Maseet by the Waqf Board, the Nihangs, and CRCI displays associational links. These links, according to political scientist Ashutosh Varshney, are instrumental in preserving interreligious peace. Such links were forged between the Nihangs, the Waqf, and the community throughout the negotiations (Varshney 2002).

References

Akhter, Andalib. 2002. "Creating History at Hargovindpur." *Islamic Voice*. www.islamicvoice.com/may.2002/secular.htm, accessed 21 September 2002.

Bok, Sissela. 1990. *Strategies for Peace: Human Values and the Threat of War*. New York: Vintage.

Bowman, Glenn. 2002. "Response to Robert Hayden." *Current Anthropology* 43(2): 219–20.

———. 1993. "Nationalising the Sacred: Shrines and Shifting Identities in the Israeli-Occupied Territories." *Man* 28: 431–60.

Brass, Paul. 2000. "Elite Groups, Symbol Manipulation and Ethnic Identity among the Muslims of South Asia," in *Nationalism: Critical Concepts in Political Science*, eds. J. Hutchison and A. Smith. London: Routledge, 35–43.

Casey, Edward. 1996. "How to Get from Space to Place in a Fairly Short Stretch of Time: Phenomenological Prolegomena," in *Senses of Place*, eds. S. Feld and K. Basso. Santa Fe, NM: School of American Research Press, 13–52.

Copland, Ian. 2002. "The Master and the Maharajas: The Sikh Princes and the East Punjab Massacres of 1947," *Modern Asian Studies* 36(2): 657–704.

Flueckiger, Joyce. 2006. *In Amma's Healing Room: Gender and Vernacular Islam in India*. Bloomington: Indiana University Press.

Friedland, Roger and Richard Hecht. 1998. "The Bodies of Nations: A Comparative Study of Religious Violence in Jerusalem and Ayodhya." *History of Religions* 38(2): 101–49.

Gilmartin, David and Bruce Lawrence, eds. 2000. *Beyond Turk and Hindu: Rethinking Religious Identities in Islamicate South Asia*. Gainesville: University Press of Florida.

Hasan, Mushirul, ed. 1998. *Islam, Communities and the Nation: Muslim Identities in South Asia and Beyond*. Delhi: Manohar.

———. 1994. "Minority Identity and Its Discontents: Ayodhya and Its Aftermath," *South Asia Bulletin* 14(2): 24–40.

Hassner, Ron. 2002. "Understanding and Resolving Disputes over Sacred Space." Stanford Center on Conflict and Negotiation, Working Paper 62.

Hayden, Robert. 2002. "Antagonistic Tolerance: Competitive Sharing of Religious Sites in South Asia and the Balkans." *Current Anthropology* 43(2): 205–31.

Hecht, Richard. 1994. "The Construction and Management of Sacred Time and Space: The *Sabta Nur* at the Church of the Holy Sepulchre," in *Nowhere: Space, Time and Modernity*, eds. R. Friedland and D. Bowen. Berkeley: University of California Press, 181–235.

Macauliffe, Max. (1909) 2000. *The Sikh Religion*. Delhi: Low Price Publications.

Malerkotla State Gazetteer. 1904. Lahore: The Civil and Military Gazette Press.

Robinson, Francis. 2000. *Islam and Muslim History in South Asia.* New Delhi: Oxford University Press.

Savarkar, Vinayat. (1923) 1969. *Hindutva, or Who is a Hindu?* Bombay: Veer Savarkar Prakashan.

Shackle, Christopher (2009). "Punjabi Sufi Poetry from Farid to Farid," paper given at *New Directions in Sikh Studies* conference, UC Santa Barbara, November 14–15.

Stewart, Tony. 2001. "In Search of Equivalence: Conceiving the Muslim-Hindu Encounter through Translation Theory." *History of Religions* 40(3): 260–87.

United States Commission on International Religious Freedom, US Dept. of State. 2003. *Annual Report.* http://www.uscirf.gov/countries/region/south_asia/india/india.html, accessed 20 December 2007.

United States Commission on International Religious Freedom, US Dept. of State. 2004. *Countries of Particular Concern: India.* http://www.uscirf.gov/countries/ countriesconcerns/Countries/India.html, accessed 20 December 2007.

Varshney, Ashutosh. 2002. *Ethnic Conflict and Civic Life: Hindus and Muslims in India.* New Haven: Yale University Press.

Chapter 3

CHTHONIAN SPIRITS AND SHARED SHRINES: THE DYNAMICS OF PLACE AMONG CHRISTIANS AND MUSLIMS IN ANATOLIA

Maria Couroucli

Χιτίρελεζ λέγανε οι Τούρκοι. Αι Γιώργη λέγαμε εμείς.
The Turks said Hitirellez, we said Saint George[1]

The coexistence of Christian and Muslim "visitors" or "pilgrims" to holy sites is a very old feature of the Balkan and Anatolian landscape; travelers and ethnographers have observed mixed religious practices since the early twentieth century. These belong to many local traditions, some going back to the time of the Ottoman conquest and others even to late Byzantine times (Hasluck 1929; Shankland 2004; Zegginis [1996] 2001: Foss 2002). The Balkans and Anatolia are lands where Islam and Christianity have met and coexisted, more or less peacefully, for more than a millennium, and many aspects of local customs echo different types of relations between religious communities (including conversions, business associations, and intermarriages). Not surprisingly, the frontier hero, often descending from two "races" (two genealogically distinct groups and, by extension, two separate "peoples"), has been a major figure in the epic poetry of the literary traditions of the Eastern Mediterranean and the Middle East since the Middle Ages. These are warriors with ambiguous identities who can be claimed by more than one community.

Pilgrimage is both an individual act and a collective practice, and this dual character makes it complex to analyse. The vast majority of visitors to shared sacred places in the broader Byzantine and Ottoman world have always been local men and women, and their devotional activities form part of a common and widespread pattern containing elements from more than one religious tradition. Oriental "pilgrimage" was not a specific state or activity, but a short episode in the longer pilgrimage of life. Therefore there was no need for a specific word to designate it (Dagron 2004: 7).[2] This Oriental Christian practice is referred to as *proskynesis*, the veneration of a personage in certain sacred places where his "presence" can be felt.[3]

Mixed or shared practices have inaccurately and anachronistically been associated with cosmopolitanism, a category that has lately come under some interesting criticism. Among other things, it has been accused of failing to incorporate an understanding of the particularity of experience and of "subsuming under the generic category of 'identity' the historical experiences and allegedly common 'cultures' of other 'groups'" (Brubaker and Cooper 2000: 30). Contemporary debates around identity and difference point to the "hollowness" of categories and to the constant "re-interpretations" of and adaptations to the "other" (Theodossopoulos 2006: 24). These also reveal the tensions and passions involved in discussing such issues as "collective representations" and national stereotypes (Kechriotis 2002; Calotychos 2003; Papagaroufali 2005; Theodossopoulos 2006). The language of identity implies the existence of an axiomatic identity, while in fact "bounded groups are a contingent, emergent property, not an axiomatic given" (Brubaker and Cooper 2000: 31). As I hope will become clear below, shared *sacra* do not imply a shared religious identity: shared *sacra* are primarily sacred 'places'.

Mixed religious practices across the vast Byzantine and Ottoman space-time have not been the result of any top-down "tolerant" or "multicultural" ideology or policy; no legal dispositions or other kinds of texts emanating from official authorities seem to uphold any such hypothesis.[4] Instead, the "tolerant" attitude of the Byzantine and Ottoman societies is best understood in relation to their intrinsic nature as political entities: empires with a long tradition of cultural pluralism characterized by the coexistence of more than one symbolic system within a relatively loosely organized society, a social order maintained for centuries over vast territories. In this context, common ritual practices are a grass-root phenomenon whose existence and perseverance can better be understood by looking into the ethnographic detail of these experiences, keeping in mind that they have not marked the memory of the "communities" involved in identical ways.

Shared ritual practices in Anatolia are highly codified social activities involving ritual objects, gestures, and postures relating pilgrims to sacred place. Here, the important participants are laymen and laywomen; rituals and devotional practices do not necessarily involve interaction with the clergy. Ethnographic and historical material sustains the hypothesis that these practices are linked to the "chthonian" character of the objects of devotion, who are deities of the underworld in the limited sense of the word (below the surface of the earth) and who are primarily linked with the local population. I use the term chthonian (*chthonios*) to signify the one who comes from the land, from the territory (*chthon*), which is not the same as from the agricultural, nourishing earth (*gaia*). Chthonian spirits have a special relation with autochthonous men and women, the earth-born, those originating from the land their ancestors have transmitted to them (Détienne 2003: 20).[5] Those Saint George's shrines that attract mixed pilgrims in the Balkans and in Anatolia are usually situated outside towns and villages, on hilltops or in the woods, next to springs and crevices. These are "liminal" places inhabited by chthonian or other spirits on the frontier between the earth and the underworld (Stewart 1991).

My research is based on both ethnographic and historical data. The first comes from my observations of contemporary mixed ritual practices in Istanbul, and the second from archival research conducted in Athens. These findings lead me to argue that sharing *sacra* is primarily a local phenomenon, whose symbolic importance is related to a specific social group within a specific space-time.

St. George's Holy Space-Time

Saint George is one of the most popular saints of Oriental Christendom, whose cult spread widely, especially after the Crusades, covering a domain stretching from Egypt to Georgia, and from the Balkans to Anatolia. Shrines dedicated to Saint George or the Virgin Mary are the two typically syncretic holy places in the Levant, and traditionally attract Muslim men and women along with Christian pilgrims (Voile 2004). One of the most important present-day "shared" celebrations of the saint is the annual festival that takes place on 23 April on Princes' Islands (*Prinkipo*) near Istanbul. My study, based on a series of observations of the pilgrimage between 1992 and 2004, has further been enlightened by documentary sources on similar "mixed" celebrations in the Black Sea region at the beginning of the twentieth century.[6]

Saint George's Day, although a "fixed" feast, has in fact been celebrated on variable dates in both Eastern and Western Christian practice. In the Orthodox world, it is often moved to the Monday following Easter Sunday because as a major holiday it cannot be celebrated during Lent (a time of fasting and penitence). In Western Christian custom, Saint George's Day has also not remained fixed. In England, the holiday disappeared from the church's official calendar during the Reformation, reappearing later as a "June festival" organized by guilds and companies. The Catholic Church has recently retrograded Saint George's Day into a simple "commemoration," following doubts about his historical existence and martyrdom (Morgan 1990; McClendon 1999). These variations of time and place in relation to the saint's celebrations add another dimension to the "betwixt and between" character of the personage, that seems to thrive on ambiguity and marginality.

Saint George as a legendary figure has its Turkish parallel, *Hidrellez* (or in old Turkish *Hidir İlyas*)—a combination of *Hidr*, who stands for springtime and new life, and *Elias*, a symbol of the sun, whose importance has been well documented in Anatolian and Balkan folklore. The earliest study of these mixed practices is Hasluck's work on Balkan popular religion; he was the first to point out similarities in popular religion between Saint George, Elias and Hidr occurring as early as the beginning of the Ottoman period:[7]

> in Turkey ... Khidr seems to be a vague personality conceived of mainly as a helper in sudden need, especially of travelers. He has been identified with various figures of the Old Testament, notably with Elias, of whom he is considered a re-incarnation, and with the Orthodox St. George, whose day, together with the associations of Lydda, he has

taken over; the characteristics he has borrowed from St. George include the reputation of a dragon-slayer, which St. George himself may have borrowed from a pagan predecessor. ... [I]t seems abundantly proved, from oriental literary sources, that the personalities of Khidr and Elias are distinguished by the learned, the former being the patron of seafarers and the latter of travelers by land. ... [H]is (Khidr's) day is regarded by seamen as the opening of their season. ... (and) he is regarded as a patron of spring, being called the "Verdant," partly in allusion to the greenness of that season, while his feast is the beginning of spring and, in Syria, the beginning of sowing. His discovery of the water of life may also have a reference to his connection with spring, while the physical conception of his functions has probably aided his confusion with Elias, the rainbringer of the Christians. (Hasluck 1929: 320–22)[8]

More recent ethnographic work in Anatolia has established a relationship between the widespread *Hidrellez* celebrations in early May and ancient Anatolian calendars, which also divide the year between the cold season and the good season (Bazin 1974; Boratav 1955; Gokalp 1978, 1980; Tsibiridou 2000; Zegginis 2001). The first is called *Kasim*, November in Turkish, and starts on Saint Dimitrios' Day in the Christian calendar (26 October Julian, 8 November Gregorian) marking the beginning of winter's agricultural labor, the return of the transhumant herds from mountains to lowlands, and the end of the fishing season. The second date (23 April Julian, 6 May Gregorian) is called *Hidrellez* and corresponds to Saint George's Day; it signals the beginning of the season for good navigation and highlands transhumance (Bazin 1974; Gokalp 1980). These dates also correspond to the cycle of the Pleiades, a star cluster that divides the year in two, disappearing from the Mediterranean winter sky at the end of April and reappearing at the end of October. In Greek mythology, the Pleiades cycle was related to Demeter, goddess of earth and agriculture, whose daughter, Persephone, married to Hades, king of the underworld, lived part of the year with her mother above the earth and part of the year below with her husband. In winter, Demeter was sad, and therefore nothing grew until spring, when her daughter would reappear and stir the earth back to life. One of the parallels between the two couples, Saint Dimitrios/Saint George and Demeter/Persephone, is of course the names themselves; Saint Dimitrios stands as the Christian—and male—mirror image of Demeter, while *Georgios* (George) is homonymous with *georgos* (farmer). Analogies between Saint George and a number of mythological figures, slayers of dragons and monsters have been well established (Anagnostakis and Balta 1994: 116–19). One of these is the ancient Greek god Apollo, another dragon slayer and life/spring/water bringer, whose shrines stand on the frontier between the world of the men and the underworld. In one version of the saint's life (ibid.), he is the offspring of a mixed marriage between an Armenian pagan and a Christian woman from Cappadocia. Here he is very much like the hero of the Byzantine epic *Digenis Akritis*, son of a Muslim father and a Christian mother. The legendary Alexander is also of "mixed" blood; according to the popular *Romance* (Veloudis 1977) he is not King Philip's son, but the fruit of the union of his mother and an Egyptian magician/god. The hero descending from two races is a frequent theme in oriental mythology; the Christians Digenis and Armouris, and the Muslim Hasan Askari, Sayyid Battal or Melik Danishmend are all of a "double" or "mixed" descent (Delehay 1909; Grégoire 1942; Melikoff 1960; Anagnostakis and Balta 1994). The same theme is present in the legend of Sheik Beddredin, founder of the order of the Semavites in Adrinople (Edirne) in Thrace (Zegginis [1996] 2001: 150). Even more similar is the legend associated with the figure of Sarï Saltïk in Albania, who was the founder of the local Bektashi order and whose cave is still a pilgrimage site today, visited by large crowds on 6 May, Saint George's Day. Sarï Saltïk is said to be a holy man who saved the life of the young daughter of a Christian prince and killed a dragon to make water available for the population (Clayer 1996). In Greek folksong, Saint George appears to protect a mixed couple and bless their marriage by abduction (Politis [1914] 1978: 72). The song points out the only possible exogamic union in the Ottoman world, the one involving a Muslim man and a Christian woman. From the Asia Minor archives comes a similar echo: "Our grandfathers used to say that Turks also feared and respected Saint George. They even loved him as a kinsman, because they considered him their son-in-law, having married the Turkish girl Fatme."[9]

St. George of Prinkipo

In present-day Turkey, 23 April is a national holiday, the Day of Children and the Republic (*23 Nisan Ulusal Egemenlik ve Çocuk Bayramı*), commemorating Kemal Ataturk's coming to power in 1920. Families spend the day outdoors, picnicking in parks and woods. It is also an important feast among the *Rum* community (the Greek Orthodox of Turkey),[10] who traditionally celebrate it in the countryside with religious services in monasteries or country chapels, followed by picnics or shared meals. The Greek Orthodox monastery of Saint George, situated at the top of the hill on Princes' Island near Istanbul, attracts an impressive and constantly increasing number of visitors, estimated at a hundred thousand people in 2004. They come from Istanbul to the picturesque town—with its beautiful old villas, seaside restaurants, and souvenir shops—by crossing the Bosporus by boat. Most of the visitors are "cultural Muslims" who belong to the Muslim majority in Turkey, while Armenians and *Rum* prefer to visit the monastery at other times—a fact that questions the nature of the day's celebration. Is this still a shared shrine? Is this pilgrimage a shared religious phenomenon? It is difficult to claim that a kind of *communitas* comes into being while apparently different and disconnected ritual practices are being performed at this particular time and place (Hertz 1928 Morinis 1992). As will be shown later, Muslims visiting the shrine partake in a traditional activity made possible and culturally meaningful to them through their sharing of a common social memory of Ottoman local traditions, when Christian and Muslim neighbors interacted on social occasions across religious boundaries.

Sacred space and ritual time are not fixed realities. For example, while Muslim feast days follow the lunar calendar, Christian holidays are fixed by using both the lunar and the solar calendar: Christmas is always celebrated on 25 December, following the solar calendar, but Easter's date depends on both the solar and the lunar cycle. Moreover, the Oriental church considers Lent as a period of fasting and prayer; celebrations of joy cannot be held during this period. Marriages, for example, are best postponed to the period following Easter, during May and June. The same seems to hold true for St George's feast, for whenever 23 April happens during Lent, the holiday is transferred to Easter Monday. When I observed the feast in 1997 the Greek Consul was the host and the great majority of participants (around two hundred people in all) arrived after mass to share the food and music. In practice, St George's shrines host different types of celebrations, depending on the specific calendar configurations: when 23 April is after Orthodox Easter, both Christian and Muslim pilgrims gather together. Thus on Princes' Islands in Istanbul, when the holiday happens during Lent, Christians do not celebrate; but the tens of thousands of Muslim pilgrims, ignoring this, visit the monastery, and monks and priests welcome them in the usual way. Priests are very pleased by the great numbers of Muslim pilgrims, since they are the proof of the "power" of the saint and of Christian shrines in general: "they have faith and when they come to us we welcome them ... we read them prayers."[11] Christian visitors are less enthusiastic about the attractiveness of the shrine among the Muslim population; they refer to the feast as "the Muslim feast" and prefer not to go "up the hill" that day.

After setting foot on the wharf, pilgrims prepare to participate in a series of ritual activities taking place in and around the shrine. Locals dressed for the occasion sell candles and bottles of oil set out on small tables, while *faytons*, one-horse carriages which take pilgrims and tourists up the hill to the clearing just below the monastery, are queued for by the pilgrims. In that clearing small stalls set up overnight offer a wide selection of votive articles and other paraphernalia day-trippers can purchase and use in order to make the most of their pilgrimage. In addition to candles and bottles of oil, there are large reels of thread, different types of small, cheap ex-votos, including miniature icons, sugar cubes, and the inevitable blue glass "eyes." Pilgrims choose according to the wish to be made—chance, school, love, marriage, house, money, or health—and the purchased ex-votos will be taken to the monastery to be "blessed" and subsequently kept as souvenirs. The thread is used right away; one end is tied to a bush at the beginning of the path, and the person making the vow unreels it as they walk up the path to the sanctuary. By noon, one side of the wide footpath leading to the top of the hill is covered with thousands of parallel lines of thread. Trees and bushes lining the path are used for other votive activities; hundreds of strips of cloth or paper tissue are hanging from their branches. A third votive gesture consists of "building houses"; on one side of the path, under trees and bushes, small stones are piled one on top of the other, producing unstable miniature constructions evoking a shelter or a hearth. A few years ago people also used construction bricks, more straightforwardly suggesting housing. They would put them on the plateau, next to the monastery walls, or along the low protection walls bordering the cliffs overlooking the sea (Fig. 3.2). The assumption seemed to be that the *Rum* saint could help the pilgrim achieve the stereotypical Istanbul *Rum* social status: a well-to-do craftsman or shopkeeper, owner of his house and shop.

On feast days, pilgrims may have to queue for one or two hours before they can enter the *Catholicon* (the monastery's church) where they must very quickly complete a series of tasks: light a candle at the narthex, proceed into the main chapel towards the *proskinitarion*, the icon stand which holds the miraculous icon in a glass frame, and pause before it, as long as the crowds allow, to say a word of prayer before exiting the chapel through its rear door. In recent years, as the masses of pilgrims have continued to grow, the priests have stopped receiving individual visitors and reading them prayers inside the church as they did up until the 1990s. The clergy's presence inside the church is more about watching over the flow of pilgrims as they move from the entrance to the exit. New restrictions on movements in and around the sanctuary are another consequence of the massive presence of pilgrims on the day of the feast. Secondary buildings are now closed to the public on feast days for security reasons; one can no longer visit the adjacent chapels (Saint Charalambos, Saint Mary and the Saint Apostles) or, most importantly, go into the *Agiasma* (holy fountain) situated at the back of the main church to drink water.[12] Outside, interaction between pilgrims and the sacred place continues: candles are lit and made to stand on nearby stones or walls; coins are rubbed against slabs of stone (if they "stick" they believe the vow has been heard); miniature keys are "tried" in the keyhole of the church door. All around people are praying, hands spread, palms up, oblivious of the crowds. Some people sit in groups, picnicking on the grass, while others stand looking down on the sea below.

According to the priests, Muslims come to Saint George because the saint can heal: "Even the imam sends these people to us priests, because they (the imams)

Figure 3.1. On the path leading to the Monastery of St. George Koudounas: pilgrims build miniature hearths, wishing for happiness in marriage. Photo M. Couroucli.

Figure 3.2. Votive constructions (representing houses) outside the Monastery of St. George Koudounas. Photo M. Couroucli.

cannot heal people. They also come to the (parish) churches. Saint George is famous for his power to help for a house and for business. They come to make *tamata* (i.e. votive offerings)." Greek Orthodox churchgoers in Istanbul share the same view. In 2004, at Trinity Church in *Pera*, near *Taksim*, a woman in her sixties told me: "many people go to Saint George at Prinkipo, because he grants everything that people ask from him: a house, work, good health, he gives everything. The saint has 'a good reputation' and the priests are very hospitable." Typical pilgrims to the island are literate women from the middle classes of Istanbul who have been brought up in the secular tradition of modern Turkey. More recent migrants from Anatolian towns and villages only go to mosques. It takes deep local knowledge and local connections for a Muslim pilgrim to penetrate a Christian sacred place. Autochthonous inhabitants of the city, those born and raised in Istanbul, whether Muslim or *Rum*, share local ways as well as a sacred map of Istanbul. Among its important reference points are the *Ayazma* (in Turkish, from the Greek *Agiasma*, "holyful") which are the holy fountains to be found in or near Christian churches which receive pious visitors on certain dates and which are known for their healing powers. On Fridays one can go to Saint Mary's Church at Vlachernai,[13] on Saturdays to Saint Dimitrios at Kurucesme, and on Christmas Eve, along with Istanbul's high society, to Saint Antoine's Catholic Church at Istiklal for midnight mass. Syncretism is part of the local culture of Istanbul, where having religious communities living side by side has given rise to a long tradition of coexistence. Saint George's celebrations in Prinkipo reflect the multicultural Istanbul of the beginning of the twentieth century, when half of the city's population belonged to the *Rum*, Armenian or Jewish "minorities," and one in five Ottoman subjects were Christian (Alexandris 1983; Berktay 1997

Keyder 2002; Stewart and Shaw 1994). This multicultural tradition of the late Ottoman period is well documented in Millas' book on Prinkipo and its history:

> At least once a year, every family goes to the sacred mountain to visit the saint, sprinkle themselves with holy water and fill bottles with it that will be kept for difficult times. Commoners would go on the saint's day, while more important families would go to Saint George for a day-trip, where they would organise open-air parties. On important occasions, a table would be set behind the monastery, the abbot hosting the feast. The Greek newspapers of Istanbul at the time often mentioned those gatherings … there were always people on Sundays at Saint George's monastery. (Millas 1988: 484)

This was Istanbul's *Belle Époque* that resonated with the cosmopolitanism characteristic of Mediterranean port cities where well-to-do urbanites of various religious backgrounds shared a particular lifestyle (Driessen 2005; Örs 2006, Yerasimos 1992). The memory of this cosmopolitan spirit seems to be the symbolic base of syncretic practices observed on Princes' Islands today.

The saint has traditionally been known to heal most illnesses, and particularly mental illness. Until the beginning of the twentieth century, incubation was still practiced inside the *Catholikon*; the sick were brought to sleep on its slab-stoned floor, waiting for the saint to appear in dream and offer recovery (Millas 1988: 468).[14] As was mentioned above, Saint George is related to agriculture and pastoralism, protecting the sheep of shepherds as well as his own flock. In the old days, the children of the island were "dedicated" to Saint George and referred to as "the Saint's little slaves" (*ta sklavakia tou Agiou*). They wore bells around their necks that were like the bells hanging from the saint's armor on the main icon—hence his Greek name *Ai Giorgis Koudounas* (Saint George with the bells). Millas, drawing from a number of travelers' accounts from the nineteenth century, mentions that children wore the amulet until just before they married or went into the army, both considered as *rites de passage* into adulthood. When the time came to get their freedom back, the "little slaves" would offer the saint a candle as tall as their own height during a ceremony in which the priest read the "liberation prayer."

Being read prayers by the priest is another devotional activity that can no longer take place during the festival; people now come on a regular Sunday to meet with the priest after the service, and very few Muslim pilgrims attempt such a transaction. Today priests give a small bell to each of those who come to the monastery to make vows, a bell they have to return, accompanied by an offering to the church, after their vows have been granted (Brown 1981; Chelini and Branthomme 1982; Maraval 2004; Sotiriou 1962). Priests and monks have many stories to tell about miraculous healings involving Turks: typically they will relate how a boy was brought back to health, how a Turkish woman was healed from mental illness, or how a Turkish man came and offered the church "a very important sum" in reciprocation for a very important miracle the saint performed for him or his family.

Shared Shrines on the Black Sea Coast

The calendric importance of the dates of Saint George and Saint Demetrios is well established in the Greek folklore of Asia Minor. In some localities, Saint George stands for both, and is celebrated both in springtime in a chapel in the countryside, and in the autumn at the parish church. The months corresponding to the feasts were both called *Agiorghita*, the time of Saint George, in local dialect. The Greek Orthodox official calendar recognizes this custom by providing two occasions for celebrating Saint George: 23 April for the commemoration of his martyrdom, and 3 November for the transportation of his relics and the consecration of his first church in Lydda.

Early-twentieth-century celebrations of Saint George in the Black Sea region were of two kinds: those taking place at parish churches in villages or towns, and those related to chapels or sanctuaries in the countryside. Ritual practices associated with a town or village parish church take place on the saint's day when *Rum* parishioners gather in church, sometimes joined by pilgrims from neighboring villages. Muslim neighbors may also attend celebrations; some documents mention "Turks" standing by as the icon is processed round the neighborhood. The saint's day is also an occasion for visits across communities. Muslims visit Christian houses and are offered traditional sweets as part of an exchange system linking well-to-do families in both communities (CEAM, PO 1–3, PO 757). Legendary miracles from Byzantine times also echo mixed practices among the elite, such as a thirteenth-century story concerning the wife of a Turkish emir from Sivas who was possessed by a demon and cured at Saint Phokas' shrine in Trebizond after spending the night in his church (Foss 2002: 146).

Shared practices per se have not been observed inside parish churches; they take place outside parishes in the countryside, in and around Christian chapels or ruins of a pre-existing chapel, or even in "natural" sacred spots (rock, tree, etc.). Muslim presence at the sanctuaries is not considered a problem by members of the Rum community. From their point of view, Turks venerate Saint George because he is strong; he can heal but also punish those who do not respect his *sacra*. Legends from the Black Sea relate how the saint manifests himself near his shrine either to punish those who have shown disrespect to his sacred place or holy day (usually Turks being struck ill or paralyzed until they undo the wrong they committed by going to the priest to pray and bring offerings) or to reward with a miracle those who acknowledged his power by treating the saint well or praying to him: "one day, a Turk went to labour the saint's field. His plough got stuck and they had to bring in a priest to celebrate to set it free." Saint George is said to be heard riding his horse at night, the soil trembles and his horseshoe leaves marks on nearby stones. Only pure people can see him and only those who believe in him can get well. Black Sea ethnographic material also provides local context about the equation Saint George=*Hidrellez*. As the saint punishes those showing disrespect, Turks would also call him *Deli Hidirellez* or *Zantayertz* (Mad Saint George).[15]

The Asia Minor archives in Athens contain descriptions of celebrations taking place in some fifty churches dedicated to Saint George in the Black Sea area. Seven of these accounts refer to parish churches, where the clergy and the official community institutions were in charge of the feast, which include meals offered to visitors. In some towns, Turks brought candles or other offerings (including agricultural goods and animals for slaughter, *kurban*) to churches.[16] In five different localities, shared practices were explicitly mentioned as celebrations taking place on 23 April in the countryside with picnics, dancing, or wrestling contests. When sanctuaries were old or abandoned, they were no longer considered consecrated, and Orthodox priests were not allowed to follow their parishioners in their practices. Many of the descriptions of votive acts performed by visitors at these sites sound strikingly like those carried out at Prinkipo today. In the countryside near Ladik, for example, Saint George's chapel had become a Bektashi shrine, attracting pilgrims from both communities:

> Saint George's day was also celebrated by Turks, they called him Hittirelez ... Turks and Greeks went there, they would tear up pieces from their clothes and attach them to the trees. Then, they would ask the saint of the tekke for grace (*haris*). They also took small stones or coins and would try to make them stick on stones. If they did, their wishes would be fulfilled. (CAMS, PO 965)

Shared Sacra, Autochthony and Traditional Culture

Shared practices are one of the most striking aspects of the Byzantino-Ottoman legacy and demonstrate a specific way of living that makes room for difference. Yet this tradition has nothing to do with modern narratives celebrating a "tolerant" and multicultural society; in Ottoman society syncretism flourished within a strongly hierarchical structure, where Greek, Armenian, and Jewish minorities enjoyed fewer rights and occupied a lower social status than the Muslim majority.[17] In Anatolia as elsewhere, Muslims visited Christian shrines within a certain system of belief where the Christian "other" is both familiar and inferior, and this is why entering Christian sanctuaries implies no ritual pollution (Couroucli 2003, 2005; Mayeur-Jaouen 2002, 2005).[18] This phenomenon of "making room for difference" died away as Christian minorities became marginalized and finally eliminated, allowing the establishment of a modern state whose national project, based on ethnic, cultural, and religious homogeneity, had no place for cultural tolerance.[19]

The common veneration of Saint George's holy places is one of the aspects of the cohabitation of different religious communities within the same territory, and one of the expressions of the ties between men and women and their locality. The Black Sea material suggests that people across religious communities venerated sacred places that were related to legends about a supernatural being with a local, chthonic nature that lived at the edge of two worlds. I have suggested elsewhere (Couroucli 2009) that this was possible because within Ottoman society the two basic principles of social organization, kinship and territory, had remained relatively autonomous. This fundamental separation served to protect the local society from the intervention of central authorities while allowing the existence of autonomous activities at the margins; shared holy places are characteristically also referred to as *vakf* (autonomous religious foundations) in both Balkan and Anatolian localities (Zegginis (1996) 2001; de Rapper 2007). In folk representations, the saint stands for the unity of the local community—of "those who share the same blood" (the *omoemi*), despite and beyond the organization of religious groups into separate communities.[20] According to the Christian legend, he is there to protect all those who appeal to him, including Muslim "others" and marginal peoples. The iconography represents him as both chthonian (belonging to the earth and springing from the soil, yet ready to attack creatures from the underworld such as dragons and snakes) and as a superman, a hero warrior riding his horse across frontiers and fighting malevolent forces (punishing wrongdoers and healing the sick). It is useful to remember that in Ottoman times Christians were not allowed to ride on horseback, because they were considered to be of inferior status; horsemen, if not Muslims, could only be supernatural beings, permanent outsiders to the quotidian world.

Inasmuch as the Anatolian local community is not a frozen social reality, shared practices are not a single, unchanging phenomenon existing from Byzantine times until the early twentieth century, even though ritual elements may remain surprisingly stable over the centuries without those who carry them out recognizing their historical depth. For example, my Orthodox informants always presented the significance of the threads pulled along the footpath to Saint George's monastery in Prinkipo as obscure, assuring me that these were "Muslim ways." The legend

Figure 3.3. On the path leading to the Monastery of St. George Koudounas: tree with pieces of white cloth and strings attached by pilgrims. Photo M. Couroucli.

about Empress Zoe, who had conceived the future Constantine VII (913–959) by wearing a string with which she had "measured" the miraculous icon of the Virgin, is obviously no longer part of local lore (Carr 2002). Shreds of cloth hanging from trees near sanctuaries are also considered "Muslim ways," although such practices are to be observed in many places in the Balkans, Greece included.

Pilgrimage to shared sacred places in the Eastern Mediterranean is a most spectacular expression of Christian and Muslim cohabitation; nevertheless, it has largely been ignored by anthropologists, who have focused more on "normal" (rather than marginal) traditions in the region, thus reinforcing local national discourses about the homogeneous character of the societies they are studying. After all, national folklore also tended to dismiss those practices as untypical of the traditional society that was the foundation of the nation. It is precisely because of their marginality and their difference, though, that the study of mixed practices around sacred places can provide valuable clues to the common experience of people who lived "together" for centuries, in or near the Holy Land, in Syria, Egypt, Anatolia or the Balkans. How did they make it? What exactly did they share? How did they avoid conflict? Did members of the different communities "cross" the boundaries, and on what occasions? What were the consequences of this crossing for the larger society? Did people live together or did they live side by side?

Recent ethnographic interest in religious practices reflects the popularity and the greater visibility of these phenomena taking place in a new context where twentieth century secular traditions are becoming things of the past: post-Kemalism[21] in Turkey, post-socialism/neo-nationalism in the Balkans, and neo-orthodoxy in Greece are some of the characteristic trends. Observing these phenomena implies addressing recent issues about multiculturalism, religious tolerance and politically correct attitudes vis-à-vis minorities, which are at the heart of contemporary political debate. My analysis tends to the conclusion that shared sacra do not necessarily lead to a shared religious identity; I showed above how their sacred character comes from the interaction between local human communities around holy sites: shared *sacra* are in fact "sacred localities."

Notes

1. The quote comes from the file for the village Ladik (near Argyroupolis/Gumushane on the Black Sea Coast) at the Centre for Asia Minor Studies, Athens (CAMS, PO 965). I wish to express my deepest thanks to the staff of the center for their help and encouragement during my research in their collection of ethnographic documents in 2005 and 2006.

2. "Le pèlerin occidental a un nom, une iconographie, une histoire. Du chrétien d'Orient qui va faire ses dévotions dans un sanctuaire proche ou lointain, on dit simplement qu'il voyage, qu'il avait fait un vœu, qu'il a accompli un acte de piété; il n'y a ni spécificité du pèlerinage ni statut particulier du pèlerin dans cette partie de la chrétienté. … Tout Oriental était un pèlerin virtuel, de court ou de long voyage; il n'était pas besoin d'un mot pour le dire." [The Western pilgrim is related to a name, an iconography, a story. When the Oriental Christian visits a sanctuary, nearby or far away, to venerate the saint, it is only said that he travels, that he has made a vow, that he accomplishes an act of devotion. There is no specificity of the act of pilgrimage or particular status attached to the pilgrim in this part of Christianity … Every Oriental was a potential pilgrim,

involving a shorter or longer journey; no specific term was needed to imply this.] (Dagron 2004: 7).

3. "More than the one who travelled, the Byzantine pilgrim is a *proskynetes*, one who venerated; the critical movement was over the threshold of access to the one venerated. The space claimed was one less of distance than of presence" (Carr 2002: 77).

4. For a more extended discussion on cosmopolitanism in relation to shared shrines in the Ottoman tradition, see Couroucli 2010: 220–39.

5. See Détienne 2003 on representations of the autochthonous character of men and gods in Athens, especially in relation to the "liminal" temple Erechtheion on the Acropolis, where the contest between Athena and Poseidon took place.

6. Most of the documents providing the historical context for this study come from the archives of the Centre for Asia Minor Studies in Athens (hereafter CAMS)—a unique and very rich ethnographic collection on the Greek Orthodox community in late Ottoman times, when religious minorities constituted an important segment of both urban and rural populations in Anatolia.

7. Hasluck refers to the writings of Cantacusenus (fourteenth century) on Hetir Elias, and of George the Hungarian (fifteenth century) on "the extraordinary vogue enjoyed by Khidr in his day."

8. Bazin (1974: 720–27) writes that the Arabic stem *h-d-r* conveys green grass, announcing spring, and the slaying of the Dragon symbolizes victory over winter. Roasted (*pefrygmena*) young wheat grains (*hydra*) are mentioned as a ritual meal in fifth-century Greek texts (Chantraine 2009: 1214, who quotes Aristophanes' *Peace*: 595). In the Greek Orthodox tradition *nea hidra* are brought to church as part of the *protogenimata* (first harvest) offerings, a tradition parallel to the Jewish ceremony of firstfruits, the day following Passover (Leviticus 2:14 and 23:13–14). *Nea Hidra* and *Heohidra* are mentioned in Korae's dictionary of modern Greek (1835) as fresh grain offerings. Greek orthodox hymns and prayers sang on 23 April celebrating St. George relate him to spring: *Aneteile* to ear, *deute euhithomen* (Spring has dawned, let's be merry) (Synekdimos "Book of Prayers" 23 April).

9. See CAMS, Agrid, Argyroupolis/Gumushane, PO 757.

10. The Orthodox Greeks of Istanbul are usually referred to as *Rum*, Romans, local inhabitants of the Eastern Roman Empire (Byzantium). The Greeks from Greece are called *Yunanli*, after the country's name in Turkish, *Yunanistan* (the land of Ionia).

11. From the church's point of view, the importance of a shrine is related to the numbers of pilgrims who visit it; early accounts of shrines mention the crowds attending them at festivals (Foss 2002).

12. Drinking water and taking a bottle back home is one of the traditional acts of devotion practiced in the various *Agiasma* of Istanbul. Muslims not only drink water from fountains situated near mosques, but also wash—a habit Christians consider improper in relation to Christian *Agiasma*.

13. In Byzantine Constantinople the "usual miracle" at Vlachernai enabled the pious to see the Holy Spirit descending on the icon (Carr 2002).

14. Saint George appears as a healer of the mentally ill both in Christian and Muslim traditions. According to Glenn Bowman, Mar Elyas monastery in Palestine is related to the nearby Saint George (Khadr) monastery, where the mad are believed to be cured (1993: 435). See also Brigitte Voile on practices of exorcism in Saint George's shrines among Coptic Christians in Egypt (2004: 145). Many references to this "specialization" of the saint are to be found in the CAMS archives from Pontos area, where the surname *deli* or *zantos* (both meaning "mad") is often mentioned.

15. See CAMS files, nos. PO 17, PO 41, PO 106, PO 132, PO 157, PO 679, PO 965.

16. See CAMS files, nos. PO 177, PO 757.

17. Furthermore, Ottoman attitudes towards religious practices follow (in time, at least) earlier traditions concerning religious mixing in the Mediterranean like, for example, the Venetian system in Crete. Here the local elites adopted the dominant religion (Latin Christianity) in a specific way: men became Catholic while women remained Orthodox. These practices did not stop after Crete was conquered by the Ottomans; on the contrary, they became a specific way of living, where a "public" and a "private" religion coexisted within the same families (Green 2000: 108).

18. The reverse situation was impossible; members of the Empire's Christian minorities were not allowed into mosques, and the sacred places of the Muslim majority only became accessible to Christian visitors when these places were converted into museums after Turkey's secularization in the 1920s.
19. The process of Turkish-state formation was analogous to that of the establishment of Balkan states in the nineteenth century, with similar consequences.
20. On the contrast between kindred (*synghenis*) as a social group and blood relatives (*omoemi*, from *aima*, blood) in local Anatolian mixed villages, see Couroucli 2009.
21. The term refers to present-day Turkish political establishment and ideology, where the ideas of Kemal Ataturk, the founder of the Turkish Republic in 1923, are less dominant. For an ethnographic analysis of modern Turkey in relation to this heritage, see Özyürek 2006.

References

Albera, Dionigi and Maria Couroucli (eds). 2009. *Religions Traversées. Lieux saints partagés entre chrétiens, musulmans et juifs en Méditerranée*, eds. D. Albera and M. Couroucli. Arles: Actes Sud; Aix-en-Provence: MMSH.

Albera, Dionigi and Maria Couroucli (eds). 2012. *Sharing Sacred Spaces in the Mediterranean*. Indiana: Indiana University Press.

Alexandris, Alexis. 1983. *The Greek Minority in Istanbul and Greek-Turkish Relations, 1918–1974*. Athens: Centre for Asia Minor Studies.

Anagnostakis, Ilias and Evangelia Balta. 1994. *La découverte de la Cappadoce au XIXe siècle*. Istanbul: Eren.

Anonymous. 2001. *Megas kai Ieros Synekdimos Orthodoxou Christianou* (Book of Prayers). Athens: Papadimitriou.

Bazin, Louis. 1974. *Les calendriers turcs anciens et médiévaux, Thèse Paris III, 1972*. Service de reproduction des thèses. Université de Lille III.

Boratav, Pertev. 1955. *Contes turcs*. Paris: Erasme.

Bowman, Glenn. 1993. "Nationalizing the Sacred: Shrines and Shifting Identities in the Israeli-Occupied Territories." *Man* 28: 431–60.

Brown, Peter. 1981. *The Cult of Saints: Its Rise and Function in Latin Christianity*. Chicago: University of Chicago Press.

Brubaker, Rogers and Frederick Cooper. 2000. "Beyond 'Identity'", *Theory and Society* 29(1): 1–47.

Calotychos, Vangelis. 2003. *Modern Greece: A Cultural Poetics*. Oxford: Berg.

Carr, Annemarie Weyl. 2002. "Icons and the Object of Pilgrimage in Middle Byzantine Constantinople," *Dumbarton Oaks Papers* 56, Washington DC: Dumbarton Oaks Research Library and Collection, 75–92.

Chantraine, Pierre. (1983) 2009. *Dictionnaire Etymologique de la langue grecque*. Paris: Klinksieck.

Chelini, Jean and Henri Branthhomme. 1982. *Les chemins de Dieu. Histoire des pèlerinages chrétiens des origines à nos jours*. Paris: Hachette.

Clayer, Nathalie. 1996. "Les hauts lieux du bektachisme albanais," in *Lieux d'islam*, ed. M. Amir-Moezzi, Editions Autrement, Collection Monde HS no. 91/92: 168–83.

Corbin, Henry. 1972. *En Islam Iranien, Aspects spirituels et philosophiques: Vol IV : L'École d'Ispahan. L'École Shaykhie. Le douzième imam*. Paris: Gallimard, 309–22.

Couderc, Paul. (1946) 1981. *Le calendrier*. Paris: PUF.

Couroucli, Maria. 2003. "Genos, ethnos, nation et Etat-nation." Identités, Nations, Globalisation, Ateliers, no. 26: 287–299 http://ateliers.revues.org/8737.

———. 2005. "Du cynégétique à l'abominable: à propos du chien comme terme d'injure et d'exclusion en grec moderne." *L'Homme* 174 : 227–52.

———. 2009. "Saint Georges l'Anatolien, maître des frontières," in *Religions Traversées. Lieux saints partagés entre chrétiens, musulmans et juifs en Méditerranée*, eds. D. Albera and M. Couroucli. Arles: Actes Sud; Aix-en-Provence: MMSH, 175–208.

———. 2010. "Empire Dust. The Web of Relations in Saint George's Festival on Princes Island in Istanbul," in *Eastern Christians in Anthropological Perspective*, eds. C. Hann and H. Goltz. Berkeley: University of California Press, 220–39.

Dagron, Gilbert. 2004 "Preface," in P. Maraval, *Lieux saints et pèlerinages d'Orient: Histoire et Géographie Des origines à la conquête arabe*. Paris: Cerf, 7–8.

Delehaye, Hippolyte. 1909. *Les légendes grecques des saints militaries*. Paris. Picard.

Driessen, Henk. 2005. "Mediterranean Port Cities: Cosmopolitanism Reconsidered." *History and Anthropology* 16(1): 129–41.

Foss, Clive. 2002. "Pilgrimage in Medieval Asia Minor," *Dumbarton Oaks Papers* 56, Washington DC: Dumbarton Oaks Research Library and Collection, 129–51.

Gokalp, Altan. 1978. "Hizir, Ilyâs, Hidrellez: les maîtres du temps, le temps des hommes," in *Quand le crible était dans la paille: mélanges en l'honneur du Professeur P. Boratav*, eds. R. Dor and M. Nicolas. Paris: Maisonneuve et Larose, 211–31.

———. 1980. *Têtes rouges et bouches noires*. Paris: Société d'Ethnographie.

Grégoire, Henri. 1942. *Digenis Akritas. The Byzantine Epic in History and Poetry* (in Greek). New York: The National Herald.

Green, Molly. 2000. *A Shared World: Christians and Muslims in the Early Modern Mediterranean*. Princeton: Princeton University Press.

Hasluck, Frederick William. 1929. *Christianity and Islam under the Sultans*. Ed. Margaret Hasluck. Oxford: Clarendon Press.

———. 1914. "Ambiguous Sanctuaries and Bektashi Propaganda," *The Annual of the British School at Athens*, vol. XX (session 1913–1914).

Kechriotis, Vangelis. 2002. "From Trauma to Self-Reflection: Greek Historiography Meets the Young Turks 'Bizarre' Revolution," in *Clio in the Balkans*, ed. C. Koulouri. Thessaloniki.CDRSEE

Keyder, Çağlar. 2002. "The Consequences of the Exchange of Populations for Turkey," in *Crossing the Aegean*, ed. R. Hirschon. New York and Oxford: Berghahn Books, 39–52.

Maraval, Pierre. 2004. *Lieux saints et pèlerinages d'Orient: Histoire et géographie des origins à la conquête arabe*. Paris: Cerf.

Mayeur-Jaouen. 2002 *Saints et héros du Moyen-Orient contemporain*. Paris: Maisonneuve et Larose.

Mayeur-Jaouen, Catherine. 2005. *Pèlerinages d'Egypte: Histoire de la piété copte et musulmane, XVe–XXe siècles*. Paris: EHESS Éditions.

McClendon, Muriel. 1999. "A Moveable Feast: Saint George's Day Celebrations and Religious Change in Early Modern England." *The Journal of British Studies* 1: 1–27.

Melikoff, Irène. 1960. *La geste de Melik Dāniṣmend: Étude critique du Dāniṣmendnāme* (Bibliothèque Archéologique et Historique de l'Institut Français d'Archéologie d'Istanbul, x–xi). Paris: Librairie Adrien-Maisonneuve.

Millas, Hercule. 1988. *Prinkipos* (in Greek). Athens: Melissa.

Morgan, Gareth. 1990. "The Mummers of Pontus." *Folklore* 101(2): 143–51.

Morinis, Alan. 1992. *Sacred Journeys: The Anthropology of Pilgrimage*. Westport, CT: Greenwood Press.

Örs, Ilay. 2006. "Beyond the Greek and Turkish Dichotomy: The Rum *polites* of Istanbul and Athens." *South European Society and Politics* 11(1): 79–94.

Özyürek, Esra. 2006. *Nostalgia for the Modern*. Chapel Hill, NC: Duke University Press.

Papagaroufali, Eleni. 2005. "Town Twinning in Greece: Reconstructing Local Histories through Translocal Sensory-affective Performances." *History and Anthropology* 16(3): 335–47.

Politis, Nicolaos. (1914) 1978. *Eklogai (Selected Greek Popular Songs)*. Athens: Bayonakis.

Rapper, Gilles de. 2007. "Les lieux partagés du religieux en Albanie: La notion de vakëf," in *Le religieux en partage: Explorations anthropologiques dans l'espace méditerranéen*, eds. D. Albera and M. Couroucli. Aix-en-Provence: Actes Sud, 53–85.

———. 2009. "Vakëf : lieux partagés du religieux en Albanie." In D. Albera, M. Couroucli (dir.), *Religions traversées. Lieux saints partagés entre chrétiens, musulmans et juifs en Méditerranée*. Arles: Actes Sud ("Etudes méditerranéennes"), 53–83.

Shankland, David (ed). 2004. *Archaeology, Anthropology and Heritage in the Balkans: The Work of Hasluck*. Istanbul: Isis.

Sotiriou, Dido. 1962. *Matomena Chomata*. Athens: Kedros (French translation: 1996. *Terres de sang*. Athens: Kauffmann).

Stewart, Charles. 1991. *Demons and the Devil: Moral Imagination in Modern Greek Culture*. Princeton: Princeton University Press.

Stewart, Charles and Rosaling Shaw (eds.). 1994. *Syncretism/Anti-Syncretism: The Politics of Religious Synthesis*. London: Routledge.

Theodossopoulos, Dimitrios. 2006. "Introduction: The 'Turks' in the Imagination of the 'Greeks.'" *South European Society and Politics* 11(1): 1–32.

Tsibiridou, Fotini. 2000. *Les Pomak dans la Thrace grecque: Discours ethnique et pratiques socioculturelles*. Paris: L'Harmattan.

Veloudis, George (ed.). 1977. *I phyllada tou Megalou Alexandrou: Diegesis Alexandrou tou Makedonos* (The Tale of Alexander the Great). Athens: Ermes.

Voile, Brigitte. 2004. *Les Coptes d'Egypte sous Nasser: Sainteté, miracles, apparitions*. Paris: CNRS.

Yerasimos, Stéphane. 1992. "Du cosmoplitisme au nationalisme," in *Istanbul 1914–1923. Capitale d'un monde illusoire ou l'agonie des vieux empires*, ed. S. Yerasimos. Paris: Editions Autrement, 11–24.

Zegginis, Eustratios. (1996) 2001. *O Bektasismos sti Dytiki Thraki* (Bektashism in Western Thrace). Thessaloniki: Pournara.

Chapter 4

THE WORK OF MENDING:
HOW PHARPING PEOPLE MANAGE AN EXCLUSIVIST
RESPONSE TO THE PROCESSION OF VAJRAYOGINĪ

Will Tuladhar-Douglas[1]

The ancient Newar[2] Buddhist deity Vajrayoginī has four distinct shrines at the corners of the Kathmandu Valley of Nepal. The two at the southwest and northeast corners, Pharping and Śaṅkhu, are the most significant. In this chapter I will consider how the communities of Pharping recognize and cope with the non-participation by Tibetans in the annual procession of Vajrayoginī. The material gathered here offers concrete evidence of the effort required to sustain an inclusivist understanding of religious boundaries when one economically powerful group within a community insists on an exclusivist understanding. This discussion will of necessity refer to key prior studies, in particular Gellner's substantial work on Newar Buddhism (1993) and Shrestha's monograph on Śaṅkhu (2002).

In my own article on the implicit intercommunal collaboration in the ritual life of the major Newar deity Būgadyaḥ (Tuladhar-Douglas 2005) I argued that Newars engage in what we might call "tacit collaboration" insofar as specific social processes requiring intentional activity, such as the formation of secret cults and the application of secrecy, allow different segments of the same society to apply several different names to a single shrine image without generating conflict. I further argued that in a society where the patrons for a particular shrine might well change their official religious affiliation, it was a good strategy for the priests to facilitate practices ensuring flexible patronage for their shrine. This makes sense in a society, such as the Newar, where there are plural sectarian identities and where the maintenance of an overt sectarian identity is only undertaken by members of a few caste groups (such as priests), while the majority of people prefer to avoid the inflexibility and work involved in taking sides.[3]

The Buddhist priests in charge of Būgadyaḥ accept that Śaiva priests, sent by the Hindu king to manage the procession, believe that Būgadyaḥ is actually a particular Śaiva saint, while knowing that this is only a provisional identity maintained by the deity for the sake of non-Buddhists. Moreover, even among Buddhists there are public, private, and secret (i.e., tantric) names for Būgadyaḥ. Each name carries an iconographic programme that may not be at all apparent from the external image. There are several secret names used by different groups in distinct worship rituals and all have distinct iconographies and associated rituals, while each is hermetically sealed off from other groups by regimes of secrecy. This muted multivocality is a specific, and rather stark, instance of a general feature of Indic shrine images, not apparent from written sources, which might be termed "polyonomy."

The purpose of my earlier article was to show that a single shrine image, even if it has a "main" sectarian name, can easily acquire several other sectarian names while its identity is in no way reducible to any one of those names. This plurality is only possible because worshippers collude in ignoring potentially divisive behavior at the site. Here however I am concerned with a complementary process. I want to show how townsfolk assert and, if necessary, repair an understanding that all religious acts in that place should work in this manner. In trying to understand this I will call upon Michael Carrither's notion of polytropy (Carrithers 2000) and will focus on a number of small local shrines that resist sectarian labeling.

About Pharping

Pharping is an ancient Newar city-state, now a town, that has several distinct communities. Informants around the bus park identify three of them readily: the Newari-speaking Newars, the Nepali-speaking Bahun-Chetris, and the Untouchables. Whereas the Bahun-Chetris are high caste and the Untouchables belong to low-caste groups such as the tailors and butchers, the Newars are divided into numerous caste groups (*thar*). A Newar informant will not identify Newars as a group but will instead list the major Newar *thar*: *Maharjan, Bālāmī, Śreṣṭha,* and *Mānandhar,* followed by the smaller Newar *thar.* Newars, who are said to be indigenous and were politically dominant prior to the consolidation of the Nepalese monarchy, make up more than half the population of the town. As we shall see, the ritual geography and processes that constitute Pharping are still Newar and render the town comparable to other Newar urban centers such as Lalitpur, Bhaktapur, or Śaṅkhu.

As with any other Newar town, Pharping's town plan is integral to its ritual life.[4] Shrines to the Eight Mothers[5] mark the entrance and exit of the old trade road,[6] a building with no other ritual use in the center of the town is still named as being the residence of the centuries-absent Newar king, and the main calendrical processions follow a specific route traversing each of the town's seven squares (*tols*). These squares create local identity both of, and within, Pharping. A woman going to do her morning *pūjā*s (ritual offerings) visits the *tol Gaṇeśa* (shrine to Gaṇeśa) or other shrines of her family's *tol*; a newborn child is taken to see that same Gaṇeśa on its first voyage out of the house; and football teams from the older parts of the town that have *tol*s all take their names from those *tol*s. Belonging to a *tol* is the key of belonging to Pharping. The historical stratigraphy of the town is neatly expressed by the clustering of low-caste families around the *Poḍe Ṭol*, named for the untouchable Newar Sweepers. *Poḍe Ṭol* has large houses built by wealthy low-caste families, both Newar and Parbatiya (Poḍe, Kāmi, Sarki) as well as some newer Mānandhars (a Newar caste usually located just below the Maharjans) who have expanded from an older cluster of Mānandhar households around the next *ṭol* uphill.[7]

There are a few villages populated by Tamang speakers (a rural Tibeto-Burman language; speakers support both Nyingma Tibetan lamas and indigenous shamans) immediately around Pharping and, while relatively few Tamangs actually live within the town, Newar informants will, if gently pressed, often mention them as members of Pharping. Certainly they make up a significant part of the economic activity of the Pharping markets and shops.

From the Pharping bus station, it is impossible not to notice the many large, colorful Tibetan monasteries dotting the surrounding hillsides, some still under construction. The Tibetans are recent arrivals; Lévi noted that there were *bhoṭiyā* pilgrims in Pharping around 1900, but he did not identify them as actually being Tibetan (Lévi 1905: II, 400). *Bhoṭe* or *bhoṭiyā* are Nepali terms for a range of Tibetic peoples, including middle hills ethnic groups such as Tamangs or Gurungs, those from the alpine regions of Nepal, such as Sherpas, and those who are actually from the various parts of Tibet (Ramble 1997). The first Tibetan monastery was constructed before 1960 and, while there are now at least twenty-six, land continues to be acquired for the construction of even more. Pharping (Tibetan: *yang le shod*) is an important site in the mythical history of the Nyingma school of Tibetan Buddhism as the place where its founder, Guru Rimpoche or Padmasambhava, established the Vajrakīla (*rdo rje phur ba*) tantras during an intensive retreat. Hence the vast majority of monasteries built around Pharping are closed retreat centers, and they are usually paired with more public monasteries located in Bodnath, to the east of Kathmandu, or with monasteries located in Tibetan refugee settlements in India. It is a sign of wealth and prestige for an incarnate lama, teaching lineage, or monastery to build a retreat center in Pharping.

The constant stream of Tibetan monks, patrons and families is now a part of Pharping life, but their economic (and visual) impact is not always acknowledged.[8] In compiling lists of Pharping residents, I found I always had to ask, "and what about the Tibetans?" before any resident would mention them. So far as I know, no Tibetan actually owns land within the limits of Pharping's old town. However, many Tibetans rent rooms or flats from local landlords, and the monasteries hold large tracts of land on the hills all around the town.

Not all Tibetans are celibate, religious, or male. Many of the male Nyingma religious in Pharping, whether officially celibate or not, take partners locally or bring them in. Nyingma Vajrayāna Buddhism, like Newar Buddhism, links celibacy and tantric practice with a partner. There are a few new families in Pharping composed of a Tibetan man and a local woman. Furthermore, there are nuns as well as monks. The only Tibetan religious in Pharping who has learned to speak Newari is a nun.

The groups labeled "Tibetans" and *bhoṭe* are not simple ethnic blocks, though many Pharping residents see them as such and in the context of conversations about the monasteries lump them together. There are Sherpa and Tamang monasteries, for example, and the population of any monastery may be made up of a mix of genuine Tibetan refugees from different parts of Tibet, Tibetans from refugee settlements in Nepal and India, *bhoṭe*s, and non-Tibetans from Nepalese ethnic communities such as Rai who would not otherwise be called *bhoṭe*. While residents of Pharping can, and usually do, distinguish between these groups when talking about those outside the monastic communities, using terms such as Sherpa, *bhoṭe*, or Tamang, the distinctions are dropped for people who dress as Tibetan lamas. All such people are called "lama" or *tibeti manche* (Tibetan). Only tourists in Tibetan lama's clothing are labeled differently—as "tourists."

For their part, the lamas have a limited awareness of the complexity of Pharping. Some of the resident refugee lamas know that Pharping has a mix of ethnicities, but none that I interviewed could name more than two or three Newar *thar*, and it was not clear that they were even aware that the Newars were a distinct community. They draw distinctions among Sherpa, Tamang, refugee Tibetan, refugee-camp Tibetan, and other groups, as well as drawing strong distinctions between Nyingma and other schools, and between incarnate lamas, celibate lamas (of whom there are fewer and fewer), and non-celibate lamas.

In comparison, Śaṅkhu is almost purely Newar. Being further north and east, it has not had the same degree of immigration from Nepali speakers (who have moved from west to east, and up-slope along the Himalayas), and as it does not have a major Nyingma pilgrimage site, it did not become a center for diasporic Tibetan activities, even though it is actually closer to the main Kathmandu Valley Tibetan settlement at Bodnath. What Śaṅkhu does have that Pharping lacks is a fully functioning Newar Buddhist monastery (*bahā*). Shrestha (2002) notes that although eight of Śaṅkhu's nine *bahā*s are defunct, one is still a thriving institution with a resident *sangha* (monastic community). By contrast, inhabitants of Pharping remember ten *bahā*s, but the one surviving institution (at the shrine of Vajrayoginī) has no resident *sangha*. The *Vajrācārya* priest who lives there is actually a member of *Bu Bahāḥ*, a monastery in Lalitpur, and he has built his home in that city.[9]

Pharping has three major shrines, all controlled by Newars: *Vajrayoginī, Dakṣin Kālī*, and *Śes Nārāyaṇ*. While *Vajrayoginī* is definitely a *Vajrayāna* Buddhist deity, *Dakṣin Kālī* (as her name indicates) is a *Śākta* deity who expects blood sacrifice, strongly patronized by the (non-Newar) *Śāh* royal dynasty; and the deity at *Śes Nārāyaṇ* is a form of *Viṣṇu*.

Worshipping Vajrayoginī

The cult of Vajrayoginī at Pharping is at least twelve hundred years old. She is a fierce tantric deity, described in textual sources as both beautiful and wrathful. Of the four Vajrayoginīs around the Kathmandu Valley, this particular one is known as the Flying Vajrayoginī (*khagamana*), although many of the Tibetans worship the image as a form of Vajravārāhī, the Adamantine Sow. As with many other important Indic deities, she has both a fixed shrine complex, with a main shrine image, and a smaller image that goes on procession (*jātrā*) annually around her domain. Her shrine is above and outside Pharping in the jungle on a mountain, and is approached along an old road that leads uphill from Pharping, past a shrine to the wrathful protective deity Mahākāla. The Mahākāla shrine marks the northwest corner of Pharping and other *jātrā*s; if approaching the shrine as part of a clockwise circulation, turn the corner here to go back down into Pharping.

Although she has both Śaiva/Śākta (*śaivamārgī*) and Vajrayāna Buddhist (*bauddhamārgī*) names, Vajrayoginī's shrine priest is unambiguously Buddhist, and no non-Buddhist professional religious have the right to perform worship at her shrine. Among locals, almost all Newars come to worship at her shrine at some point during the year. A visit to her shrine is required for a new bride who has married into a Pharping Newar family. Newars from outside Pharping are also frequent patrons; high-caste Buddhist families—Tulādhars, Śākyas, and Vajrācāryas —and their *guthi*s (local caste-based endowed ritual societies) that come from Kathmandu and Lalitpur for their own annual rituals at her shrine. Tibetans, both lay and ordained, worship at the shrine. Bahun-Chetris and Untouchables also patronize Vajrayoginī, although the Bahun-Chetri tend to gravitate towards the other two major shrines in Pharping. People in Pharping remember the day some twelve years ago when a determined delegation of Untouchables marched to the Vajrayoginī shrine and were pleased to find that the old sign banning them had been taken down. In brief, we can say that every resident of Pharping can visit Vajrayoginī and, for most Newars and Tibetans, frequent visits are a duty.

The Procession

The annual procession, by contrast, draws all the residents of Pharping (and more than a few spectators from nearby villages) together for a three-day festival. On the first day, the smaller image, together with her priest, descends from her main shrine to the town where, during the rest of the year, it rests in an antechamber hidden from casual view by the incumbent priests. With the help of several men under the direction of the Vajrācārya priest, this image is first lowered down through a hatch in the floor of her secret room. She is then put onto a palanquin and carried, accompanied by music, down the road into town. Twenty years ago this road was isolated, but now it is crowded with Tibetan cafés and shops aimed at tourists visiting the new monasteries that have been built on the hillside. The image passes the *Mahākāl* shrine and descends into *Śeṣ Nārāyaṇ Tol*. This *tol* is unusual in that all the families that are from, or descend from, high Buddhist castes have houses there.[10] Vajrayoginī is then placed in a shopfront on the square that is set aside for her. She will stay there for the following two days. A steady stream of people, including representatives of all the major families in Pharping, arrive to offer a public worship. At times when the site is crowded they queue up outside the shrine and sit in their finest clothes on the steps of the shops opposite, with their offering plates carefully set in front of them. The Maharjans have a *guthi* especially for performing this *pūjā*. At night, *bhajan* groups (singers of devotional songs) from certain *ṭol*s perform nearby.

The procession on the third evening combines spectacular individual mortification with opportunities for girls to display their finery (and boys to capture them with digital cameras). The leaders of the *jātrā* are one or more men who have undertaken to perform the vow of measuring the road with their bodies (*dhalaṃ dhanegu*). In the cases I have observed these men have all been Maharjans, but they and others insist that anyone can undertake this vow. Surrounded by family members and wearing only white cloth on their heads and bodies, these men lie full length on the ground, arms extended and hands together. Their supporters then place small oil lamps at the furthest reach of their hands. The men then stand and take three steps to the oil lamp, and again stretch out full length on the ground. In this way they will, over the following three or four hours, cover the entire procession route.

The business of managing these pilgrims is time consuming and slow, and the remainder of the procession forms up behind them (see figure 4.1). The procession falls neatly into four parts. First there are the prostrators together with their support teams. Next comes the two groups of musicians (*bhajan samiti*) who had played and sung near the deity for the previous two nights, bracketing a gang of wildly dancing young men. Third comes along a double file of women in their finest clothes. This is by far the largest element of the procession. Every woman of Pharping, whether born or married there, should walk in this double file a few times in her life. In recent years the organizers have taken to laying a long white cloth down along the route for the women to walk on which distinguishes them clearly from the prostrators, who after a few minutes are muddy, sweaty, and smeared with damp red *ṭīka* (ritual powder). Finally Vajrayoginī herself comes surrounded by her entourage. First is yet another set of musicians, followed by more young male dancers, and then the official escort of a troupe of "guards"— flautists in antique uniforms. They are followed by a censor and a yak-tail-whisk bearer, and then finally Vajrayoginī herself, borne on a heavy palanquin supported by eight or more men.[11]

The place of Vajrayoginī in the devotional life of Pharping is at least partly expressed by the contrast between the male renunciants, wearing the white cloth of ascetics and undertaking an arduous pilgrimage that involves sprawling in the mud, and the long ranks of women strolling upright in their most attractive clothing on a white cloth that protects them from it. In the old Sanskrit meditations devoted to her, she is both sexually attractive and wrathful, and one of the very few female deities to appear on her own. For Pharping she is a protective deity, a major esoteric Buddhist deity and a women's deity.

As with other major ritual events, the *mūl jātrā* (a week-long yearly festival dedicated to Hariśankar) and the *Kārttik pyākhā* (a fortnight-long sequence of ritual dramas performed every twelve years), everyone in Pharping is assumed to attend either as a performer or an actively engaged spectator. Despite this the Tibetans do not, as far as I can tell, attend the late-night *pyākhā* nor make a point of watching the *mūl jātrā*. They do take part in a high-profile and organized way in the annual Buddha Jayanti procession (Tuladhar-Douglas 2004) as a way of signaling their Buddhism. However in the case of Vajrayoginī, Tibetans distinguish between performing rituals at the shrine and participating in the festival; Tibetans do not participate in the *jātrā*.

Data

I was puzzled by the absence of the Tibetans at the Vajrayoginī celebration. Tibetan religious are not part of the entourage around Vajrayoginī, and Tibetan women do not walk in the women's procession. In informal conversations with Pharping residents (conducted in Newari with Newars, and Nepali with others) I found that a typical answer to the question, "do the Tibetans take part in the Vajrayoginī *jātrā*?" was something like "of course!", but then, after consideration or further questioning, "but I haven't actualy seen them there." This reflects the conflict between the strongly held belief that everyone in Pharping should, and does, take part in the *jātrā*, and the empirical fact that the Tibetans simply do not. I set up a series of semi-structured interviews, keeping close track of the social position of the respondents. My goal was to construct a complete grid recording the responses of members of each social group to a question about every other social group's participation in the Vajrayoginī *jātrā*. Although I did not collect information from Tamang informants, I was otherwise able to gather a fairly complete, if coarse-grained, conspectus for the various groups of Pharping (see table 4.1) which seemed, with significant variations, to indicate that Tibetans did not take part in the Vajrayoginī *jātrā*.

Two Views

The Maharjans have very close relations with the Tibetans through running the construction businesses that actually build the monasteries. They are also the largest nominally Buddhist Newar *thar*. Some Maharjans have learned to speak Tibetan in order to further their business interests while at least one family has sent a son to become a monk. When I asked, one evening in a busy Maharjan contractor's shop, if Tibetans took part in the *jātrā* of Vajrayoginī, the answer came back that they definitely did take part. I pushed the point, and said that I had seen scant evidence of this. The shop owner, who is an old friend and has done very well out of the Tibetan construction trade, pushed back. *Bālāmha Phampi mī he kha*—"They certainly are good Pharping people," he said, "and they do come for the *jātrā*." Did they, I asked, know the route of the *jātrā*? Did they know the names of the seven *ṭols* of Pharping? Other Maharjans in the shop reacted to this; knowing the names of the seven town squares through which a procession must pass is a strong marker for Pharping identity. No, he conceded, they did not understand Pharping that way, the way Pharping people do. They did give a lot of business to Pharping. They were part of Pharping! Other Maharjans I interviewed more briefly were equally firm in their belief that the Tibetans did definitely take part in the *jātrā*.

A milder, but more pervasive, refusal to notice the Tibetans lack of participation emerged as I interviewed other Pharping residents. Every respondent knew that everybody *could* take part in the Vajrayoginī *jātrā* and almost every respondent said, when asked initially, that the Tibetans *did* take part. It was only when I asked if they had ever actually seen any Tibetans take part that respondents (other that Maharjans) would, after reflection, give an answer qualified in terms of personal knowledge. Yet this never became a generalization: "No, I haven't seen them there myself" did not lead, as it might have, to "They never take part, do they?"

Tibetans themselves, by contrast, simply denied that they took part, and responded to the query with incomprehension or explicit criticism. In 2005, I interviewed one Tibetan monk in a shop, together with two Bālāmī Newars. This monk was not ethnically Tibetan. He was a Nepali *bhoṭe* from near Ilam who had ordained as a Tibetan monk. Bālāmīs tend to patronize Śaiva institutions but, as with most Newars, see no need to draw a line between religions. This monk often stayed the afternoon in the shop, and the couple with him during this interview worked closely with the monk in an incense business. When I asked about the absence of Tibetans in the Vajrayoginī *jātrā*, this monk was sharply critical of the *jātrā*. He asserted that *jātrā*s "were Hindu." It was wrong for a Buddhist to take part, and therefore no Tibetan monk could be involved. The Bālāmīs were startled by this claim and objected, as did I, but the monk was unconvinced. If a Buddhist deity had a *jātrā*, he said, it was an example of bad Hindu influence on pure Buddhist rituals. This was not the first time I had heard Tibetan lamas criticize Newar Buddhists for being "Hindu," but this particular criticism of a highly respected deity was unusual.

His response was more direct than some. In 2006 I interviewed three long-established refugee lamas sitting together, drinking tea and watching the Vajrayoginī *jātrā*. I asked them if Tibetans ever took part. When they said no, I asked first if lamas had ever taken part—no—and if any Tibetan girls had ever taken part in the women's procession, to which the answer was also no. I asked if Tibetans ever took part in any Newar *jātrā*s. Yes, they do, was the reply, followed by the question "have you ever been to Svayambhū and seen the Tibetan women walking there?" This confused me for some seconds. Svayambhū is an ancient Newar stūpa sacred to Mañjuśrī, and while one often sees Tibetans walking around it carrying out the ceremonial '*khor ba*, there are no Newar *jātrā*s there. It transpired that the lama was referring to the '*khor ba* practice which women often do. It is a morning or evening routine of walking along a long path, making a clockwise circumambulation of the entire hill on which the stūpa sits. It certainly is a social ritual, and one which acts powerfully to construct a sense of place, but it is distinctively Tibetan. Unlike the Nepali monk, who took an intolerant line in defense of a "pure" Buddhism that excludes Hinduism, these lamas did not direct a modernist[12] criticism at the Vajrayoginī *jātrā*; they simply could not conceive of a Tibetan taking part in a Newar procession. It was, literally, unthinkable, and the closest they could come to it was remembering Tibetans doing a Tibetan ritual near a site that Tibetans know Newars hold to be sacred.

While it might be objected that Tibetan lamas would not take part in a Newar procession, or a procession dominated by women, these do not seem to be reasons for their absence, nor were they ever mentioned. Important Tibetan lamas, both celibate and lay, do in fact take part in a shared *jātrā*, that of Buddha Jāyanti. This involves all the Newar *thar* in Pharping and many other groups as well; and although Tibetan lamas do participate, that participation is not without conflict (see Tuladhar-Douglas: 2004). As for Tibetan women participating in a Pharping Buddhist procession, the Buddha Jāyanti procession includes women although they are not a focus of the procession in the way that they are for the Vajrayoginī procession.

Managing the Discontinuity

What interests me here, then, is not whether or how sacred sites are shared, but how a specific process of sharing is performed and understood by the actors who make it happen. The refusal of the Tibetans to take part in the *jātrā* creates an uncomfortable discontinuity of practice. Most Pharping residents simply overlook it, though most will not actually deny the Tibetan absence if it is pointed out. The two groups closest to the ethnic dividing line, the Maharjans on the "inside" and the Tibetans on the "outside", have diametrically opposed answers. It falls to the Maharjans to assert and repair the inclusive social order that the Tibetans test by their principled refusal to participate.

My interviewing activities had the potential to damage this order by impolitely calling attention to an otherwise easily overlooked discrepancy. By deliberately noticing the Tibetan behaviour, I was not being a good Pharping person—and my interlocutors had to clean up after me. Recall that, even though non-Maharjan informants did acknowledge, when pressed, that they had not actually seen Tibetans take part in the procession, this never led to a general claim that they woud not or could not. Rather, the general understanding that anyone could take part was protected by refusing to draw conclusions from the behavior exposed by my questions. Maharjan informants, who felt some obligation to defend the Tibetans, responded more forcefully to my tactless querying by a direct refutation of the undesirable inference.

Michael Carrithers, studying Jains and Hindus in Gujarat, Western India, has characterized the state of affairs there as a "polytropy": "people turn towards many sources for their spiritual sustenance, hope, relief or defence" (Carrithers 2000: 834). It is an eclecticism, a pluralism, a refusal to police boundaries and, by turns, convivial or quarrelsome. Polytropy is a term that describes a social fabric woven from the plural religious orientation of families and individuals. It can be seen as complemetary to shrine images having many names, each allowing a different form of worship, which I have elsewhere (Tuladhar-Douglas 2005) called polyonomy. These two processes make for a resilient pluralism of the sort observed in Pharping and, I suspect, Gujarat.

Contrary to Carrithers, I suspect that polytropy by itself is probably not enough to explain this pluralism. Boundaries do exist, both in allegiance to deities and in the naming of shrines. An individual is respectful of many, perhaps all, deities but has specific allegiances through lineage to one, through caste to another, through locality to yet another. So too a specific shrine image may have a dominant name, with others asserted or remembered as acts of resistance; or the image may simply sustain a wide range of names in different registers. Certain shrine images, as I will discuss below, may have names that—for their particular sociohistorical context—are a refusal of sectarian identity.

The complex caste and ethnic composition of Pharping may go some way to explain why polytropy is the ordinary state of affairs there. All residents, save the Tibetans, know that it is originally, and perhaps essentially, a Newar town. Its defining rituals, shrines and their officiants are all Newar. Yet almost half of the inhabitants are non-Newar *Parbatiya*, divided between the low or untouchable *thar* that live mostly below the main road and the higher Bahun-Chetri *thar* families, some of whom live in the old town and some in the upper part of town, outside the old core. None of the main ritual processions go into the low-caste Parbatiya areas. There are also a few Tamang living at the edges of Pharping, and several Tamang villages around Pharping. This means that the crowded vegetable market in the center of Pharping or the throng gathered in a town square for a procession is highly diverse. If there were to be exclusivist rivalries, then Tamangs, Tibetans, and some Newar castes (including the priest at Vajrayoginī) would line up on the Buddhist side.[13]

Instead what I found was the assertion that to be a good Pharping person was to take part in, to join in, to help sustain the polytropy. Carrithers argues that it is *pūjā*, the act of worship itself, that creates polytropy. I am not so sure that this is enough. Certainly *pūjā* is important. Countless times in my fieldwork I have gone to one shrine or another for reasons that had far more to do with asserting social bonds ("they're going in, so should we") or a sense of place ("we're at this end of town, we should stop at the local Gaṇeśa") than any particular reverence for the deity of the shrine. Yet there are also attitudes and gestures that sustain the integrity of the woven cloth, so to speak. Firmly believing that the whole town ("Pharping people") shares a willingness to join in is itself also part of creating that cloth. So too is claiming that people who do not join in are "nonetheless" good

Pharping folk. It is both a constant series of gestures (*pūjā*s, visits, ways of walking) and a social attitude. In fact, a polytropy is just as carefully constructed in its social setting as is an exclusivist, bounded definition of religion. The difference may be that a polytropy requires a strong sense of place.

The Importance of Place

In his exposition of polytropy, Carrithers anchors it in the practice of *pūjā*. He makes four points:

1. Polytropy is a wholly and thoroughly social concept, denoting that the consumers of religion actively turn to persons.
2. Polytropy covers many qualities of religious relationship, from the occasional request … from a distant god to the god who one visits daily.
3. These relationships … are hierarchical and manifested through … *puja*.
4. Polytropy is a dynamic process.

(Carrithers 2000: 834–35)

Looking over my notes I have been struck by an emphasis on place. My Maharjan informants asserted that the Tibetans really did take part in the *jātrā* by stating that they were "good Pharping people." I noted above that a child born in Pharping, or a football team, or a woman performing the *nhikā* (daily worship) on behalf of her household all enact their membership in Pharping through the local shared shrine of the town square. Annual participation in *jātrā*s constructs, in a precise and orchestrated way, membership both in one's local square and in the town as a whole. This is especially true for the intricate *Hariśaṅkhar jātrā*, involving seven separate *rath*s (carts) being pulled on various days from each of the *tol*s through the circuit of all of the *tol*s until the cart returns to its origin.[14] So too, in the Vajrayoginī *jātrā*, the deity descends from the mountain above and outside Pharping, down the old road, past the wrathful protective deity Mahākāla. After two days of worship, she travels on a palanquin as the culmination of a long procession around all seven *tol*s in the correct order, then leaves the town by the same road and returns to her forested mountain home.

For a resident of Pharping, then, life-cycle rituals, football season rituals, annual rituals and daily rituals all not only require performers to act as Pharping people but simultaneously construct them as Pharping people. The rituals all take place around shared sites that create a sense of shared locality within the town, which in turn creates a sense of belonging to the town. What all these small, local shared shrines have in common is that they belong to deities (most often Gaṇeśa) who are believed by Pharping people to have no sectarian identity.

This requires some explanation. There is a well-known late Purāṇic tradition that locates Gaṇeśa in the family of Śiva, and almost all descriptions of Hinduism for the Western classroom give Gaṇeśa as a "Hindu" god. This is certainly not how he is understood by Newars. He is the god of beginnings, propitiated at the outset of every *pūjā* regardless of whether one is formally Śaiva, formally Buddhist, or (as with most Newars) not encumbered by the question. Certainly people know the Hindu stories, especially now that Indian television force-feeds a far less nuanced version of them, but Buddhist Newars, who might be expected to assert a counternarrative, do not. Gaṇeśa is simply the Remover of Obstacles (*vighnāntaka*), the god of beginnings, and the pre-eminent locality deity. Every *ṭol* in Pharping has its Gaṇeśa. The morning *pūjā* is a chance to be seen to be a good member of the locality and exchange a bit of gossip. While the *nhikā* performed by an individual within his or her home may reflect sectarian affiliations, the public act that creates the social identity of the place and gives its residents their sense of place, refuses them.

In Pharping, defence of polytropy is an inherent aspect of maintaining the social fabric of Pharping itself. It would not make sense to go to the trouble of repairing the polytropy except inasmuch as it is part of Pharping, and the agents who create Pharping are themselves created of Pharping.

As is clear from other studies of Newar society (Gellner 1993), this practice is not specific to Pharping. For Newars, polytropies are local, and it is possibly precisely because individuals are grounded in the ritual construction of a shared locality that each participant feels a profound sense of place. What is especially interesting about the Pharping case is that historically newer Nepali-speaking populations who have settled in and around Pharping have, at least to some extent, accepted and been folded into the Newar ritual process of creating Pharping and its polytropy.[15] The rules may be Newar in appearance, but each morning the locality deities watch a heterogeneous population make their offerings. Some Parbatiya Nepalis—who do not include Buddhism in their polytropies and polyonomies elsewhere in Nepal—live within the old core of Pharping, belong to one of the seven *ṭols*, and worship the local deities. A far larger number commute in, just to take part in the Vajrayoginī *jātrā* and other formal Newar rituals.

So far, this integrative process has failed to include the recently arrived Tibetans. I am currently researching the specific genealogies of their intolerance, but at a minimum we can say that there simply is no shared sense of place. The Tibetan claim to Pharping is based on a foundation myth for the Nyingma school and on events in the life of their founding figure, Padmasambhava. Very few Tibetan lamas know that Padmasambhava, twelve hundred years ago, worked with Newars in Pharping to found the Nyingma school. For the Tibetans, implicitly or explicitly, Pharping is part of a Tibetan geography of the Himalayas that has gained stridency in exile; their identity, whether individual or corporate, owes nothing to modern Pharping town and its hybrid Newar pasts.

There may be general conclusions to be drawn here about the relationship between a socially cohesive sense of place and the possibility of sharing sacred sites. While, in this case, I have argued that the tendency to defend a shared understanding of the Vajrayoginī *jātrā* arose together with a sense of place constructed through microlocalities, it is also true that, for all Newars, Vajrayoginī is part of their total geography, one of four Vajrayoginīs that ring the whole of the Kathmandu Valley. All four of these shrines (all five, if we include Guhyeśvarī in the center) are examples of shared shrines, and the narratives and namings that allow for sharing at this broader level are part of Newar identity as a whole. Something similar is true for shared pilgrimage sites such as Mount Kailash (Śaiva, Jain, Buddhist) or Lake Rewalsar (Śaiva, Sikh, Nyingmapa) that are located within a common Indic sacred geography.

The opposite condition, the *dis*location experienced by diaspora populations and industrialized families moved about as a result of enforced labour mobility, may in turn explain the failure of sympathetic imagination that underlies one sort of inability or refusal to envisage a shrine as mutually sacred. If a family does not have the time to settle in one place for long enough to appropriate and then transmit a sense of place, how can they ever learn to share it?

Hard Work

In closing I wish to draw from this study some conclusions on the likely outcome of an antagonistic encounter between an inclusive, polytropy-and-polonomy style of managing religious identities, and an exclusive and perhaps modernist style of asserting a single identity (see Hayden 2002). In brief, when the dominant mode is tolerance, then striking a sectarian posture is hard work; but when there is a powerful economic or political group that practices intolerance, it becomes hard work to maintain the inclusivist stance, especially along the zone of contact. It requires common effort, and the willingness to expend that social effort only makes sense once we see that the identity of a Pharping person is derived from a sense of place built through successive acts that depend on the refusal of simplistic intolerance, single allegiances and single identities. Intolerance is a threat to the fabric within which each person's identity is discovered.

It is the very effort involved in sustaining and repairing the fabric that explains why exclusivist behavior tends to be disavowed or resisted by those who practice polytropic inclusivism. In Pharping the entire community must collude, albeit implicitly, to make good the damage caused by the Tibetan refusal. If the community understands itself to be acting as a whole, bar one troublesome part, then each actor's agreement to understand their participation as an element of a holistic community itself constitutes that whole. It is this agreement which is central; in the case described above, the Tibetan's non-participation created a vulnerability but did not in itself cause real damage—the damage was done when I inquired about their non-participation. Some of the work of repair is evident in the Maharjan claim that, despite non-participation, the Tibetans were good Pharping people.

How well this intercommunal fabric will withstand the shears of the next fifty years is very hard to say, for it is under attack from several quarters. With the changes of the 1991 People's Movement and the establishment of a parliamentary monarchy,[16] Christian missionaries have gained a foothold in the area. The appeal of conversion to Christianity is that it gives the convert cash at the same time as it frees his or her family from ritual obligations. The missionaries are perceived to be heavily subsidized—stories of recent converts being given free air tickets to the United States circulate constantly. Converts, and by extension their families, are freed from the need to get up for the morning *pūjā*, the need to sponsor expensive lifecycle rituals, the need to pay dowry and to maintain a long succession of post-funeral rituals. The appeal of conversion pits individual wealth against collective effort and, as we have seen, it takes coordinated social effort to maintain the inclusive Pharping. On another front, the remittance economy now provides most of Pharping's wealth. This, too, furnishes a powerful narrative of wealth and an eventual promise of escape, although rather than liberating the local kin of remittance workers from their social obligations, it requires them to display ostentatiously their improved ability to act within Pharping rules, by using money from elsewhere until they too can finally escape the stage. Finally the Maoist movement, which is particularly strong in Pharping, has added its own critique of burdensome ritual duties and bogus ideologies preserving caste, class and religion, and its advocates proclaim revolution as yet another means of escape from the ritual cycle and the fabric of obligations that maintains it.

Yet a Newar removed from this fabric feels its lack most keenly. In conversations with Newars who have traveled outside Kathmandu Valley, or those now living in the United Kingdom, I have found that one of the most common expressions is grief at the absence of the most local and ordinary forms of public religion. "There are no Gaṇeśas here" they say, and go on to bemoan the lack of a sense of place,

Figure 4.1. Prostrating Maharjan, ringed by family and supporters, leading the *jātrā*. Photo W. Tuladhar-Douglas.

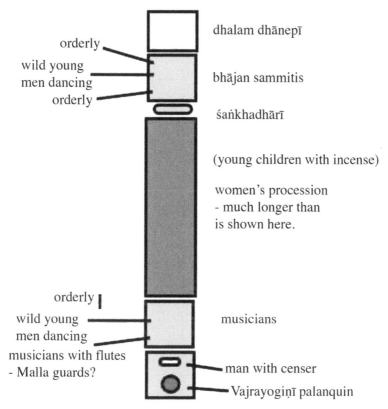

orderly

wild young
men dancing

orderly

dhalam dhānepī

bhājan sammitis

śaṅkhadhārī

(young children with incense)

women's procession
- much longer than
is shown here.

orderly

wild young
men dancing

musicians with flutes
- Malla guards?

musicians

man with censer

Vajrayoginī palanquin

Figure 4.2. Structure of the Vajrayoginī procession in 2005 and 2006. Diagram by W. Tuladhar-Douglas.

the fact that there is nowhere to meet the neighbors, no shared shrines, no polytropy, and, most literally, no "place" to raise children correctly as Newars. This concern, which I have heard voiced numerous times, points directly to my supposition that dislocation prevents the transmission of inclusive religious behavior.[17] The palpable sense of relief at returning home suggests that the

Table 4.1. Table correlating informant views (columns by group) about participation in Vajrayogini jatra (rows by group) with observed participation (final column). Table by W. Tuladhar-Douglas.

Group attending \ Respondent group	Bahun-chetri	Tuladhar	Srestha	Jyapu	Balami	Manadhar	Damai-Sarki	Tibetan	Observed by ethnographer?
Bahun-chetri	attend and perform vrata	attend and perform vrata	attend and perform vrata	yes	yes	yes	yes	yes	yes, especially eligible girls
Srestha	attend and perform vrata	attend and perform vrata	yes, do puja	yes	yes	yes	yes	yes	yes, especially eligible girls
Jyapu	attend and perform vrata	attend and perform vrata	yes, have guthi	yes, have guthi	yes	yes	yes	yes	yes, including vrata
Balami	attend and perform vrata	attend and perform vrata	attend and perform vrata	yes	yes	yes	yes	yes	yes, including vrata
Manadhar	attend and perform vrata	attend and perform vrata	attend and perform vrata	yes	yes	yes	yes	yes	yes, including vrata
Damai, Sarki	attend and perform vrata	attend and perform vrata	attend and perform vrata	?	yes	yes	yes	yes	yes, including vrata
Tibetan	yes/few	no/few	no/few	yes	no	no/few	no/few	no	no

international Newar community will be closely tied to a thousand small localities scattered throughout the Kathmandu Valley for at least a generation to come.

Notes

1. My thanks to Pharping informants, my family—especially Bhavana Tuladhar-Douglas—and the participants in the ASA panel on shared shrines organized by Glenn Bowman. The fieldwork for this article was carried out between 2002–6. It was written for a 2006 conference and revised for publication in 2007. Subsequent developments have not been discussed.
2. The Newars are the indigenous inhabitants of the Kathmandu Valley, with a complex urban society built up through repeated historical in-migrations and organized around caste, religion, and locality groups. Their wealthy mercantile city-states, never politically united, were colonized by the nascent Gorkhali empire in the eighteenth century, and modern Newar culture has developed inside an oppressive Nepali-speaking state that was officially a Hindu monarchy until 2007. Although their language is one of the only Tibeto-Burman languages to have a classical literate tradition, only half or fewer of the roughly million people calling themselves 'Newar' now still speak the language. Good introductions to Newar society include Toffin (1984), Levy and Rājopādhyāya (1992), and Gellner (1993).
3. On this see the discussion by Gellner (1993: 68ff.). A Bālāmī informant in Pharping expressed this clearly, saying "We Bālāmīs were here before there was any talk about 'Bauddha' or 'Śaiva.'"
4. See Gutschow and Kolver (1975) on Newar space and ritual.
5. The Eight Mothers (*Aṣṭamātṛkāh*) are a collection of wrathful female deities, led by Gaṇeśa in a wrathful form, who mark the limit between urban space and wild (*jāṅgala*) land. They appear and dance (as masked dancers) in the twelve-yearly autumn ritual dance (*Kārttik pyākhāṃ*). Where the mild Gaṇeśa marks the centers of the *tol*s, the Eight Mothers guard the perimeter of the town.
6. The old path leading from the Valley is now rarely traveled, but a Mahālakṣmī shrine is still present; the southbound path leading, eventually, to the Tarai and India is still used by people walking to nearby villages such as Lamagaū. The Mahālakṣmī shrine there is well known. Both shrines are at small fords on the downhill paths leading from the plateau on which Pharping sits.
7. In fact, the vast majority of low-caste families are now Nepali-speaking Parbatiya incomers who live outside the seven *tol*s, below the new metalled road built about ninety years ago for the Nepali king.
8. These monasteries also attract small groups of wealthy visitors from Eastern and Southeastern Asia, Europe and North America. These, as well as people who come on day trips in tour buses and occasional resident foreigners, are politely called "tourists."
9. His father was also the priest at *Vajrayoginī*; but prior to his father a different lineage were the incumbents. They, and even the lineage before them, were also from Lalitpur monasteries, though not *Bu Bahāḥ*.
10. These families have contested status as "Pharping people." There is one family of Tulādhars (who, although resident in Pharping for six generations, are still not fully localized) and one house is owned by the Vajrācārya incumbent at Vajrayoginī, built for him when he took up the post. The previous lineage of Vajrācāryas, who lost the priesthood when their son married a Mahārjan, also have a house there. Most of the other households in the *tol* are Mānandhar or Śreṣṭha.
11. In 2005, an outsider who dressed as a Hindu priest and who had been staying near Dakṣinkālī, placed himself, carrying a conch, into the *jātrā* just before the women. This was not regarded as problematic by onlookers; he had been inserting himself into town life in various ways.
12. The term "modernist" here refers to Buddhism as a self-consciously reformist and carefully bounded world religion, such as the movements promulgated by, among others, Dharmapala and Ambedkar.
13. David Gellner (2005) studied polytropy in the Newar case and showed that "modernist" or "exclusivist" stances against polytropy were adopted, for example, by Buddhist activists. In

Pharping, however, even faced with pointedly Hindu gestures by Śreṣṭhas and Bahun-Chetris such as aggressive *bhajan* groups who take over public rest houses, cover them with Hindu posters, then bar and lock them, the countermovement of a strident Buddhist modernism of the sort recorded by Gellner has not occurred.

14. B. Tuladhar-Douglas is currently studying the intricate organization of this *jātrā*. Families who have moved to a different part of Pharping will return to their original *ṭol* to help with the rituals and the pulling of that locality's cart.

15. Historically, small groups of certain low-caste Parbatiya groups such as the *Jog* have been a part of Newar urban sites for several hundred years.

16. While the 1991 People's Movement did not lead, as many had hoped, to the disestablishment of Hinduism as the national religion, it did lead to legislation allowing missionaries to practice inside Nepal for the first time in centuries.

17. In Tuladhar-Douglas (2010), I have tried to link this sense of place to a performance of place that links human and non-human persons through social construction of the landscape.

References

Carrithers, Michael. 2000. "On Polytropy: Or the Natural Condition of Spiritual Cosmopolitanism in India: The Digambar Jain Case." *Modern Asian Studies* 34(4): 831–61.

Gellner, David. 1993. *Monk, Householder, and Tantric Priest: Newar Buddhism and its Hierarchy of Ritual.* New Delhi: Foundation Books.

———. 2005. "The Emergence of Conversion in a Hindu-Buddhist Polytropy: The Kathmandu Valley, Nepal, c.1600–1995." *Comparative Studies in Society and History* 47: 755–80.

Gutschow, Neils and Bernhard Kölver. 1975. *Bhaktapur: Ordered Space Concepts and Functions in a Town of Nepal.* Vienna: Franz Steiner Verlag.

——— and Manabajra Bajracharya. 1977. "Ritual as Mediator of Space in Kathmandu," *Journal of the Nepal Research Centre* 1: 1–10.

Hayden, Robert. 2002. "Antagonistic Tolerance: Competetive Sharing of Religious Sites in South Asian and the Balkans." *Current Anthropology* 43(2): 205–31.

Lévi, Sylvain. 1905. *Le Népal: Étude Historique d'un Royaume Hindou.* Paris: Ernest Leroux.

Levy, Robert and Kedar Rājopādhyāya. 1992. *Mesocosm: Hinduism and the Organization of a Traditional Newar City in Nepal.* Delhi: Motilal Banarsidass.

Ramble, Charles. 1997. "Tibetan Pride of Place: Or, Why Nepal's Bhotiyas Are Not an Ethnic Group," in *Nationalism and Ethnicity in a Hindu Kingdom: The Politics of Culture in Contemporary Nepal*, eds. D. Gellner, J. Pfaff-Czarnecka and J. Whelpton. Amsterdam: Harwood Academic Publishers, 379–413.

Shrestha, Bal Gopal. 2002. *The Ritual Composition of Sankhu: The Socio-religious Anthropology of a Newar Town in Nepal.* Kathmandu: Centre for Nepal and Asian Studies.

Toffin, Gérard. 1984. *Religion et société chez les Newars du Népal.* Paris: CNRS.

Tuladhar-Dougas, Will. 2004. "Historical Studies of Pharping, I: The Celebration of Buddha Jayanti," in *Five Mountains and Three Rivers: Musashi Tachikawa Felicitation Volume*, eds. S. Hino and T. Wada. Delhi: Motilal Banarsidass, 549–70.

———. 2005. "Why It Is Good To Have Many Names." *Contemporary South Asia* 14(1): 55–74.

———. 2010. "Collusion and Bickering: Landscape, Religion and Ethnicity in the Central Himalayas." *Contemporary South Asia* 18(3): 319–32.

Chapter 5

EFFICACY, NOT CONFESSIONALITY: ON RITUAL POLYTROPY IN CHINA

Adam Yuet Chau

Introduction: Religious Polytropy versus Ritual Polytropy

In his article "On Polytropy: Or the Natural Condition of Spiritual Cosmopolitanism in India: the Digambar Jain Case," the anthropologist Michael Carrithers lays out the etymology of his newly minted word "polytropy": "I coined the word from the Greek *poly*, 'many', and *tropos*, 'turning', to capture the sense in which people turn toward many sources for their spiritual sustenance, hope, relief, or defence" (Carrithers 2000: 834). According to Carrithers, one of the consequences of living in a religiously plural society such as that found in India is that each person is necessarily surrounded by, and encounters on a daily basis, holy persons and deities of different religious traditions. People will have developed a general reverential attitude towards all these holy persons and deities, all the while being conscious of the differences between these sources of power and authority. Even though certain elite members of each religious tradition (be it Hinduism, Jainism, or Islam) might advocate purist worship and frown upon or condemn indiscriminate "turnings," it seems that the overwhelming majority of Indians, sometimes including the protesting elites themselves and their family members, are in practice polytropic.

Despite polytropic practice, a typical Indian by ethnic and caste affiliation still has a more or less definite religious affiliation. A Hindu is a Hindu, and no matter how many gurus and deities of other religious traditions he or she "turns to," there is usually no question about his or her core or fundamental religious identity. This might be evidenced by the way an Indian is treated after death. An Indian might be religiously polytropic when alive, but somehow he or she is expected to die a single-faithed person with his or her funeral ritual being presided over by a priest (or multiple priests) of one religious tradition. One might have been a spiritual cosmopolitan while alive, but one dies a Hindu or a Muslim or a Jain, and there is no ambiguity or fuzziness about that.

On the other hand, most Han Chinese throughout China's long history have not had confessional religious identities, with the exception of very small pockets of groups claiming Muslim, Protestant, Catholic, Jewish, and millenarian/sectarian identities.[1] The overwhelming majority of Han Chinese would not call themselves Daoist, Buddhist, or Confucian, and there has not been a convergence between ethnic and religious identities as often is the case in India (one suspects that religion has played a significant role in the construction of ethnicity in India and many other places in the world). In their everyday life the Chinese are not dissimilar to the paradigmatically polytropic Indians characterized by Carrithers. They enshrine Daoist, Buddhist, or other kinds of deities on their domestic altars alongside the tablets for their ancestors in a seemingly indiscriminate manner; and they too approach in a seemingly opportunistic manner deities or religious specialists—of whichever persuasion—to exorcise evil spirits, ward off bad fortune, produce a good marriage partner or a long-awaited male descendant, deliver good fortune and blessing for the family or cure for a difficult illness, find a lost motorcycle, or resolve a life dilemma. A person with a particularly difficult problem will go to a Daoist temple, then a Buddhist temple, then a spirit medium, and then even a Catholic church or a Muslim mosque if the problem is resistant to other interventions. To him or her what matters is not which religious tradition the particular temple or specialist is affiliated with—which often is not clear anyway—but how efficacious (*ling, lingying, lingyan*) the deity or specialist is in responding to his or her requests. Typically, a person will make a vow promising that, if the problem is solved, he or she will bring offerings or money, help with the temple festival by contributing labor or materials, or spread the name of the deity far and wide. For temple festivals that hire opera troupes, a devotee and supplicant can also promise to sponsor a number of opera performances.

Depending on the extent of engagement one has over time with these various temples, deities, and specialists, one develops a network of more or less enduring and meaningful relationships with them which might be maintained for generations (cf. Roberts, Chiao and Pandey 1975; Roberts, Morita and Brown 1986). Less efficacious deities and specialists are visited less often and are gradually dropped from the network, while newly discovered, more efficacious ones are added. The temples and specialists might, and do, vie with one another for clientele and donations.[2]

In contrast to the commoner majority, more or less coherent religious group identities did develop among the elite religious practitioners such as members of the Buddhist sangha, the Quanzhen Daoist monastic order, and Confucian academies.[3] One key element all these three traditions shared was reliance on canonical texts; indeed, it is these texts that made them into "Great Traditions" (Redfield 1956).[4] These elite religious practitioners' main goal was self-cultivation, and their penchant for textual exegesis and philosophical reflections necessarily attracted them to one another's textual resources. As a result, historically there was frequent and serious trafficking of people and ideas between these three Great Traditions (see, for example, Mollier 2008). So at the level of discourse and practice each of these three Great Traditions became rather syncretistic. But one has to remember that the elite members of these religious traditions with stronger sense of religious identities were a very small minority. And even these identities were strictly speaking more akin to professional identities than confessional identities, so a Confucian scholar-ritualist could learn to become a Daoist priest in a process culminating in the Daoist ordination ritual, which was more like additional professional accreditation than a statement of religious conversion. In other words, one accrued more religious identities rather than converting from one to another (more can be found on conversion in the Conclusion).

Below the elite religious practitioners in terms of level of sophistication there were all kinds of religious service providers such as *fengshui* masters, diviners, fortunetellers, spirit mediums, magical healers, householder Daoist priests, Buddhist ritual masters, and Confucian ritualists who provided their specialist services for a fee. There were also sectarian village-based volunteer ritualists who provided ritual services to fellow sect members and other villagers for free.

There is usually one kind of specialist for each occasion. For finding the best site for houses and graves one needs a *fengshui* master; for divining one's luck and fortune one consults a fortuneteller; for exorcising evil spirits one can hire a spirit medium or an exorcist. But the one ritual occasion that is the most significant in the Chinese world is the funeral, and it is what the Chinese do ritually at the funeral that will be the focus of this chapter. Unlike standard funerals in most societies, where a religious specialist belonging to the same religious group as the deceased presides over the funeral, in China the host household can hire either Daoist priests or Buddhist monks to perform the funeral ritual (each group of ritualists following different liturgical programs).[5] But what is most interesting is that rich people in late imperial and Republican times would hire as many groups of religious specialists as possible to accrue karmic merits and other spiritual benefits for the deceased (and, by association, his or her kin) as well as to assert the family's social status and prestige. These religious specialists could include groups (always in groups) of Buddhist monks, Buddhist nuns, Daoist priests, Tibetan Buddhist lamas, and lay sectarian practitioners. So, unlike the shared or mixed sacred site situations analysed in most of the other chapters in this volume, the Chinese funeral exhibits the sharing of the same ritual event by groups of religious specialists belonging to different religious traditions. Modifying Carrithers' expression, I would like to call this condition "ritual polytropy."[6]

Death-related Concerns

At a Chinese funeral there are five mutually related yet distinct concerns.

First, what to do with the body of the deceased? This question can be called the "geo-corporeal concern," for it deals with transferring the body of the deceased, in a coffin, out of the home to the grave site, and then burying the body in the ground. The host household (*zhujia*) hires a *yinyang* master to take care of these procedures. The *yinyang* master (usually referred to as the "geomancer" in the Chinese Studies literature) is entrusted with the task of "siting" the best location and orientation for the house of the living (*yangzhai*) as well as the dwelling of the dead (*yinzhai*). He (always a male) is also responsible for aligning the coffin properly (with his geomantic compass), arranging in-grave utensils, and appeasing the earth god for having disturbed him with the digging of the grave.

Second, what to do with the soul of the deceased? This question can be called the "salvation concern," for it deals with the passage of the soul through hell and its prospect of reincarnation or "going onward to Western Paradise" (*shang xitian*) (cf. Cohen 1988). Traditionally, Buddhist monks would most commonly be hired to take care of these aspects (but see below). The rite they conducted is called "doing the merits" (*zuo gongde*) and involves chanting scriptures to accrue more merits for the deceased so that he or she would receive less severe punishments in the courts of hell and be reincarnated into better stations of life. This rite usually includes feeding the hungry ghosts the night before the burial.[7]

Third, what to do with the inauspicious impact of the death (labeled "death pollution" in the symbolic anthropology literature)? This can be called the "pollution concern." Traditionally Daoist priests specialize in exorcising evil influences and restoring communal or household peacefulness, but a *yinyang* master can equally be employed for this purpose.

Fourth, how to enact proper relations between the people who have converged to the time-space of the funeral (descendants, agnatic and affinal kin, friends, neighbors) within this particular ritual context (i.e., funeral)? This can be called the "ritual-social propriety concern," for it deals with the ritually proper enactment of social relationships between the mourners and the deceased, between the host family and the other mourners, and between the host family and the guests (including the hired professionals). The chief director (master of ceremony) is in charge of ensuring ritual propriety among all present: the stylized wailing, the graded mourning clothes, the funeral music, the prostrations and kowtows, the proper sequencing of ritual phases, and so forth. Traditionally a Confucian scholar would be invited to recite stylized elegies and to dot the ancestral spirit tablet (*chengzhu*), thus making the deceased into a proper ancestor.

Fifth and last, how to cater to the guests' needs and treat them well? The success of the funeral rests on addressing satisfactorily all five concerns, but it is the guest-catering aspect that the host family worries about the most. The host family's worries are justified because the guests will evaluate the event primarily based on their perceptions of how well the host has treated them (e.g., by gestures of respect, and the quality and quantity of food, drinks, and cigarettes distributed). The guests give little attention to the intricacies of the symbolic actions conducted or orchestrated by the ritual specialists relating to the other four concerns.

Why do the Chinese put so much emphasis on funerals? Death in itself is not ontologically more significant than, say, birth, and the various symbolic and social significances piled onto death are of course cultural constructs. Religious specialists play a large role in constructing these significances. Over China's long history,

Confucian, Buddhist, and Daoist thinkers and ritualists have all contributed to the elaboration of death-related cosmologies and ritual procedures. In time these became so complicated that only professionals could handle them, which of course suited the professionals' interests. Furthermore, people who had had a death in their family could hire professionals to take care of the rituals while they could focus on the mourning. The death rituals are meant for the deceased and spiritual beings, and thus are not meant to be understood by laypersons (who are not really interested in understanding their esoteric symbolisms). Indeed, many of these ritual procedures and symbolisms are esoteric and professional secrets. Another consequence of the elaboration (or over-elaboration) of death rituals in China is that a dead person seems to have three souls (though this is never conceptualized consciously by people), one staying with the corpse in the grave, one residing in the ancestral spirit tablet, and one going through the courts of hell and eventually being reincarnated (see Cohen 1988). The history of Chinese death ritual is a long and complicated one. It underwent its classical formulations in pre-dynastic times (when a proper and codified funeral was only reserved for members of the royal household and the aristocracy), was subsequently profoundly influenced by the advent of Buddhism which in turn spurred the Daoists to come up with their own full-blown funerary liturgical structure (with much borrowing from Buddhist funerary liturgy). In the Song Dynasty there was a neo-Confucian backlash against both Buddhist and Daoist ritual practices which resulted in a Confucian ritual formulation (see Brook 1989). By late imperial times, the three kinds of death rituals (Buddhist, Daoist, and Confucian) had all become acceptable and were variously employed by all Chinese, depending on the family's wealth and the availability of specialists. Throughout this history the service of the *yinyang* master has always been indispensable because he deals with burial matters.

How Many "Sheds" of Scriptures?

Despite some regional variations, death rituals achieved a remarkable degree of standardization in late imperial China (see Naquin 1988; Watson 1988; Watson and Rawski 1988; Sutton 2007). The standard funeral procedure was as follows:

- Dressing the corpse (*xiaolian*) [immediately after the death occurs]
- Public notice of death and reporting the death to the local gods (*baomiao*) [immediately after the death occurs]
- The encoffining of the corpse (*dalian*) [usually on the third day after death]
- The third-day reception (*jiesan*) [right after encoffining]
- The beginning of the condolence-receiving period (*kaidiao*) [which will last until the coffin leaves the home]
- Completing the tablet (*chengzhu*) [during the condolence-receiving period]
- Sending off the deceased (*songlu*)
- The burial procession (*fayin*) [when the coffin leaves the home for the burial site or the temporary storage place]

– The burial (*zang*) [may take place right after the funeral procession or a long time afterwards]

Even though the linear sequence of the funeral was quite standardized, the timing of some of the actions was very flexible. Poor people buried their dead as quickly as possible because they could not afford good coffins that could hold in the stench of the decaying corpse, and did not have a lot of guests who would come to pay respects to the deceased. Wealthy households in old Beijing, and north China in general, usually kept the coffin (tightly sealed of course) unburied for a long time in an ostensible display of filial piety and social status. Sometimes the auspicious date that the *yinyang* master determined for the burial could be years after the death.

Many of the guests who came to pay respects brought money and gifts, and specified how many "sheds of scriptures" (explained below) they would sponsor to help accumulate karmic merits (*gongde*) for the deceased. The typical dwelling in old Beijing was the so-called courtyard compound (*siheyuan*), referring to the layout of the dwelling complex: a squarish courtyard surrounded on all four sides by one-storey houses (each consisting of multiple rooms), all belonging to the same family and closed in by continuous walls. Wealthier families had multiple courtyards along a south-north axis, all flanked by houses. One would always enter a courtyard compound through the main entrance in the southern wall and proceed inward towards the north through the front courtyard and then the second courtyard, and so on. The rooms towards the back/north side were inner living quarters, while the rooms towards the front/south side were the more public quarters (e.g., reception hall, kitchen, servants' quarters).

Let us consider a hypothetical case of a death which has occurred in a wealthy family living in a courtyard compound with two courtyards. The deceased would be put in the coffin with the appropriate encoffinment procedures, and then the coffin rested in the main hall to the north of the back courtyard. The back courtyard would be used for all the mourning and ritual activities, while the front courtyard would be filled with tables and chairs for catering to guests. Four groups of religious specialists would be hired to chant scriptures: Tibetan Buddhist monks (lamas), Daoist priests, Buddhist monks, and Buddhist nuns—summarized in the Chinese expression *fan, dao, chan, ni* (see Anonymous; Liu 1996; Jin 1996). Each group of religious specialists and their performances were traditionally referred to as a "shed" of scriptures. Three of the four "sheds" might be gifts from relatives and friends (of course they had to pay these specialists). A "shed shop" (*pengpu*) would be hired to construct temporary covered scaffold platforms, similar to an opera stage (hence the expression "sheds of scripture") over the top of the houses flanking the back courtyard to the south, east, and west (the coffin was at the north side). Sheds, even though made of fir poles, wood boards, straw sheets, colored sheets of cloth, and decorated with removable sculptures along the roof ridges (see Liu 1996: 67–68), looked, from a distance, like palaces raised high above the neighboring one-storey courtyard compounds. The groups of monks, nuns and Daoist priests would ascend to these platforms and chant from above the visitors who gathered in the courtyard below to pay their respects to the deceased. The Buddhist monks would chant from the shed-platforms facing north, the Daoists and the Buddhist nuns would take the side shed-platforms, with the Daoists on the east side facing west and the nuns on the west side facing east (Anonymous). Lamas by tradition usually did not chant from above the ground (though this is not a steadfast rule), so they would be offered a place at ground level in the courtyard below (and in front of) the monks (ibid.). Typically the religious specialists would take turns to chant, even though sometimes they would be asked to chant simultaneously so as to increase the spectacle (and also perhaps make sure that they would finish the liturgical program in time). The liturgical programs could be shorter or longer depending on how long the religious specialists had been hired to chant. According to the principle "the more the better," the same liturgical programs could be repeated over and over again with the same set of scriptures.

Buddhist funerary rituals are premised upon the ideas of karmic merits and demerits, and reincarnation. Each person born is said to be a reincarnated soul from a previous life, carrying the weight of accumulated karmic merits and demerits from previous lives. His or her actions in this life also affect how the soul will be reincarnated again after death. The soul of a really terrible person would go straight to the Buddhist hell to suffer all kinds of punishments, while the soul of a supremely meritorious person would go straight to the Western Paradise. Most souls get way-stationed in a limbo for a period lasting up to forty-nine days before being reincarnated. During this liminal period the soul is believed to benefit from the merit-accruing effects of sutra chanting (including messages of repentance on behalf of the deceased), and a better reincarnation can be achieved as a result of "liturgical assistance" and "karmic bribery." This is why sutra chanting is sponsored during funerals.[8] The forty-nine days are broken down into seven seven-day periods, each of which requires liturgical intervention, and each period culminating on the seventh day, until the seventh seventh day (*qiqi*), which is a sort of liturgical finale. The program also includes a "feeding the hungry ghosts" ceremony aimed at "delivering the souls from the hells, nourishing them with food blessed by the Buddha for alleviating their pain, and making them able to be preached to, converted, and eventually saved" (Goossaert 2007: 335). This generous act, of course, also accrues merit for the deceased and members of the host family.

The Tibetan Buddhist funerary rituals are premised upon similar karmic principles, though there are many more Tantric exorcistic elements. In old Beijing there were numerous Tibetan Buddhist monasteries. The Tibetan monasteries were patronized by the Manchu Qing imperial household and palace dignitaries, such as eunuchs and high officials. The lamas would however "do funerals" for anyone who could afford the fee (the lamas' services were the most expensive among the various kinds of ritualists). As a group they had the highest prestige among religious specialists during Qing times (because of imperial patronage), and their presence at a funeral testified to the high status of the host household.

Instead of accruing karmic merits for the deceased and members of the host family, the Daoist priests would call upon the Daoist high deities to intervene to ensure the welfare of the deceased. The deceased is actually posthumously ordained and granted a Daoist deity title so that he or she can escape the sufferings in hell courts (Goossaert 2007: 337). Mirroring the Buddhist "feeding the hungry ghosts" ceremony, the Daoists also engage in a more general salvationary ceremony for all suffering souls, which shows strong Tantric influences (ibid.: 246–55).

The meanings of the specific contents of these funerary rituals, including the chanting of sutras and scriptures, ritual drama, gestures and mudras (stylized hand gestures) are not of concern to most of the people present at funerals (but see Goossaert 2007: 252), though many enjoy the spectacle. These rituals require highly specialized knowledge and skills, and host households and guests are happy to leave them to the specialists. A host household only needs to ensure that these specialists appear to be doing their jobs properly (e.g., not dozing off while chanting or obviously omitting segments of the ritual).

One indispensable ceremony during the funeral in the late imperial era was the dotting of the spirit tablet (*chengzhu*) (see Chang 1997: 139). A wooden tablet would be prepared to host or "seat" the spirit of the deceased and to be installed on the family altar and later in a clan or lineage hall where it would be regularly worshiped. On the face of the tablet was written the title and posthumous name of the deceased with the character 主 (meaning host or master, the traditional term used to refer to the ancestral tablet) written with the dot, on the top part, left "undotted." The host family would invite an accomplished Confucian scholar to add the dot to the character (hence the name of the ceremony). The dotting of the spirit tablet would be one of the most ritually potent moments during the funeral. The "ink" used for dotting the tablet was actually blood from the pricked middle finger of the eldest son of the deceased, he being the chief host of the funeral and chief mourner (Chang 1997: 139) (though it is not clear if this practice was widespread). Accompanied by a few other well-regarded Confucian scholars who served as assistants, the "tablet dotter" (*hongtiguan*, literally "official of grand inscription") took a seat at a specially prepared desk, faced southeast, took an empowering breath, breathed onto the brush while visualizing the image of the deceased, completed the character 主 by adding the dot, and thus literally transferred the spirit of the deceased into the wooden spirit tablet (ibid.). Unlike the troupes of religious specialists (i.e., the lamas, monks, nuns, and Daoist priests), Confucian scholars were not hired, although gifts (which may very well have included cash) appropriate to the invitation were prepared, thus allowing the Confucian ritualists (who were usually amateurs) to appear morally superior to the professional specialists.

Ritual Polytropy at General Wu Peifu's Funeral

To give a sense of the degree of ritual-polytropic excess into which funeral rituals in old Beijing could spiral, I will describe the funeral of General Wu Peifu, a retired warlord of the Republican period (1912–1949). Wu Peifu was one of the major warlords during the fights for post-dynastic supremacy in the 1910s and 1920s, and was famous for refusing to cooperate with the Japanese invaders who wanted him to be a figurehead leader in the Japanese-occupied areas. General Wu died in his Beijing residence under suspicious circumstances in December 1939 during the Japanese occupation of the city. His death made him into a patriotic martyr, and his funeral was one of the grandest ever in the city, rivaling those of imperial family members (Rawski 1998). My source is an account of Wu's funeral based on contemporary newspaper reports of the funeral proceedings (Chang 1997: 123–60).

The funeral took place at the home of the Wu family. Wu died on 4 December 1939; the encoffining (*dalian*) and the funerary program began on the 5th; and the third-day reception (*jiesan*) and sending off of the spirit of the deceased (*songlu*) took place on the 6th, when ten sheds of scriptures were chanted to help deliver the deceased. Two sheds of sutras were chanted by lamas from Yonghegong and Longfusi (the two most famous Tibetan Buddhist temples in Beijing), two sheds of Daoist scriptures chanted by Daoist priests from Baiyunguan and Dongyuemiao (the two most famous Daoist temples in Beijing), five sheds of sutras were chanted by Buddhist monks from Tanzhesi, Jietaisi, Guangjisi, Fayuansi, and Nianhuasi (all famous Buddhist temples in Beijing), and one shed of sutras was chanted by Buddhist nuns from Cuifeng'an (a famous Beijing nunnery).[9] Each temple sent troupes of thirteen members, so altogether there were about a hundred and thirty lamas, monks, Daoist priests and nuns chanting all day long. There were so many troupes of religious specialists that the platforms on all three sides had three levels to accommodate them. Numerous troupes of musicians performed at crucial junctures of the funeral. All of these religious professionals and musicians then participated in the grand sending-off procession in the evening, displaying through the town the grandeur of the funeral to the entire Beijing citizenry. Traffic along the way came to a standstill because of the large number of bystanders watching the spectacle. A large quantity of "paper offerings"[10] were burnt at the conclusion of the procession. And finally the lamas, monks, and Daoist priests simultaneously put on a spectacular show of "feeding the hungry ghosts" (*yankou*) at the Wu residence.

Between the date of the sending-off and the date of the eventual burial,[11] the Wu family hosted multiple sheds of scriptures (mostly sponsored by relatives, friends, and colleagues) at every crucial juncture, especially on the last day of each of the seven seven-day periods:

- The first seventh; six sheds (13 monks from Changchunsi, 15 monks from Jiaxingsi, 15 monks from Hongci Guangjisi, 13 lamas from Yonghegong, 13 monks from Nianhuasi, 17 lay Buddhists from Pushan lianshe);

- The twelfth day commemoration (occasioned by the visit of an important Japanese commander); six sheds (13 monks from Nianhuasi, 15 monks from Yijiaosi, 9 female Daoist priests from Lianhuashan Subsidiary Branch Temple, 15 monks from Nianhuasi for *yankou*, 13 monks from Hongci Guangjisi);
- The second seventh; number of sheds not given in source;
- The third seventh; number of sheds not given in source;
- The fourth seventh; three sheds (13 Daoist priests from Baiyunguan, 13 nuns from Cuifeng'an, 13 monks from Nianhuasi);
- The fifth seventh; six sheds (13 lamas from Yonghegong, 13 monks from Hongci Guangjisi, 13 monks from Nianhuasi, 13 monks from Chengshousi, 13 Daoist priests from Baiyunguan, 13 nuns from Cuifeng'an);
- The sixth seventh; five sheds (Daoist priests from Baiyunguan, monks from Guangjisi, Tanzhesi, Nianhuasi, and Chengshousi);
- The ceremony to dot the spirit tablet (*chengzhu*), presided over by invited prominent Confucian scholars;
- The seventh seventh; main ritual presided over by Confucian scholars, supplemented by three sheds (Buddhist, Tibetan Buddhist, and Daoist); more than 400 members of the Japanese Tenrikyo sect branches in Beijing and North China conducted a ceremony;[12]
- Opening condolences (*kaidiao*) of the seventh seven-day period; eight sheds (13 lamas from Yonghegong, 13 monks from Nianhuasi, 13 Daoist priests from Baiyunguan, 13 monks from Changchunsi, 13 monks from Huajiasi, 13 monks from Tanzhesi, 13 monks from Jiaxingsi, 21 monks from Yongtaisi and Yanshousi);
- Last night to keep company of the soul of the deceased (the night before the sending-off procession); 11 sheds (troupes from Yonghegong, Baiyunguan, Tanzhesi, the Zhengyitang of the World-Saving New Religion (*Jiushi xinjiao*),[13] Dongyuemiao, Huoshenmiao, Hongci Guangjisi, Lianhuashan Subsidiary Branch Temple, Chengshousi, Cuifeng'an and Nianhuasi);
- One-hundredth-day commemoration; seven sheds (scripture chanting by lamas from Yonghegong, monks from Tanzhesi, Changchunsi and Nianhuasi, Daoist priests from Dongyuemiao and Baiyunguan);
- One-year-anniversary commemoration; 12 sheds (13 lamas from Yonghegong, 13 Daoist priests from Dongyuemiao, 13 monks from Guangjisi, 13 monks from Fayuansi, 13 monks from Yijiaosi, a second group of 13 monks from Fayuansi, 13 monks from Chengshousi, a third group of 13 monks from Fayuansi, 13 female Daoist priests from Lianhuashan Subsidiary Branch Temple, 13 nuns from Cuifeng'an, 13 monks from Nianhuasi).[14]

As this grand old-Beijing funeral (or funeral series) shows, ritual polytropy in China can be carried to extreme heights. It might be difficult to find in the historical and ethnographic record any comparable instances of ritual polytropy approaching such an extensive and extended sharing of "sacred space," and such a mixing of different religious traditions and personnel, other than perhaps in some ritual situations in the New Age Movement in late-twentieth/early-twenty-first-century United States, which I will address in the conclusion.

Conclusion: Efficacy, Not Confessionality, in a Confucian-Buddhist-Daoist Ritual Polytropy

The Chinese lived in a Confucian-Buddhist-Daoist polytropy. But there is a significant qualitative difference between Chinese "ritual polytropy" and the traditional "religious polytropies" found in India and other South Asian countries such as Nepal (see Gellner 1992, 2005; Carrithers 2000; Nawa 2007). In traditional Nepal and India, Hindu-Buddhist (or Hindu-Islamic or Hindu-Jainist) polytropy was based on people having relatively unambiguous religiocultural identities (based on caste or ethnicity or geographical region). It is true a Hindu might do *puja* to all figures of authority and deities of any tradition, but he was still a Hindu (even without the boundary-closing modern census identity); a Newar Buddhist might fully participate in a Hindu festival but he was still a Buddhist. Being a Hindu, a Jain or a Buddhist was following a path, embodied in the teaching (*dharma*). Although following a *dharma* was not as strong as confessing one's faith in the sense of belonging to one of the Abrahamic religions, it was nonetheless a form of confessionality. There is no doubt that a distinction existed between the virtuosi and the laity in terms of the ability to live out fully one's *dharma*, but even members of the laity would aspire to fulfill more of the requirements of the *dharma* in their old age or in the next life.

In China, on the other hand, with the exception of the small minority of clerics and certain sectarians, no one was known as a Confucian, a Buddhist, or a Daoist, and anyone was free to employ a Confucian, Buddhist, or Daoist to conduct rituals (especially funerals), sometimes even to gather all types of ritualists together in one ritual space (i.e., "ritual polytropy"). It was the efficacy of the rituals (and the ritualists) that mattered, not the religious identity of the people (if that was even discernible). We can call this an "efficacy-based religiosity." Here we need to explain briefly why Buddhism "behaved" so differently in China compared to, say, South Asia, Southeast Asia, and Tibet. Chinese Buddhism penetrated into Chinese society, not by making Chinese people into *dharma*-following lay believers, but by providing ritual (primarily funerary) services to them. Had Western missionaries attempted to merely provide the Chinese with Catholic priests or Protestant ministers as yet another of the many troupes of ritualists, and not force them to adopt an entire Christian confessional framework, it would have been a lot easier for the Chinese to accept them; it would have meant simply adding one more tradition (and form of efficacy) to the existing ritual polytropy.[15]

Even the Chinese state historically has not been interested in asking the Chinese people what religions they belonged to. The late imperial state, for example, was only interested in knowing how many Daoist and Buddhist clerics there were so that it could issue licenses and bring them under tighter control (see Goossaert 2000). The People's Republic of China (PRC) party-state followed a similar mechanism and attempted to bring all Daoist and Buddhist clerics under the supervision and control of two nationwide organizations (with subordinate branches at provincial, prefectural, and municipal levels): the National Daoist

Association and the National Buddhist Association (see Goossaert 2008). Significantly, even though the PRC party-state was otherwise obsessed with counting and categorizing—for example the registration of fifty-five officially recognized minority nationalities, the elaborate class background labels, and the household registration system—it did not attempt to put the majority of the Chinese people into discrete categories of religious identity (e.g., Daoist or Buddhist), as for example Indonesia did shortly after independence.[16] Several factors might have informed such a seeming disinterest. First, the party-state might have simply followed late-imperial models of dealing with religious specialists in administrative terms rather than treating the lay population in religious terms. Second, the party-state might have understood the vague religious orientation of the Chinese too well to bother asking about their religious identity. Third, the party-state might have feared that registering the national population along such religious lines would give the Daoist and Buddhist associations too much power or political clout. Finally, the party-state might have thought it useless to register people's religious affiliation when religion (understood as largely "feudal superstition") was supposed to be eradicated. It is often assumed that the modern Chinese regimes have been too atheistic to allow the Chinese people to profess any religious identity—both the Nationalist and the Communist/Maoist regimes have been strongly anti-traditionalist and anti-religion—but the truth might be that the Chinese would not readily profess any religious identity even if they had not been faced with anti-religion pressures. In other words, the Chinese might have been "indifferently religious" or "non-religious"—if we understand "being religious" as being confessionally religious—even without "Godless Communism." While the overwhelming majority of Chinese people failed to adopt a confessional religious identity during the modern era, the Indians and Nepalis embraced such identities during the same period, undoubtedly spurred in part by census taking and state policies, but equally strongly by the importance of traditional religious identities.

The differences between Chinese and South Asian religiosity and the implications of these differences for conversion cannot be overemphasized. Even though rituals are important for South Asians, it seems that Hinduism and Buddhism are both *dharma*-based or path-based religions. Theoretically one can only take one path or follow one *dharma*; in other words, Hinduism and Buddhism are theologically predisposed to create and foster exclusivist religious identities (except when Buddhism "behaved" very differently in China, as explained above). This would potentially facilitate conversion to other exclusivist religions such as Islam, Protestantism, or Catholicism, because these can be conceived as different, and for the converts, truer paths/*dharmas*. Conversion from one *dharma*-based religion to another *dharma*-based religion requires a change in the contents of one's symbolic universe but not the abandonment of the familiar *dharma*-based religiosity. In other words, while I agree with Gellner that modern Nepali conversions have been catalyzed by "the Western view of religion as a single, overarching religious identity recorded unambiguously in a census, which is different from, and equal to, all other similar identities" (Gellner 2005: 776), I believe this "unique and exclusive religious attachment" (ibid.) is not entirely modernist or Western in origin. *Dharma*-based religiosity (and ethnic-religious makeup) had prepared the grounds in India and Nepal for the Western modernist schema of religious categories and identities. In other words, there has been "elective affinity" between the traditional *dharma*-based religiosity found in South Asia and modernist confessional religious identities.

Contrarily, as a result of the efficacy-based religiosity in China, there was no such thing as conversion between any of the three main ritual traditions (Confucian, Buddhist, and Daoist) in traditional China. For the Chinese, conversion to Protestantism or Islam would entail not only changing the *contents* of one's symbolic universe but more radically changing from the traditional efficacy-based religiosity to a *dharma*-based religiosity. The Chinese case suggests that certain indigenous religious cultures might be predisposed to resist religious conversion as well as modernist categorizing schemas (such as surveys and censuses soliciting information on people's "religious affiliations," which may harden people's religious identities).

Even though religions in the Western world have been known historically for their strong confessionality, the twentieth century has witnessed the development of spiritual movements against traditional adherence to organized, confession-based religions. This culminated in the New Age Movement of the last quarter of the twentieth century in the United States and many other parts of the Western world. The most fundamental tenet of this loosely coherent movement is that one should search for spiritual sustenance in all kinds of religious traditions, be they Hindu, Japanese, Chinese, Tibetan, Native American, Afro-Caribbean, Pagan, Judaic, Islamic, or Christian. On the bookshelves of a typical New Ager one may find the Bible, the Qur'an, Buddhist sutras, the Daodejing (a Daoist classic), the autobiography of the Dalai Lama, yoga manuals, the Don Juan series by Carlos Castaneda, and so forth. His or her personal altar can be equally eclectic, mixing Buddha statues with Marian images, Indian incense with Tibetan prayer flags, Hopi *kachinas* with voodoo dolls, and so on. Critics of the New Age Movement have labeled this pick-and-choose style eclecticism "cafeteria spirituality" (Batstone 2001: 228), but New Agers insist that what matters is not where a particular religious tradition comes from but whether or not one "clicks" or "connects" with the tradition or aspects of the tradition. One can click or connect with multiple traditions as long as one benefits spiritually from all of them. In fact, since each tradition has something unique to offer, one should incorporate as many traditions as possible in one's spiritual portfolio (Batstone 2001: 228).

This eclectic New Age philosophy combined with multiculturalism to give birth to multifaith religious services in which religious specialists from different traditions converge in one space to preside over a congregational service. In such services a Baptist minister, a rabbi, a Baha'i, an imam, or a Tibetan Buddhist lama either sermonizes and/or conducts rituals for the whole congregation, one after the other.[17] This situation uncannily resembles the ritual polytropy in China described above, though there is a crucial difference. While the Chinese ritual polytropy is premised on the maximization of efficacy (including the maximization of social prestige) and a broad disregard for the specific contents performed by the religious specialists, the New Agers' engagement with the various religious traditions is far more serious and personal, betraying a strong legacy of the *dharma*-based religiosity that not only characterizes Hinduism and Buddhism (except as it is practiced in efficacy-based religious cultures such as China) but also traditional monotheistic religious traditions such as the Abrahamic religions.

Notes

I thank Glenn Bowman for having invited me to join the initial panel on shared shrines at the 2006 annual meeting of the Association of Social Anthropologists of the UK and Commonwealth (ASA). I am very grateful for valuable comments on earlier drafts made by Michael Carrithers, Isabelle Charleux, David Gellner, Vincent Goossaert, Paul Katz, and Daniel Overmyer. I have also benefited from comments from the ASA panel audience as well as conversations on this topic with Joseph Askew, Brigitte Baptandier, Peter Flügel, John Lagerwey, Susan Naquin, Caroline Osella, and Vladimir Uspenskiy. I thank Nicolas Standaert for sharing with me his manuscript *The Interweaving of Rituals: Funerals in the Cultural Exchange between China and Europe* (2008, University of Washington Press), which served as an important source of inspiration. I also thank Glenn Bowman for his editorial help in making the chapter and my arguments much clearer.

1. By "sectarian" I am referring to the mostly Buddhist-inspired millenarian cults that developed around charismatic leaders that demanded exclusivistic membership adherence. Their occurrence was sporadic in Chinese history and they were often targets of state crackdowns.

2. The form of competition may include Buddhist temples against Daoist temples, Daoist temples against spirit mediums, Buddhist temples against other Buddhist temples, Daoist temples against other Daoist temples, householder Daoist priests against other householder Daoist priests, spirit mediums against magical healers, etc.

3. The religious situation in China is very complex, given the history of severe modernist interventions from the late Qing, Republican, and Communist regimes as well as the vastly different trajectories in the various "Chinas" (the People's Republic of China, Taiwan, Hong Kong, and the Chinese diasporic communities). Most of the processes involving religious change or specific historical events discussed in this article happened in the past and are thus described in the past tense, but since some of these dynamics have continued into the present or have been revived in the post-Mao era, I have often reverted to the present tense to emphasize the continuity. The reader is advised to consult two excellent recent edited volumes on the issue of Chinese religion and modernity (Yang 2008; Ashiwa and Wank 2009), and my own edited volume on the revitalization and innovation of religion in reform-era China (Chau 2011a).

4. It goes without saying that different strands of socioreligious practices only gradually cohered into these distinct traditions through the efforts of a large number of people. Confucius did not found Confucianism, nor did Laozi Daoism, and Buddhism did not arrive in China in one flat-pack. Also, by invoking the notion of "Great Traditions" I do not intend (nor did Robert Redfield in his original conception of the great and little traditions) to portray them as existing independently of less elite forms of religious practices. On conceptualizations on "modalities of doing religion" that attempt to go beyond the "three teachings" paradigm (Buddhism, Daoist, and Confucianism), see Chau 2006, 2011b, and 2011c.

5. In Japan, the two major religious traditions, Shinto and Buddhism, have worked out an admirable division of labor (and, one may add, share of income), in which the Shinto priests are in charge

of matters relating to life-stage rites of passage and marriage, while the Buddhist monks take care of the funeral and after-death matters (see Suzuki 2000, chapters 2 and 6).

6. In the employment of religious specialists one observes a major difference between "Indic" religious polytropy involving respect and veneration for the superior "holy person" or religious specialist, and Chinese ritual polytropy in which specialists are hired, and little if any respect or honor is paid to them. Chinese ritual specialists, though indispensable because of the ritual role they play, were traditionally considered marginal to society and accorded no special respect as a group (although obviously famous ritualists from well-known temples were accorded due respect). In fact, they were sometimes looked down upon, in part because of a persistent strand of Confucian literati's anticlerical stance and in part because of the religious specialists' obvious dependence for their livelihood on selling their services in an often competitive ritual market.

7. Hungry ghosts are spirits of dead people who are without descendants to give them offerings on a regular basis. They roam around and try to snatch offerings destined for others. Hungry-ghost feeding rituals were invented to take care of them so that they will not cause trouble. The so-called "ghost month", i.e., the seventh month in the Chinese lunar calendar, is a period dedicated to feeding hungry ghosts. But most Daoist and Buddhist funeral rituals have incorporated hungry-ghost feeding liturgies so that the hungry ghosts will not fight over the offerings meant for the spirit of the deceased.

8. Special sutras dedicated to merit-generation are chanted at funerals.

9. I have not translated the names of these temples into English as these are details unnecessary for this chapter. But readers who know Chinese can consult the Chinese character list at the end of the chapter for the original temple names in Chinese. For scholarly works on old Beijing temples and monasteries, see Goossaert 2007 and Naquin 2000.

10. A funeral goods shop was hired to manufacture various votive objects from bamboo strips, wooden sticks, and paper, which were to be burnt at the end of the funeral to accompany the deceased to the other world. These objects included representations of houses, horses, sedan chairs, servants, and other things thought to be useful to the deceased in the nether world. See Scott (2007) on paper offerings.

11. The Wu's was an unusual case where, for various reasons, the coffin was temporarily stationed, after the burial procession, in a temple, and was not put in the ground until seven years later.

12. Tenrikyo is a syncretistic Japanese New Religion founded in the nineteenth century. It came into China in the early 1930s, following the Japanese control of Manchuria (Wilson 1995: 263–64).

13. This is a new syncretistic religion Wu Peifu cofounded. Many such religions were founded during the Republican period, which the China historian Prasenjit Duara has called "redemptive societies" (Duara 1997).

14. The temple name of one of the twelve sheds is not given.

15. For a historical study of the "interweaving" of Chinese and Catholic funeral rituals, see Standaert (2008).

16. The post-independence Indonesian state required by law that all citizens belong to a religion (*agama*). The Chinese Indonesians were therefore forced to declare to be Buddhists, Catholics, or Muslims (Daoism or Chinese popular religion not being recognized in Indonesia).

17. This multifaith New Age spiritual orientation should not be confused with interfaith dialogue, in which the participants have strong denominational identities but are willing to come together to explore common grounds. I thank Caroline Osella for pointing this out to me.

Chinese Character List

Names of temples:

Baiyunguan	白雲觀	Lianhuashan xiayuan	蓮花山下院
Changchunsi	長椿寺	Longfusi	隆福寺
Chengshousi	承壽寺	Nianhuasi	拈花寺
Cuifeng'an	翠峰庵	Pushan lianshe	普善蓮社
Dongyuemiao	東嶽廟	Tanzhesi	潭柘寺
Fayuansi	法源寺	Yanshousi	延壽寺
Hongci Guangjisi	弘慈廣濟寺	Yijiaosi	翊教寺
Huajiasi	華嘉寺	Yonghegong	雍和宮
Jiaxingsi	嘉興寺	Yongtaisi	永泰寺
Jietaisi	戒台寺		

Stages in funeral (in temporal sequence):

xiaolian	小殮	kaidiao	開吊
baomiao	報廟	chengzhu	成主
dalian	大殮	fayin	發引
jiesan	接三	zang	葬
songlu	送路		

Other Terms:

bai	拜	shang xitian	上西天
fan, dao, chan, ni	番, 道, 禪, 尼	siheyuan	四合院
fengshui	風水	Wu Peifu	吳佩孚
gongde	功德	xuyuan	許願
hongtiguan	鴻題官	yankou	焰口
Jiushi xinjiao	救世新教	yinyang	陰陽
ling	靈	yangzhai	陽宅
lingyan	靈驗	yinzhai	陰宅
lingying	靈應	Zhengyitang	正一堂
pengpu	棚鋪	zhu	主
qiqi	七七	zhujia	主家
Quanzhen	全真	zuo gongde	做功德

References

Note: The names of Chinese authors writing in Chinese are presented family name first, followed by their given names, without commas separating the two.

Anonymous. 2008. "Laobeijing de sangyi quan guocheng" (The Entire Funeral Process in Old Beijing). http://www.humancn.com/html/249/11/11784/1.htm, accessed 28 March 2011.

Ashiwa, Yoshiko and David L. Wank (eds.). 2009. *Making Religion, Making the State: The Politics of Religion in Modern China*. Stanford: Stanford University Press.

Batstone, David. 2001. "Dancing to a Different Beat: Emerging Spiritualities in the Network Society," in *Religions/Globalizations: Theories and Cases*, eds. D. Hopkins, E. Mendieta and L. Lorentzen. Durham: Duke University Press, 226–42.

Brook, Timothy. 1989. "Funerary Ritual and the Building of Lineages in Late Imperial China." *Harvard Journal of Asiatic Studies* 49(2): 465–99.

Carrithers, Michael. 2000. "On Polytropy: Or the Natural Condition of Spiritual Cosmopolitanism in India: The Digambar Jain Case." *Modern Asian Studies* 34(4): 831–61.

Chang Renchun. 1997. *Jinshi mingren da chubin* (Grand Funerals of Famous People in Recent Times). Beijing: Yanshan chubanshe.

Chau, Adam Yuet. 2006. *Miraculous Response: Doing Popular Religion in Contemporary China*. Stanford: Stanford University Press.

——— (ed.). 2011a. *Religion in Contemporary China: Revitalization and Innovation*. London: Routledge.

———. 2011b. "Modalities of Doing Religion," in *Chinese Religious Life*, eds. D. Palmer, G. Shive, and P. Wickeri. New York: Oxford University Press, 67–84.

———. 2011c. "Modalities of Doing Religion and Ritual Polytropy: Evaluating the Religious Market Model from the Perspective of Chinese Religious History." *Religion* 41(4): 533–554.

Cohen, Myron L. 1988. "Souls and Salvation: Conflicting Themes in Chinese Popular Religion," in *Death Ritual in Late Imperial and Modern China*, eds. J. Watson and E. Rawski. Berkeley: University of California Press, 180–202.

Duara, Prasenjit. 1997. "Transnationalism and the Predicament of Sovereignty: China, 1900–1945." *American Historical Review* 102(4): 1030–51.

Gellner, David. 1992. *Monk, Householder, and Tantric Priest: Newar Buddhism and Its Hierarchy of Ritual*. Cambridge: Cambridge University Press.

———. 2005. "The Emergence of Conversion in a Hindu-Buddhist Polytropy: The Kathmandu Valley, Nepal, c.1600–1995." *Comparative Studies of Society and History* 47(4): 755–80.

Goossaert, Vincent. 2000. "Counting the Monks: The 1736–1739 Census of the Chinese Clergy." *Late Imperial China* 21(2): 40–85.

———. 2007. *The Taoists of Peking, 1800–1949: A Social History of Urban Clerics*. Cambridge, MA: Harvard University Asian Center.

———. 2008. "Republican Church Engineering: The National Religious Associations in 1912 China," in *Chinese Religiosities: Afflictions of Modernity and State Formation*, ed. M. Yang. Berkeley: University of California Press, 209–32.

Jin Yunzhen. 1996. "Beijing sanxiang tezhong hangye" (Three Special Professions in Beijing), in *Huiyi jiu Beijing* (Remembering Old Beijing). Beijing: Yanshan chubanshe, 67–70.

Liu Yeqiu. 1996. "Shuoshuo ban sangshi" (Talking about Organising Funerals), in *Huiyi jiu Beijing* (Remembering Old Beijing). Beijing: Yanshan chubanshe, 54–59.

Mollier, Christine. 2008. *Buddhism and Taoism Face to Face: Scripture, Ritual, and Iconographic Exchange in Medieval China*. Honolulu: University of Hawaii Press.

Naquin, Susan. 1988. "Funerals in North China: Uniformity and Variation," in *Death Ritual in Late Imperial and Modern China*, eds. J. Watson and E. Rawski. Berkeley: University of California Press, 37–70.

———. 2000. *Peking: Temples and City Life, 1400–1900*. Berkeley: University of California Press.

Nawa, Katsuo. 2007. "Some Unintended Consequences of Ritual Change: The Case of Funerals in Chhangru, Byans, Far Western Nepal," in *Political and Social Transformations in North India and Nepal: Social Dynamics in Northern South Asia Vol. 2*, eds. H. Ishii, D. Gellner and K. Nawa. New Delhi: Manohar, 263–88.

Rawski, Evelyn S. 1998. *The Last Emperors: A Social History of Qing Imperial Institutions*. Berkeley: University of California Press.

Redfield, Robert. 1956. "The Social Organization of Tradition," in *Peasant Society and Culture*. Chicago: University of Chicago Press, 40–59.

Roberts, John, Chien Chiao, and Triloki Pandey. 1975. "Meaningful God Sets from a Chinese Personal Pantheon and a Hindu Personal Pantheon." *Ethnology* 14(2): 121–48.

———, Saburo Morita, and Keith Brown. 1986. "Personal Categories for Japanese Sacred Places and Gods: Views Elicited from a Conjugal Pair." *American Anthropologist* 88(4): 807–24.

Scott, Janet Lee. 2007. *For Gods, Ghosts and Ancestors: The Chinese Tradition of Paper Offerings*. Seattle: University of Washington Press.

Standaert, Nicolas. 2008. *The Interweaving of Rituals: Funerals in the Cultural Exchange between China and Europe*. Seattle: University of Washington Press.

Sutton, Donald S. (ed.). 2007. Special Issue on "Standardization, Orthopraxy, and the Construction of Chinese Culture--A Critical Reappraisal of James L. Watson's Ideas," *Modern China: An International Quarterly of History and Social Science* 33(1) (January 2007).

Suzuki, Hikaru. 2000. *The Price of Death: The Funeral Industry in Contemporary Japan*. Stanford: Stanford University Press.

Watson, James L. 1988. "The Structure of Chinese Funerary Rites: Elementary Forms, Ritual Sequence, and the Primacy of Performance," in *Death Ritual in Late Imperial and Modern China*, eds. J. L. Watson and E. S. Rawski. Berkeley: University of California Press, 3–19.

——— and Evelyn S. Rawski (eds.). 1988. *Death Ritual in Late Imperial and Modern China*. Berkeley: University of California Press.

Wilson, Sandra. 1995. "The 'New Paradise': Japanese Emigration to Manchuria in the 1930s and 1940s." *The International History Review* 17(2): 249–86.

Yang, Mayfair Mei-Hui (ed.). 2008. *Chinese Religiosities: Afflictions of Modernity and State Formation*. Berkeley: University of California Press.

Chapter 6

SAINTS, SITES AND RELIGIOUS ACCOMMODATION IN SRI LANKA

Rohan Bastin

> In fact, things are more complicated because the imperial Stranger
> himself needs surviving Autochthons and because the citizen
> Autochthon calls on strangers in flight—but these are not all the
> same psychosocial types, any more than the polytheism of the
> empire and the polytheism of the city are the same religious figures.
> — Gilles Deleuze and Félix Guattari, *What is Philosophy?*

My chapter examines a plural religious site as it featured in the event of the 1995 papal visit by John Paul II to Sri Lanka. By examining certain features of this event, which drew together threads of different religious traditions, I show how a syncretic moment for refashioning religious intolerance was made possible through the reproduction of an encompassing order of religious significance. The very factors and agents that seek to drive the different Sri Lankan religious traditions apart effectively drew them together around an important and highly complex concept of religious potentiality (in Sinhala, *haskam*). I have examined this concept of potentiality at length elsewhere in a study of a major site of Sri Lankan Hindu and Buddhist interaction called Munneśvaram (Bastin 2002). My interest here is to explore *haskam*'s workings in the circumstances of a dynamic process of structure and event involving "the structural relays between lower and higher levels of sociocultural order" (Sahlins 2005: 6) mobilized in the papal visit. These processes cannot be explained using either/or categories such as tolerance and intolerance, competitive sharing and antagonism, or practice and ideology as, for example, Robert Hayden (2002) attempts in a comparison between Indian and Balkan examples of shared shrines. Instead, events, and specifically religious events involving the sacred in its transgressive potentiality, are situations of chaotic blending in and through which certain types of religious singularity are constituted in their territorializing effect. By this I mean the combined effect of boundary-marking and boundary-transgression that occurs in the context of shared shrines and shared *sacra*. These critical interstices in the territorializing movement of sovereign spaces relate to the nature of the sacred itself. The sacred is thus not simply something set apart and forbidden, but the force and movement of violation itself (Caillois 1959; Bataille 1987). It is, to use Deleuze and Guattari's (1994) terminology, the double movement of territorialization: the transgressing deterritorialization as well as the reordering reterritorialization. What I demonstrate in the following is how such a process—an unresolved double-movement— occurred in the event of the papal visit to Sri Lanka for the beatification of a seventeenth-century Catholic priest.

The matter at hand is the role that syncretism plays in the formation and reformation of religious singularities. Syncretism, as diversity of worship, and anti-syncretism, as a dimension of that worship which refuses interaction, are essential features of religious practice because they are concerned with the problem of boundaries and the prevalence of transgression. Robert Hayden (2002) is right to note that the issue is one of tolerance and intolerance. However, his analysis of Indian and Balkan shared shrines poses that issue in either/or terms, and thereby neglects the capacity of tolerance and intolerance to combine in the reproduction of the religious field. Such a field I suggest has the form of a singularity when more accurately it is a multiplicity of singular differences that coalesce according to forms of attraction.[1] Critically, such a field identifies transcendent powers of creation and destruction as the essence of its concern. In other words, syncretism and anti-syncretism are inherent features of the sacred (as, for example, Latin *sacer* or Polynesian *tapu*). For example, royal incest, mythical boundary-transgressing stranger-kings and trickster figures are well-known archetypes of the power that derives from transgression and, above all, the ambiguity of this power—its Janus face of consistency and chaos or "chaosmos."[2] Put another way, syncretism is about playing with fire, albeit in a Promethean sense. It lies at the heart of the paradox of being human and being sacred: the paradox of becoming. This means that the transgression of boundaries is occurring constantly in any religious field but, at the same time, it means that such transgression is always remarkable. As Marit Brendbekken describes it in relation to contemporary Haitian Vodou, the process is "a structured hybridisation of something being always already hybridised" (Brendbekken 2003: 62).[3]

Notwithstanding its prevalence, the double-sided and oscillating nature of religious power—its inherently syncretic nature—is both celebrated and repressed (or structured in Brendbekken's usage) to different degrees, both within and between different religious traditions. These are the different forms of attraction constituting religious singularities of greater or lesser extent. For example, broadly compared, polytheistic Tamil Śaivism encompasses difference in a hierarchical holistic totality (Dumont 1980), where monotheistic Islam is more synthetic and thereby homogeneous and sublimating. Sri Lankan Buddhism and Roman Catholicism in their own ways combine aspects of both. However, looked at more closely and historically one can discern that considerable differences in these orientations to difference and multiplicity also exist *within* these religious traditions. For, as Deleuze and Guattari declare in the epigraph above, the polytheism of the empire and that of the city are not the same (Deleuze and Guattari 1994: 86–87). Both "empire" and "city" describe modalities of power, and not religious singularities per se or even the religious authorities who determine the nature and content of authentic tradition (doxa). Such modalities penetrate and encompass these singularities and authorities, and thus impact profoundly on both the nature of heterogeneity and orientations towards it. This establishes the generative schemes or enabling conditions for actions or practices— the singular differences—that reproduce the larger multiplicity identified as this or that religion along with its internal structure. And from these practices occur events such as the 1995 visit by that "Imperial Stranger" John Paul II to Sri Lanka that I interpret in the following. In doing so, I wish to make a case for the study of the events (structured occurrences) over the contexts (shared shrines) in which they occur. This is not simply an insistence on the study of practices at shrines (Stirrat 1992) rather than the study of events—those practices that constitute ideas, or ideational singularities (Deleuze 2004: 64) and have the status of cause and effect in the shaping of practice. Put simply, practices occur, but not every occurrence is an event, because, as Sahlins (2005) demonstrates, the modalities of power and the associated "structural amplification" vary considerably when a temporal moment becomes, as it were, momentous.[4] It follows, though, that sites of the sacred, as I am defining it as a "chaosmos," are themselves event-sites more likely to inspire future events that realize and reproduce their potentiality.

St. Anthony's Church, Kochikade, and Other Sri Lankan Shared Shrines

The Catholic church dedicated to St. Anthony in the old inner part of Colombo known as Kochikade is widely regarded as a site of miraculous power (Sinhala *haskam*) by Catholics and other Christians, as well as by Buddhists, Śaivites and, to a small extent, Muslims. The church was built near a point on the foreshore in Kochikade adjacent to the Pettah, the thriving trading hub of Colombo port. The point is where, in 1740, an Indian-born Catholic priest named Father Anthony planted a wooden cross in order to force back the sea and create a beach upon which local fishermen could dry their nets. The priest was in hiding from Dutch Protestant persecution at the time and, in return for this miracle, he received the support of the local population and ultimately the acquiescence of the Dutch authorities. A small wooden statue of St. Anthony was later imported from Goa and installed on the spot where the cross was planted. This statue is regarded as imbued with the power of the saint to intervene in daily life and solve problems, and this places the Kochikade church in an elite grouping of Sri Lankan religious sites imbued with power or *haskam*, and attracting a plurality of worshippers across ethnic and religious lines. Every day, but especially on the first Tuesday of each month, large numbers of men and even larger numbers of women visit the church, queue in gender-specific lines to stand before the famous statue, and, mostly if Catholic, attend the masses given in Sinhala, Tamil, and English. On the rear wall behind the altar, either side of a large statue of the saint, in large brass letters are the two English words "Priest" and "Victim." These terms relate to the central message of overcoming adversity through faith and prayer that is elucidated in the sermons and readings, as well as in the various individual entreaties sometimes overheard as they are quietly spoken by devotees offering special yellow candles to the saint as well as to other members of the Roman Catholic hierarchy.[5] This is the common thread that connects the various plural religious sites in Sri Lanka—the alleviation of personal misfortune and/or the request for a special favor. St. Anthony's at Kochikade is thus very similar to the popular plural pilgrimage church of St. Anne at Talawilla, where a Marian statue was washed up and a Marian apparition occurred during the Portuguese period (sixteenth to seventeenth century). British observers in the mid-nineteenth century first noted the popularity amongst non-Christians of the St. Anne shrine, as well as the incidence there of *bhakti*-like self-mortifying worship (Stirrat 1992: 32).

Catholic saints are the key figures in syncretic religious traditions involving Christians, most famously in Caribbean Vodou where historical factors, including a largely autonomous native clergy, enabled what Leslie Desmangles (1992) describes as a symbiosis of traditions and combination of religious figures for a relatively socially homogeneous worshipping community.[6] Symbiosis or syncretism of this kind is less explicit in Sri Lanka where shrines such as the St. Anthony church at Kochikade are heavily controlled by specific religious authorities, with clear lines of management as well as distinct ethnic and religious affiliations. While this situation differs from private shrines where innovative blending can be more apparent (Bastin 2003; Stirrat 1992: 189ff.), it holds for other religious centers, both Śaivite and Buddhist, widely regarded as sites of miraculous power and popularly attended across ethnic, religious and, albeit less importantly, caste lines.[7]

One of these sites is the Munneśvaram temple complex, a site of highly competitive religious interaction between Sinhala Buddhists and Tamil Śaivites in an area well known for its ethnic mix (Bastin 2002). Through the ownership of the two main temples by Tamil Śaivite priests, the ostensible religious form of each temple is explicitly Śaivite. This form, which comprises architecture, imagery, and ritual, grew increasingly distinctive as religious revitalization movements— Buddhist and Śaivite—intensified their sense of ethnic particularity and religious orthodoxy through the nineteenth and twentieth centuries. Rebuilt from the 1870s, Munneśvaram's main temple became a distinctly Śaivite temple run by Tamil Brahmin priests observing a full Śaivite ritual calendar and attracting a growing Tamil (Sri Lankan and Indian) clientele. This served to alienate many of the surrounding Sinhala Buddhist villagers for whom the temple had previously served as a politico-religious center. As I demonstrate in my longer study, though, the distinctive aesthetic form that alienated local worshippers served to empower the temple as a Śaivite complex in the island-wide Buddhist domain. Munneśvaram's special location, a marginal yet powerful position, did not alienate the broader mass of devotees. It actually empowered the sense of religious potentiality (the *haskam*) of the temples and their deities, because the Buddhist revitalization movement declared Munnesvaram's kind of practices to be corruptions of pure Buddhism, and thus part of illusory but nonetheless thoroughly real existence. This was especially so at the second temple for the goddess Kali, owned and run by non-Brahmin Tamils, a temple renowned especially for sorcery and its wild possibilities. Nationally, therefore, Munnesvaram was not a traditional center, but a marginal place and, appropriately, a Tamil Saivite place. Outsider Buddhists began to flock to the temple.

The overall religious aesthetic, consisting of design and rite as well as the worshipping body, is thus syncretic or symbiotic in the sense that it contains a diverse worshipping body, largely Saivite and Buddhist but also Catholic and Muslim, whose worshipping practices such as bodily comportment in the temple along with language and other subtle indicators vary from each other, while at the same time they appear to be attending a distinctively singular Tamil Saivite temple. Hence my emphasis on the relative homogeneity of the Vodou worshipping community attending shrines of distinctively heterogeneous form in contrast to the more singular form of the Sri Lankan shrines complemented by a more heterogeneous community.

Inclusion of the crowd is thus critical to an appreciation of the blending, especially in contexts where the crowd is intrinsic to the idea of divine (and/or demonic) presence. In Sri Lanka, such a concept is evident in the value placed on bearing witness in Saivite and Buddhist religious experience—the value of the gaze. Divine presence is constituted and reconstituted in and through ritual, with special emphasis on this gaze (Bastin 2005b). For example, Saivite and Buddhist statues are consecrated through completion of their eyes, either by painting (Buddhist) or carving and painting (Saivite). A Saivite temple as a whole is opened by having its "eye" (Sanskrit *nethra*) opened as this is an essential metaphor for originating consciousness and the cosmogony that the temple celebrates. Worship (Sanskrit *darsan*) is the act of seeing the divine gaze (Eck 1985). Much of the ritual spectacle derives from this principle. In Buddhism, the gaze is also worked out aesthetically in Buddhist eye-painting ritual (Gombrich 1966) and more broadly in deity worship (Kapferer 1997: 128f.) as well as ideas of demonic possession (*yaksa disti*, "demon gaze") (Kapferer 1983: 50).

The value placed on the gaze and, with it, the act of worship informs the relational nature of the cosmos which I characterize as hierarchical and encompassing. In using the concept of hierarchy, I am referring to the arguments of Louis Dumont (1980, 1986) and especially to their treatment for the Sri Lankan context by Bruce Kapferer (1983, 1988, 1997). Hierarchical orders are holistic or totalizing schemes of value by which society and cosmos are conceptualized and imagined. They do not describe straightforward empirical realities but rather the imaginary institution of society, laid out as a cosmological order. They are thus ideological but also bear an unconscious or underlying prereflexive logical structure or *habitus*. This logic or, in Kapferer's terms "ontology" (Kapferer 1988: 79–84; 1997: 288), informs inter alia orientations to identity and difference such as in the ideological pairings of pure and impure, divine and demonic, and status and power. As Dumont demonstrated in his comparative analysis of modern and non-modern values, the issue of whether the pairings are dyadic (where pure and impure share an identity in difference) or hierarchical (where pure encompasses impure, as the whole is larger than the sum of its parts) is a matter of ontology or what he termed "structure." In the former, the pairing is dialectical; in the latter it is hierarchical. Importantly, dialectical ontologies prefigure synthetic homogeneities and sublimation, whereas hierarchical ontologies preserve the possibility of the other, the unencompassed. Difference is thus preserved in identity, not sublimated by it—a point underlined by religious inclusiveness in South Asia, especially in that broad range of practices conventionally glossed as "Hinduism." For historical reasons I employ the more accurate term "Śaivite" to describe Sri Lankan Hinduism, but this is not to deny its hierarchically inclusive nature, which I contrasted above with Islam. I would now characterize the latter as displaying a dialectical synthesis compared to the former's tendency to encompass. I reiterate, though, that the differences between the two are not reducible to simple tolerance and intolerance.

Devotees who worship Śaivite deities are thus part of those deities. Their participation in worship influences the uniqueness of local forms of those deities.[8] In this relationship, or better ensemble of relationships, people do not lose or surrender their distinctiveness but continually negotiate it and, at Munneśvaram and elsewhere, bring their concerns to the attention of the gods as Buddhists, as Catholics, or as Śaivites—and even, on occasion, as Muslims (for whom surrender to a relatively more sublimating religious order is valued). Devotees' backgrounds potentially affect how they relate to the deities they participate in creating in all of these deities' local specificity. They do so through their general bodily dispositions (based on factors like diet or other observances) as well as the kinds of offerings they make and favors they seek. Even a person's caste works upon the mutability of divinity, shaping the nature of the deities and establishing each temple as a unique expression (a part) of a transcendent entity (the whole). The paradox of every temple being the center of the world is thus resolved in the singular identity of each temple being made possible through the general characteristics of each temple. One does not face a single Mount Meru as one faces Mecca, because each temple is Mount Meru—the *axis mundi* that one circumambulates in a discrete and localizing manner rather than facing or surrendering towards it.[9]

The important point about plural shrines in the Sri Lankan context, therefore, is that they are neither syncretic, in the straightforward sense of blended religious traditions evident, for example, in the juxtaposed images of saints and deities in Vodou, nor syncretistic in the sense that such juxtaposition is deliberate and enduring, but are both syncretic *and* syncretistic in the diversity of worshippers who, in my argument, are part of the nature of the deities themselves. What I will suggest in the following is that this quality or feature of hierarchical ontology functions for the Catholic saints in Sri Lanka as it does for the Śaivite and Buddhist deities.[10] Moreover, it can also function in this way for a living person such as the Pope. For both Buddhism and Catholicism in their own ways share the principles

I have outlined here by way of a contrast between Śaivism and Islam. I emphasize that the contrast is deliberately broad in order to elucidate how these religions interact. Lest I be read as dismissing Islam as a singular totality, I would hope my approach offers a way into its diversity as well as the tensions informing that diversity.

A further point about Munneśvaram and its history of interaction, before I return to the papal visit It is significant that Munneśvaram is not simply the site of Śaivite and Buddhist interaction. Christian Jesuit missionaries completed the destruction of the surviving Munneśvaram temple statue in 1606. Through actions by Portuguese troops in 1578 and 1602, the building was already in ruins with sections of it used to build the fortifications in the nearby town of Chilaw, but the statue remained until the Jesuits set at it with iron bars. They report how they thus exorcized the Devil who had held sway over the neighborhood "as from a citadel" causing various freakish disturbances (Cagnola S.J. 1610, in Perniola 1991: 305–6).[11] While such fanatical iconoclasm appears to reject any participation in the existing (non-Christian) cosmology, and indeed seeks to destroy it, it does not remove a sense of religious potentiality but actually empowers it, albeit in certain directions that would later resonate with Buddhist attitudes. In a broadly similar way, the revitalization of the new Munneśvaram in the 1750s, which was built over the church to St. Peter that had been erected over the temple site, and its distinctively Śaivite renovations commencing in the 1870s and continuing to this day, directed Munneśvaram's aesthetic form and thereby invigorated its *haskam*, albeit again in particular ways.[12] What these various moments in the history of a shared site reveal is the capacity for different actions, both tolerant and intolerant, syncretic and anti-syncretic, to serve the formation and reformation of the religious domain. These were the kinds of processes evident when John Paul II visited Sri Lanka in 1995.

Papal Visit to Sri Lanka, 1995

Pope John Paul II (*regnum* 1978–2005) has been described as the pilgrim pope on account of his visiting over 120 countries during his reign. His practice of kissing the ground upon landing in a country (later replaced, when age intervened, with his being presented with, and kissing, a platter of earth) combined humility with a deterritorializing gesture emblematic of the purpose of his travel. This was not pilgrimage in the strict sense, but extensive travel reflecting the continually negotiated place of Catholicism in a continuously re-centering postcolonial world (Beatty 2006). John Paul certainly kissed a lot of earth but, more than that, he swelled the ranks of the saints by 482 and future saints (1,338) through dramatically hastening the complex process whereby one becomes a saint and by welcoming large numbers of candidates for sainthood, especially from what had been outposts of European empires.

The process of becoming a saint is long and bureaucratic. A special Church committee reviews nominations of dead people and this begins the usually long wait until the person is officially declared a saint. Unless the nominee is a martyr or has the waiting period waived by the Pope (as John Paul II did for Mother Theresa of Calcutta), at least five years separates their death and the commencement of the process through declaring the person "Blessed." After proof of a miracle or certainty of martyrdom as cause of death, the nominee will be beatified and deemed "Venerable." Finally, after a further miracle, the person can be canonized as a "saint." Typically, miracles are cures from life-threatening illnesses after a plea has been made to the deceased Blessed or Venerable person. The overall beatification and canonization "procedure" (as distinct from the idea of sainthood) is strictly controlled by the Church bureaucracy, and dates back to the sixteenth century with important centralizing modifications in the eighteenth century. In 1983, early in John Paul's reign, the beatification and canonization process was accelerated through a 75 percent reduction in the number of miracles needed for elevation. This led, for example, to the beatification of Jadwiga of Kraków in 1987 and her canonization in 1997; Jadwiga or Saint Hedwig having been a medieval Magyar queen of Poland who became, in John Paul's reign, the patron saint of queens and, significantly, of Europe—the new Europe of the Treaty of Rome and the collapsing Eastern Bloc.

In January 1995 a Qantas airliner brought the Pope and his entourage from Australia to Sri Lanka as the last stage of a three-stop beatification journey involving the Second World War-martyr Peter ToRot in Papua New Guinea, the nineteenth-century educator-nun Mary McKillop in Australia, and the seventeenth-century Goan missionary Joseph Vaz in Sri Lanka. Catholics as well as non-Catholics eagerly anticipated the event in every country, but in Sri Lanka, where I was researching Catholic-Buddhist interaction, the Pope's visit sparked controversy after it became widely known that John Paul II had described Buddhism as a pessimistic and atheistic religion. Outraged calls to ban him from the country were modified to a simple boycott by the Buddhist clergy. Strikingly, there was a strong sense that there would be violence; that this difference of opinion would not simply remain unchallenged by physical action in a country where riots and the brutal state suppression of political opposition, including street demonstrations by Buddhist monks, were legion.

In 1959 a Buddhist monk had assassinated the prime minister. While that event led to a subsequent diminution of political practice by the clergy, subsequent ethnic conflict and two left-wing insurgencies within the dominant Sinhalese population had led to renewed engagement (Seneviratne 1999; Bastin 2009).[13] The open air mass to be held on Colombo's Galle Face Green to commemorate Joseph Vaz's beatification seemed a likely time for violence to erupt. In the end, amidst tight security, nothing more than the monks' boycott occurred. What I wish to argue, albeit speculatively, is that events surrounding the Pope's arrival conspired to silence the monks.

John Paul's description of Buddhism as pessimistic had been made in a book published a few months earlier. *Crossing the Threshold of Hope* (1994) was written in response to a series of written questions posed by an Italian journalist, Vittorio Messori, whose questions included one about Buddhism's growing popularity in Western countries. While upholding the liberal ecumenicalism of the early 1960s' Second Vatican Council (or Vatican 2), John Paul voiced his concern about Catholics leaving the church and pursuing other religions. He characterizes Buddhism as a "negative soteriology":

> The "enlightenment" experienced by Buddha comes down to the conviction that the world is bad, that it is the source of evil and of suffering for man. To liberate oneself from this evil, one must free oneself from this world, necessitating a break with the ties that join us to external reality—ties existing in our human nature, in our psyche, in our bodies. The more we are liberated from these ties, the more we become indifferent to what is in the world, and the more we are freed from suffering, from the evil that has its source in the world.
>
> Do we draw near to God in this way? This is not mentioned in the "enlightenment" conveyed by Buddha. Buddhism is in large measure an *"atheistic" system*. We do not free ourselves from evil through the good which comes from God; we liberate ourselves only through detachment from the world, which is bad. The fullness of such a detachment is not union with God, but what is called *nirvana*, a state of perfect indifference with regard to the world. *To save oneself* means, above all, to free oneself from evil by becoming *indifferent to the world, which is the source of evil.* This is the culmination of the spiritual process (His Holiness John Paul II 1994: 48).

And he explains why it remains outside Catholic ecumenicalism:

> The Second Vatican Council has amply confirmed this truth. To indulge in a negative attitude toward the world, in the conviction that it is only a source of suffering for man and that he therefore must break away from it, is negative not only because it is unilateral but also because it is fundamentally contrary to the development of both man himself and the world, which the Creator has given and entrusted to man as his task (His Holiness John Paul II 1994: 50).

What John Paul II claimed to identify was a basic difference between Buddhism and Christianity insofar as the key ideal of the former is rejection of the world while the key ideal of the latter is celebration of the world as expressive of divine will. As a characterization of Buddhism, it is not completely wrong. While Buddhist deities do exist, they do so as Buddhists sharing the orientation towards release from the world that John Paul describes. However, the Buddhist ideal of perfect generosity flows from this ideal of non-attachment. Buddhism is not all gloomy renunciation or flight from the world, and this is something John Paul missed. Many Buddhists found that offensive, especially in light of the years of competition and conflict between Christians and others in Sri Lanka.[14]

In this foreboding climate before the Pope's arrival, a miracle occurred in the area of my research roughly forty-five kilometres south of Colombo. Two weeks before the papal visit, a statue of Mary spoke to two children asking them to come inside the church they were passing. Nothing further was said, but the miracle that all could observe was that where, prior to this occurrence, Mary's eyes had been blue, they were now brown. Mary, the patron saint of Sri Lanka, had ceased to be a blue-eyed European and had become brown-eyed like the vast majority of the Sri Lankan population. The miracle caused an enormous stir right around the country. People, predominantly but not exclusively Catholic, flocked to the church almost immediately. While the numbers peaked quickly in the first month before dropping off to a trickle that continues to this day, there remained a sense that the site is indeed a new Sri Lankan site of *haskam*—or marvelous divine presence. *Haskam*, etymologically linked to the Sanskrit *āścarya* or marvel, demarcates ordinary and localized centers of religious worship from the miraculous places of extraordinary religious potentiality at which radical slippage between states of existence can occur. *Haskam*, moreover, does not acknowledge religious boundaries. It magically irrupts into existence and demonstrates the artificial nature of religious categories, as well as the impermanence of our given existence.

Commencing two weeks before the Pope's visit and continuing throughout the visit amidst the furore of the Buddhist monks' boycott, the miracle of the Marian apparition and her spontaneous indigenization via a change of eye-pigmentation seemed to be too good to be true. The miracle did not simply deflect attention away from that "scoundrel" religious leader coming from the West, but it also reterritorialized Catholic Christianity via Mary, the patron saint of Sri Lanka, who had, in effect, performed a spontaneous auto-eye-opening or reconsecration. It was added to when the Pope arrived. As his motorcade made its way through Colombo from the airport, it passed the church to St. Anthony at Kochikade. According to reports, the Pope saw the church and instantly demanded that he go inside to pray. The motorcade unexpectedly halted and the crowd lining the streets were treated to the sight of the Pope, with his unprepared security personnel running in all directions, making his way into the church. As it was a Sunday afternoon, the inner city and the church were relatively quiet. The Pope prayed for a short while and then left.

St. Anthony of Padua was the favored saint of the Franciscan order of which the Pope was a part. The Franciscans enjoyed a monopoly over missionary activities in the first decades of Portuguese control over Colombo and did a great deal to promote St. Anthony there, as they did elsewhere. He is arguably Sri Lanka's most important saint after Mary. I say "arguably" because St. Sebastian, the martyred Roman soldier who was pierced with arrows but not killed, enjoys greater visibility (Stirrat 1977, 1981, 1992). The two are like brothers replicating the brothers Pillaiyar and Murugan in the Tamil Śaivite pantheon (who are known as Gana Deviyo and Kataragama Deviyo in the Sinhala Buddhist pantheon). Where Pillaiyar is the ascetic who bears a mango in his left hand, Murugan is the warrior.[15] In a similar way, where Anthony is the tonsured Franciscan who bears the infant Jesus in his left hand, Sebastian is the Christ-like martyred soldier.[16] Both saints are associated with divine intervention and, along with the dragon slayer Saint Michael, feature in a range of unofficial and unsanctioned religious practices connected to sorcery and exorcism.[17] It is with the people associated with such practices that I was able to elicit the link between these saints and the Śaivite and Buddhist deities. For the vast majority, however, the saints and the deities are discrete entities. Whereas the Śaivite and Buddhist connection is absolutely clear, the Catholic and Śaivite/Buddhist connection is more an interpretation backed by a few informants and noted by scholars (Mosse 1994; Stirrat 1992). Nevertheless, the saints are all part of the general *haskam* or miraculous power generally acknowledged by the Catholic Church in Sri Lanka and, especially, by devotees from all religious backgrounds. The *haskam* of St. Anthony is closely linked to his church in Kochikade where, as stated at the beginning of this chapter, Father Anthony planted the miracle-making cross.[18] The church thus shares a further feature in common with major shrines like Munneśvaram in being the arrival point of divine power in the land and its cosmology.

When Pope John Paul II espied the church as he was driving past and instantly demanded that he break his journey to go inside to pray, he was demonstrating that the *haskam* associated with the church was also recognized by the Pope. The event in itself was deemed to be miraculous. For many, there was a suspicion that it must have been staged.[19] For here was the Pope, survivor of an assassination attempt in 1981, traveling into territory made hostile by his opinions about Buddhism, in a country renowned for its political unrest along religious and communal lines, who suddenly gets down from his car because he has intuitively sensed the religious potentiality of the place. The following day, the newspapers were full of descriptions of the extraordinary event, and it had taken over all discussions of the visit amongst the people with whom I worked.

John Paul's act of recognition played out the logic of vision associated with Hindu and Buddhist religious potentiality that I have discussed elsewhere as a double movement between deity and devotee (Bastin 2005b). It also resonated with Mary's eye-catching act of recognition of two weeks earlier, indeed so much so that the idea of a conspiracy seemed to me to be too good not to be true. I have noted the parallel or symbiosis by identity between Saints Anthony and Sebastian, and the Śaivite and Buddhist gods Pillaiyar/Gana Deviyo and Murugan/Kataragama. I will now go a bit further and note the parallel between Mary and the Sinhala Buddhist virgin goddess Pattini—a relation previously noted by Gananath Obeyesekere (1984: 476–82). Part of the Pattini mythology relates to how she controls the entry to Sri Lanka of minor deity/demons (*devatta*) who are hierarchically transformed from their demonic side to their divine side via the mediation of the goddess. Kali at the Munneśvaram complex is an example (Bastin 2002: 53–54), but other figures like Devol Deviyo and Suniyam are also hierarchically transformed in their arrival myths by the goddess (Kapferer 1997: 320n27; Bastin 2002: 58n22).

For some scholars and even participants, the ambivalence of the *devatta* figures is difficult to grasp because they tend to imagine pantheons as consisting of either/ or categories. As I argue above, Hindu and Buddhist relational hierarchies differ.[20] An excellent account utilizing and thereby explicating Deleuzean categories concerning difference and repetition, as well as modalities of power, can be found in Kapferer's (1997) study of Sinhalese sorcery and particularly of the greatest exemplar of the *dēvatāvā* role—Suniyam. Critically, Kapferer describes Suniyam as condensing "the forces of human self-creation and self-destruction" (Kapferer 1997: 57); forces that exist always and everywhere and thereby propel the development and innovation of symbolic orders stressing precisely this idea of ambivalence and mediation. This is the context in which the Pope's visit gained meaning (i.e., became an event). I suggest that what occurred was that Mary mediated the demonized Pope's entry to the country and the Pope then recognized Christian *haskam* in the form of the St. Anthony church, whose creation story and main statue also convey miraculous deterritorialization. The mediation was done in the form of the miracle of Mary's apparition and eye-colour change. The equivalence to a demonic status derived from John Paul's remarks about Buddhism as a negative soteriology as well as from his outsider status. The deterritorializing surrender by John Paul was completed when he prayed to St. Anthony. The result was a broad celebration of *haskam* or religious potentiality that served to defuse the sense of threat the visit had instilled. John Paul was, in effect, hierarchically mediated and could now go about his business of beatifying Joseph Vaz. The miracles worked to deflect attention onto the Pope's visit and away from the issue of the Buddhist boycott. They inspired an upsurge of religious attention, Catholic, but also Buddhist, in the area where I was working. By visiting Kochikade, John Paul had extended the logic of his deterritorializing kissing-the-earth by situating himself alongside the vast numbers of devotees who habituate the church. It no longer mattered that he thought Buddhism was depressing, for he had deterritorialized himself as the Pope from Rome and reterritorialized himself as a man of faith, acknowledging the presence of God in one of the country's most sacred (and *haskam*-rich) sites. Central to his action was surrender to the greater issues of religious faith of most religious devotees—self-creation and self-destruction. I stress too, that these acts of surrender sit within the logic of papal Catholicism, especially the self-abnegating traditions that John Paul championed. He was not, in my view, acting out of character.

I am likening this surrender to the arrival myths of certain deity/demons in Sinhala Buddhism, because I am struck by the parallel between Pattini and Mary, and especially the mediating role these mother goddesses play in both the Buddhist and Catholic belief systems.[21] I am also struck by the commonalities between Saints Anthony and Sebastian and the gods Gana Deviyo and Kataragama. I argue that these elements, which I stress I am drawing together, make the actions of the Pope constitutive of the idea of deterritorialization. In other words, the papal visit became an event, more accurately the interplay of structure and event or what Sahlins (1981) describes in relation to another "Imperial Stranger" (Captain Cook) as a "structure of the conjuncture." Following Sahlins, such a process does not simply repeat itself rather than generate transformative power. This is what Sahlins (2005) more recently describes as structural amplification, noting the importance of internal competitive tensions that amplify the process of interpretation and transformation (see Kapferer 2010a). To illustrate this, I turn to another element of the papal visit—the suppression of radical elements within the Sri Lankan Catholic clergy.

The Attack on an Asian Liberation Theology

The volatile papal visit was defused through a series of actions, some of which may have been orchestrated, mobilizing a certain cultural logic or *habitus* which was both ontological and ideological, and thus historically contingent. These actions resulted in the deterritorialization of the "imperial stranger"—the Pope—through his incorporation into the active domain of Sri Lankan religious practice. At the same time, other forces and processes were at work to reterritorialize the contemporary Catholic Church's assertions of religious orthodoxy and to silence internal opposition.

Through my research I came to know a small number of young Sinhalese Catholic clergy who were active in different social development programs.[22] They were progressives committed to taking inspiration, albeit a very careful inspiration, from Latin American liberation theology. They did not talk about it in these terms. Indeed, they would become guarded when I asked them what they thought about liberation theology. One young priest explained that Asia's situation was not Latin America's and that, therefore, their work was thoroughly original and could as easily inspire people in Latin America as Latin America had inspired them. However, the other reason was the actions of the Vatican to silence liberation theology. The Church had, under John Paul II, campaigned aggressively in South America and filled senior positions with conservatives. The Vatican team of John Paul II and his chief inquisitor,[23] Cardinal Ratzinger, was aggressively stamping official Catholicism with a conservative line seeking to suppress the spirit of rebellion in liberation theology just as it had sought to encourage rebellion against the communist states of Eastern Europe. The Church was strongly opposed to centralized secular states, but also strongly opposed to any decentralization of the Church's sovereignty, which is what liberation theology in part represents.

Cardinal Ratzinger, who would later succeed John Paul II and become Pope Benedict XVI, excommunicated the Sinhalese priest most publicly associated with Sri Lankan liberation theology, Father Tissa Balasuriya, in 1997.[24] That measure was already taking shape during the papal visit and needs some background. Balasuriya created the Centre for Society and Religion in 1971 at a time of heightened peasant militancy and state oppression associated with the Janatha Vimukthi Perumuna (JVP, or People's Liberation Front). Through the center's journal *Logos*, Balasuriya had published a series of works on Catholicism and social justice. *Mary and Human Liberation* was published in 1990 at the height of the second JVP insurgency.[25]

Mary and Human Liberation was an attempt to rethink Marian devotion in order to place Catholicism more firmly in the pluralism of Asian religion. For

Balasuriya, a priest of the Order of Mary Immaculate schooled by the Marist Brothers,[26] the figure of Mary is especially important. He seeks to liberate her from traditional theological understanding which sees her as resolving the issue of the feminine developed in relation to Eve and Original Sin and to insert her instead into an argument that the exigencies of Asian religious pluralism, political secularism, and social inequality require a reconfiguration. He contends that Asia must create its own theology commencing with the humanity of Mary and her being a woman. Among others, he cites the feminist author Mary Daly and the historian Marina Warner. He associates Jesus with a social liberation movement and Mary as the mother of a victim of state oppression. The connection to the conditions at the time could not be plainer; the suppression of the second JVP insurgency between 1989 and 1991 resulted in the disappearances and deaths of, conservatively, about forty thousand Sinhalese, mostly by government-controlled paramilitary death squads.

The divinity of Jesus and the assumption of divinity by Mary are not questioned, but Balasuriya does question the traditional use of Mary to legitimate acceptance of suffering meted out by oppressors (colonial and otherwise) (Balasuriya 1990: 110ff.). He urges a reconsideration of Mary's role in order to enable a dialogue with other Asian religions as well as with secularist and Marxist movements in Asia (Balasuriya 1990: 61). In short, Balasuriya calls for a greater localization of Catholic theology accompanied by a decentralization of Catholicism to enable the religion to engage more parochially with other religions in facing the social issues of diverse contexts. One could say, therefore, that Balasuriya is in effect calling for Mary's blue eyes to turn brown.

The Sri Lankan bishops' conference headed by Bishop Malcolm Ranjith first condemned Balasuriya's book in 1994. Balasuriya was excommunicated at the behest of Cardinal Ratzinger in early 1997 and reinstated in early 1998 after admitting to having been ambiguous about Mary's status. The result could be called a draw, because Balasuriya never quite recanted and the Vatican never gave in to Balasuriya's many supporters from around the world. The point, though, is that the debate over *Mary and Human Liberation* was raging in 1995 when the Pope visited and when I was interviewing young priests about social reform in Sri Lanka. It was not surprising, therefore, that when asked about their values the clergy with whom I was working were guarded. One of the main areas where these clergy were active was in initiating grass roots dialogue between Sinhalese and Tamil Catholics living in different parts of the country. The peculiarly straddling status of Catholicism in Sri Lanka was something they felt could be encouraged in the spirit of reconciliation and cooperation that was then sweeping the country following the election of Chandrika Kumaratunga to the executive presidency on a peace platform in 1994. This peace with the Tamil Tigers was already unraveling in early 1995, but the efforts of the young priests were admirable.

Within two weeks of the Pope's visit, all of these priests had been transferred and their networks disrupted. The activities of the Pope, his unscheduled stops to pray at St. Anthony's Kochikade, the public mass for beatifying Joseph Vaz, and so on, resembled a side show relative to what I can only speculate must have been going on in the backroom meetings between members of the entourage and the Roman Catholic leaders of Sri Lanka. Shortly afterwards, at the annual church festival of the main church in Kalutara, the Archbishop of Colombo's sermon sounded like a warning to people to behave and protect the unity of the Church in Sri Lanka. There was, in short, a dramatic change of tune to something much sterner and less compromising. The full force of the papal visit struck me at this moment, as did the comment of one of the entourage members to a journalist's question about the Buddhist monks' boycott. He replied to the effect that they were treating the matter as pertaining very much to local issues that did not relate to the Pope. The Vatican thus engineered a massive undoing of efforts to establish a plural dialogue, not only within the Church but across ethnic lines and between the Church in Sri Lanka and the other religions taking place at the grassroots. It would go on to excommunicate an important figure who was involved in linking this grassroots development with an international network. Meanwhile, Mary had appeared and spoken. Her blues eyes had turned brown. The Pope had stopped miraculously at an important plural church and prayed, and Joseph Vaz the seventeenth-century missionary had progressed another step down the road to sainthood. It was business as usual.

Conclusion: Events and Conjunctures

The papal "road show" that came to Sri Lanka in 1995 was a complex machine working to reassert central orthodoxy. It did so through an intricate web of miracles, some conventional and possibly planned, others unconventional, possibly planned, but I do not think expected. Planned or not, these miracles played out a logic that served to manifest religious potency and, above all, the deterritorializing potency that is the heart of the religious. In this sense, the miracles were transgressive or violating, and thus sacred. They irrupted into established semantic domains and in this regard shared similar qualities with syncretic practices. However, unlike Haitian Vodou, which preserves an explicit sense of symbolic juxtaposition within an encompassing cosmology and, importantly, a relatively homogenous worshipping community, in Sri Lanka the symbolic traditions keep pulling apart, as do the worshipping communities who, nevertheless, hold to a largely encompassing idea of religious potentiality or *haskam*.

Sri Lankan society in the late twentieth century displays intensely labile dimensions connected to its place in the world economy, its structural dependency and, above all, its ethnic conflict and broad political instability. The predicament for the Roman Catholic Church in world affairs is, I suggest, broadly similar, and the hastened canonization procedures as well as the extensive traveling undertaken by Pope John Paul II reflect this predicament. For this reason texts like *Crossing the Threshold of Hope* and *Mary and Human Liberation* both display urgency, while being poles apart in their vision of Catholicism's place in the world. The papal visit and the miraculous syncretism it inspired enabled a momentary synergy of these urgencies. They were like ships in the night, which then drew apart into a paroxysm of boundary-marking and antagonism—the enabling conditions for the next convergence, the next set of miraculous transgressions that would demonstrate both their mutuality as well as their inherent difference. So when John Paul II's successor, Cardinal Ratzinger, denounced syncretism as part of his election speech (Beatty 2006: 334n9), he was opening the field to future mixture and future intolerance—the nature of the sacred.[27]

Notes

1. See (DeLanda 2000) for a discussion of some of the different forms of coalescence in geology, biology, and linguistics. His account expands on the ideas of Deleuze and Guattari (1987). For a critique of De Landa's holism, see Kapferer 2010b: 205ff.

2. The term derives from Deleuze (2004). See also Deleuze and Guattari (1994); DeLanda (2002); Kapferer (2006). On Deleuze and Guattari's (1987, 1994) concept of the double movement of territorialization, see Kapferer 1997; Bastin 2005a.

3. Brendbekken's study concerns the contemporary configurations of Vodou, noting considerable variation in the understanding of the relationship between Catholic saints and the Vodou spirits (Brendbekken 2003: 67n33), while being critical of anthropological nominalism (see, for example, Stewart 1999). Vodou is, perhaps, the most celebrated example of syncretism or symbiosis (Desmangles 1992) and I touch on it briefly as a contrast to the Sri Lankan context.

4. Kapferer describes the event as: "a singularity in which critical dimensions can be conceived as opening to new potentialities in the formation of social realities or what post-structuralists, especially of a Deleuzian persuasion (see Deleuze 2004; Deleuze and Guattari 1987), would describe as the continual becoming of the social as a complex emerging and diversifying multiplicity that is enduringly open and not constrained within some kind of organized, interrelated totality of parts, either as real (existent), imagined, modeled, or projected" (Kapferer 2010a: 1–2).

5. I use the term hierarchy here in its original Church Latin sense of sacred order of divinity and saints and not in the more specialist Dumontian sense employed elsewhere in the chapter. The yellow color in St. Anthony candles derives from the original use of tallow, but interestingly remains the color of choice, given its importance in the iconography of the broad class of Sinhala Buddhist guardian deities with whose character I am suggesting the Catholic saints Anthony and Sebastian's characters resonate.

6. Desmangles (1992: 10) identifies two levels of symbiosis: by ecology and by identity. Ecological symbiosis comprises both spatial and temporal features with the spatial juxtaposition of Catholic, African and new elements in the Vodou shrines as well as the temporal juxtaposition of special worship days in the calendar. Symbiosis by identity is "a system of identification or transfiguration by which, on the basis of the similarities between African and Catholic myths and symbols, the saints were identified with African gods" (ibid.). Haitian history is critical, according to Desmangles, especially the historical formations of violence and resistance connected to slavery, the suppression of non-Catholic religion, rebellion and plantation capitalism in the post-independence context. Importantly, from independence in 1804, the Roman Catholic Church struggled to maintain its authority over a largely native clergy and this paved the way for innovations in organizational structure and religious practice. Brendbekken's (2003) more recent work demonstrates the ongoing and divergent nature of this process as different types of missionary enter the scene.

7. Caste-specific churches are neither exclusive nor common. They reflect settlement patterns more than deliberate strategies. I imagine Kochikade, for example, would have initially been a fisher caste church, but in the conditions of its urban popularity this would have changed rapidly.

8. Such a relational ontology has also been noted extensively. It is very well described by Richard Davis (1992) as well as in Frederick Smith's (2006) recent compendious study of divine and demonic possession. See also David Mosse's (1994) use of the concept for examining Hindu-Christian interaction.

9. This phenomenon of localization is skillfully argued by David Shulman (1980) in his classic study of Tamil Śaivite temple myths.

10. David Mosse (1994) argues in a similar way for Catholic saints in south India, noting, as I have said, the importance of a Dumontian relational theory of divinity and also the shifting status and identity of boundary-marking saints and lower-order Śaivite deities. Elsewhere, Mosse (1996) argues for the ideology of pure and impure as transcending Hindu categories, and thereby demonstrating what I would call (following Kapferer) a hierarchical ontology.

11. Father Cagnola, S.J., *Jesuit Annual Letter*, Cochin, 5 December 1610. Translated by S.G. Perera, S.J., 1916, and reproduced with revisions in V. Perniola, S.J. (1991) *The Catholic Church in Sri Lanka: The Portuguese Period*. Volume 2: 1566–1619, pp. 304–5. Also cited in Bastin 2002: 1.

12. A very important additional factor here about the site was that revenues from the client villages in the region came to the holders. The Munneśvaram *pattuva* (district) funded the Jesuits and later the Portuguese administration. In my argument, this wealth should be construed as an element of the temple's divine power, not as separate to it.

13. Inspired by events such as the Papal visit, but more especially by the ongoing civil war, the Tamil threat to national sovereignty, and the perception of heightened evangelism by new Christian churches, the militancy of the *Sangha* (the Buddhist community of monks, nuns, novices, and laity) has intensified since 1995 (Bastin 2009; Deegalle 2006; Frydenlund 2005). For a brief account up to the late 1990s, see Seneviratne 1999, 2001.

14. Tambiah (1992) notes how the struggle between the Catholic Church and the Buddhist post-independence government heavily influenced the rise of Buddhist militancy (see also Stirrat 1992). Young and Senanayaka provide an important complement to these works in eighteenth-century Sinhala stories featuring Jesus as a demonic carpenter-ghost (Young and Senanayaka 1998). This struggle between Sinhala Buddism and Christianity has a long history. It is also worth noting that the demonic Jesus in the eighteenth-century text shares significant characteristics with a Sinhala Buddhist demon concerned largely with promoting falsehoods and illusions.

15. The myth attached to this iconography is that the mango represents the prize Pillaiyar won for circumnavigating the universe faster than his brother. Where Murugan set off around the universe, Pillaiyar simply walked around his parents and claimed the prize. Pillaiyar is thus the clearer of obstacles and considered to be less passionately impetuous than his warrior-king brother.

16. Noting no clear iconographic thread, Stirrat links St. Anthony to Murugan/Kataragama rather than to Pillaiyar/Gana Deviyo and reports how some Catholic devotees occasionally insist on how the deities and saints are identical (Stirrat 1992: 189, 214n12). With St. Sebastian the connection is especially evident in the statuary, where the saint is often represented as a Roman soldier at the boundary of a church and a Christo-mimetic martyr inside. This contrast resonates with the "doubleness" of Sinhala Buddhist guardian deities that I describe.

17. These practices are difficult to learn about because they are strongly discouraged by the church authorities (see Stirrat 1981). With the late Chandra Vitharana, I have recorded the oral text of a lay Catholic exorcist. David Mosse's (1994) account of Catholic saints in a south Indian village also highlights the ambiguous identity with lower-order sorcery deities.

18. The area derives its name from the major Indian port of Cochin and its link to longstanding communities of Malayalee traders. Significantly, Cochin also has strong connections with Portuguese Catholicism, Catholic fishing communities, and St. Anthony worship. Father Anthony who founded the church hailed from Cochin. In the modern city of Cochin, known as Ernakulam, stands a St. Anthony church with a reputation and plural worship similar to its Sri Lankan counterpart.

19. John Paul II had made a habit of making unscheduled stops that, with photographers mysteriously on hand, enabled excellent photo opportunities. His 1983 visit to the tomb of El Salvador's Archbishop Romero appeared on the front page of the New York Times (Hanson 1987: 6). Andrew

Beatty's (2006) account of John Paul's 2002 visit to Mexico reveals a political waltz of competing organized spontaneities as the Vatican negotiated its place in contemporary Mexico, while the conservative Mexican president negotiated a place for religion in an avowedly secular state.

20. Dumont notes, but initially underplays, this relational feature of the Tamil Śaivite pantheon in his structuralist account of the deity Aiyanar (see Dumont 1986: 228–30).

21. The incidence of Marian apparitions is extensive and expanding, with several excellent historical accounts highlighting the links between apparitions and the larger social, political, and doctrinal context (e.g., Perry and Echeverria 1988). For example, the Lourdes apparition of a forget-me-not blue-eyed Mary in 1858 occurred in the aftermath of the Counter-Reformation dispute over Mary's connection to sin (Warner 1976: 249). Marpingen in Germany in 1876 reveals a similar situation with the additional element of an intense struggle between church and state (Blackbourn 1993). The apparitions that occurred in Miami, Florida, in 2000 were linked directly to the Elián Gonzalez controversy (Sahlins 2005: 11).

22. See also David Mosse (1994: 325) who describes a similar social reform movement among Tamil Catholics in south India. The Church countenanced these actions throughout the 1980s, but reined them in during the mid-1990s.

23. Strictly speaking, the label "inquisitor" was dropped in 1908 when the name of the Roman Inquisition was changed, and it later became the Congregation for the Doctrine of the Faith in 1965. Ratzinger's assumption of the directorship of that office reveals, nonetheless, continuity with the inquisition.

24. For a partisan discussion of the events, see Basil Fernando *Power vs. Conscience: The Excommunication of Tissa Balasuriya* (1997). For other documents, see the special issue of the journal *Logos*, volume 35, numbers 2 and 3, 1997.

25. I am not linking Balasuriya to the JVP except to indicate that his concern for social justice had developed in a climate of popular unrest and brutal state oppression. Nor am I suggesting that Balasuriya is the only radical voice within Sri Lankan Catholicism. The young priests I knew, like the men and women in my research area involved in social development programs, were all cynical about and frightened by the state and its repressive practices. An early victim was a colleague of Balasuriya's, Father Michael Rodrigo, who was assassinated by an unknown assailant (probably army) in November 1988. Rodrigo worked a remote parish in the southeast of the island and had been accused a few days earlier of supporting the JVP. The parish was part of the diocese of Bishop Leo Nanayakkara until his death (from natural causes) in 1982, when the Church disbanded it. The history of this diocese will be documented elsewhere, because its role in the development of what I call a "Sri Lankan liberation theology" after the JVP insurgency of 1971 is highly significant.

26. The Order of Mary Immaculate and the Marist Order emerged in France amidst the doctrinal upheavals concerning Mary's nature and status that consumed the Jesuits and the Dominicans in the first half of the nineteenth century, thus playing an important role in the Counter-Reformation revival of Catholicism in Europe (Warner 1976: 249–52). In this regard, Tissa Balasuriya is heir to a long tradition, but a tradition that many Catholics would have thought had been resolved already. Liberation theology is, however, itself heir to another long tradition in Christianity, namely the tradition of heresy or freedom of thought accompanying the localization of Catholic orthodoxy.

27. In his measured comments on Ratzinger's speech, Balasuriya (2005) reiterates his liberation theology position on dismantling Catholicism's imperial past. He does not address the issue of syncretism.

References

Balasuriya O.M.I., Tissa. 1990. "Mary and Human Liberation." *Logos* 29(1, 2). Colombo: Centre for Society and Religion.

———. 2005. "The Inauguration Sermon of Pope Benedict XVI." *Social Justice* (the monthly Journal of the Centre for Society and Religion) 191: 9–12, 27.

Bastin, Rohan. 2002. *The Domain of Constant Excess: Plural Worship at the Munneśvaram Temples in Sri Lanka.* New York and Oxford: Berghahn Books.

———. 2003. "Sorcerous Technologies and Religious Innovation in Sri Lanka," in *Beyond Rationality: Rethinking Magic, Witchcraft and Sorcery*, ed. B. Kapferer. New York and Oxford: Berghahn Books, 155–74.

———. 2005a. "Hindu Temples in the Sri Lankan Ethnic Conflict: Capture and Excess." *Social Analysis* 49(1): 45–66.

———. 2005b. "The Hindu Temple and the Aesthetics of the Imaginary," in *Aesthetics in Performance: Formations of Symbolic Construction and Experience*, eds. A. Hobart and B. Kapferer. New York and Oxford: Berghahn Books, 89–108.

———. 2009. "Sri Lankan Civil Society and its Fanatics." *Social Analysis* 53(1): 123–40.

Bataille, Georges. 1987. *Eroticism*, trans. M. Dalwood. London: Marion Boyars.

Beatty, Andrew. 2006. "The Pope in Mexico: Syncretism in Public Ritual." *American Anthropologist* 108(2): 324–35.

Blackbourn, David. 1993. *Marpingen: Apparitions of the Virgin Mary in Nineteenth-Century Germany.* New York: Alfred A. Knopf.

Brendbekken, Marit. 2003. "Beyond Vodou and Anthroposophy in the Dominican-Haitian Borderlands," in *Beyond Rationality: Rethinking Magic, Witchcraft and Sorcery*, ed. B. Kapferer. New York and Oxford: Berghahn Books, 31–74.

Caillois, Roger. 1959. *Man and the Sacred*, trans. M. Barash. Glencoe, Illinois: The Free Press.

Davis, Richard H. 1991. *Ritual in an Oscillating Universe: Worshipping Siva in Medieval India.* Princeton: Princeton University Press.

Deegalle, Mahinda. 2006. "JHU Politics for Peace and a Righteous State," in *Buddhism, Conflict and Violence in Modern Sri Lanka*, ed. M. Deegalle. London and New York: Routledge, 233–54.

DeLanda, Manuel. 2000. *A Thousand Years of Non-Linear History.* New York: Swerve Editions.

———. 2002. *Intensive Science and Virtual Philosophy.* London: Continuum.

Deleuze, Gilles. 2004. *The Logic of Sense.* London: Continuum.

Deleuze, Gilles and Félix Guattari. 1987. *A Thousand Plateaus: Capitalism and Schizophrenia*, trans. B. Masumi. Minneapolis: University of Minnesota Press.

———. 1994. *What is Philosophy?* trans. H. Tomlinson and G. Burchall. New York: Columbia University Press.

Desmangles, Leslie G. 1992. *The Faces of the Gods: Vodou and Roman Catholicism in Haiti.* Chapel Hill: The University of North Carolina Press.

Dumont, Louis. 1980. *Homo Hierarchicus: The Caste System and its Implications*, revised edition. Chicago: University of Chicago Press.

———. 1986. *Essays on Individualism: Modern Ideology in Anthropological Perspective.* Chicago: University of Chicago Press.

Eck, Diana L. 1985. *Darśan: Seeing the Divine Image in India*, second revised and enlarged edition. Chambersburg, Pennsylvania: Anima Books.

Fernando, Basil. 1997. *Power vs. Conscience: The Excommunication of Tissa Balasuriya.* Hong Kong: Asian Human Rights Commission.

Frydenlund, Iselen. 2005. *The Sangha and its Relation to the Peace Process in Sri Lanka: A Report for the Norwegian Ministry of Foreign Affairs.* Oslo: International Peace Research Institute.

Gombrich, Richard. 1966. "The Consecration of a Buddha Image." *Journal of Asian Studies* 26(1): 23–36.

Hanson, Eric O. 1987. *The Catholic Church in World Politics.* Princeton: Princeton University Press.

Hayden, Robert M. 2002. "Antagonistic Tolerance: Competitive Sharing of Religious Sites in South Asia and the Balkans." *Current Anthropology* 43(2): 205–19, 226–29.

John Paul II, His Holiness. 1994. *Crossing the Threshold of Hope.* New York: Alfred A. Knopf.

Kapferer, Bruce. 1983. *A Celebration of Demons: Exorcism and the Aesthetics of Healing in Sri Lanka.* Bloomington: Indiana University Press.

———. 1988. *Legends of People, Myths of State: Violence, Intolerance, and Political Culture in Sri Lanka and Australia.* Washington: Smithsonian Institution Press.

———. 1997. *The Feast of the Sorcerer: Practices of Consciousness and Power.* Chicago: University of Chicago Press.

———. 2006. "Virtuality," in *Theorizing Rituals: Issues, Topics, Approaches, Concepts*, eds. J. Kreinath, J. Snoek, and M. Strausberg. Leiden and Boston: Brill, 671–84.

———. 2010a. "Introduction: In the Event—Towards an Anthropology of Generic Moments." *Social Analysis* 54(3): 1–27.

———. 2010b. "Louis Dumont and a Holist Anthropology," in *Experiments in Holism: Theory and Practice in Contemporary Anthropology*, eds. T. Otto and N. Bubandt. Oxford: Wiley-Blackwell, 187–209.

Mosse, David. 1994. "Catholic Saints and the Hindu Village Pantheon in Rural Tamil Nadu, India." *Man* (New Series) 29(2): 301–32.

———. 1996. "South Indian Christians, Purity/Impurity, and the Caste System: Death Ritual in a Tamil Roman Catholic Community." *Journal of the Royal Anthropological Institute* 2(3): 461–83.

Obeyesekere, Gananath. 1984. *The Cult of the Goddess Pattini*, Chicago: University of Chicago Press.

Perniola S.J., V. 1991. *The Catholic Church in Sri Lanka: The Portuguese Period.* 4 vols. Colombo: Tisara Prakasakayo, vol. 2: 1566–1619.

Perry, Nicholas and Loreto Echeverria. 1988. *Under the Heel of Mary.* London: Routledge.

Sahlins, Marshall. 1981. *Historical Metaphors and Mythical Realities: Structure in the Early History of the Sandwich Islands Kingdom.* Ann Arbor: The University of Michigan Press.

———. 2005. "Structural Work: How Microhistories Become Macrohistories and Vice Versa." *Anthropological Theory* 5(1): 5–30.

Seneviratne, H.L. 1999. *The Work of Kings: The New Buddhism in Sri Lanka.* Chicago: Chicago University Press.

———. 2001. "Buddhist Monks and Ethnic Politics: A War Zone in an Island Paradise." *Anthropology Today* 17(2): 15–21.

Shulman, David D. 1980. *Tamil Temple Myths: Sacrifice and Divine Marriage in the South Indian Saiva Tradition.* Princeton: Princeton University Press.

Smith, Frederick M. 2006. *The Self Possessed: Deity and Spirit Possession in South Asian Literature and Civilization*. New York: Columbia University Press.

Stewart, Charles. 1999. "Syncretism and its Synonyms: Reflections on Cultural Mixture." *Diacritics* 29(3): 40–62.

Stirrat, R.L. 1977. "Demonic Possession in Roman Catholic Sri Lanka." *Journal of Anthropological Research* 33: 122–48.

———. 1981. "The Shrine of St. Sebastian at Mirisgama." *Man* 16: 183–200.

———. 1992. *Power and Religiosity in a Post-Colonial Setting: Sinhala Catholics in Contemporary Sri Lanka*. Cambridge: Cambridge University Press.

Tambiah, Stanley Jeyaraja. 1992. *Buddhism Betrayed? Religion, Politics, and Violence in Sri Lanka*, with a foreword by Lal Jayawardena. Chicago: University of Chicago Press.

Warner, Marina. 1976. *Alone of All Her Sex: The Myth and Cult of the Virgin Mary*. London: Picador.

Young, R.F. and G.S.B. Senanayaka. 1998. *The Carpenter-Heretic: A Collection of Buddhist Stories about Christianity from 18th Century Sri Lanka*. Colombo: Karunaratne and Sons.

Chapter 7

THE GHRIBA ON THE ISLAND OF JERBA OR THE REINVENTION OF A SHARED SHRINE AS A METONYM FOR A MULTICULTURAL TUNISIA

Dora Carpenter-Latiri

This chapter examines the case of the Ghriba synagogue on the island of Jerba (or Djerba) in Tunisia, where a historic Jewish community continues to live alongside the Muslim majority population. The synagogue, like its community, dates back to at least the first century AD and came to international attention in 2002 when it suffered an attack by al-Qaeda.

Claims exist for the synagogue's being to some degree a shared shrine, and here I draw on approaches both from anthropology and my own discipline of linguistics, more specifically discourse analysis, to consider the reality of such propositions. I will look at actual practice at the shrine, and perspectives on it, as well as the attitudes of those associated with it, including members of local communities, persons involved in the tourist industry, pilgrims, and government spokespersons. My chapter will show that although the practice of sharing the shrine of the Ghriba does exist, it is a marginal practice rather than a popular one. I will analyse the convergence of participants, the media, and officials in the construction of the discourse of the Ghriba as a mixed shrine, and draw parallels with nostalgic discourses about multicultural Tunisia.

Jerba, a Mosaic of Populations

Jerba is an island in the Mediterranean off the southeast coast of Tunisia. Throughout the history of the island there have been exchanges with Libya, the Near East, the Western Maghreb, and Southern Europe. It has been both somewhere accessible and somewhere to withdraw to. Historically, the island's Muslims are descended in part from the Ibadites, a heterodox branch of Islam emerging from Kharijism which found refuge in the tenth century in inaccessible places such as the Mzab in Algeria, and in Jerba. There are still Berber-speakers on the island since in Tunisia the Berber-speaking population has survived in isolated, remote areas. They are a minority group in Tunisia (1 to 2 per cent of the country's population) but relatively well represented on Jerba. In Tunisian Arabic, Berber is called *jerbi* (i.e., "Jerbian"). Jerba also has a black community, who are descendants of slaves freed in the nineteenth century.

In Jerba, Jews claim to come from two groups.[1] The first group are the descendants of the Cohanim from the first diaspora; they are the founders of the Hara Seghira ("small Jewish quarter" in Arabic) and of the Ghriba synagogue. A second group, *b'nai Israil* (sons of Israel) is settled in Hara Kbira ("large Jewish quarter" in Arabic). In the 1970s the Hara Seghira was renamed Er-Riadh ("the gardens"), and the Hara Kebira Es-Sewani ("the orchards"). The locals—and taxi drivers—use both names, although the Jews strictly use the old names.[2]

The island of Jerba is made up of a number of communities (Muslim Arabs,[3] Jews, Blacks, and Berbers) each with their own identity and particularities (Mourali and Heyer 2001). This striking situation on the island is to some extent typical of the whole of Tunisia; the country is sometimes described as a mosaic society made up of a sum of regional and tribal particularities (Camau 1989: 26–31). Unlike the rest of Tunisia, the specificity of Jerba is to bring out in a restricted space the contrasts between the communities and to manifest, by their greater relative representation, the silent minorities, in particular the Jewish one.

Jews and Muslims on the Island of Jerba: Milestones in History and Symbolic Chronology

The Jewish presence in Tunisia has a long history, predating the arrival of Islam and nourishing a double religious and local identity. It is hard to establish with any historical certainty the date of their first arrival. There have probably been Jews on the island of Jerba since at least the time of the destruction of Jerusalem's Second Temple in AD 70. The Pentecost story in the Bible mentions Jews from "the districts of Libya around Cyrene"—a large stretch of North Africa taking in present-day Libya and southern Tunisia, and sometimes also called Cyrenaica (Acts of the Apostles 2:10–11).

Since the 1990s when the Ghriba festival began being promoted internationally, discourses on the origins of the Jews in Tunisia have multiplied in local and international media (see below on the changes in the ritual practice). Oral tradition reported in both scholarly accounts (Valensi and Udovitch 1984) and tourist documentation (Tmarzizet and Perez 1993) gives only vague and varying historical indications. All versions do however agree on putting the origin of the Jewish presence in Jerba between the time of Moses' successors, when monotheism—shared by both Jews and Muslims—was established, and the Arab-Muslim conquest, a moment differently recalled by both the island's Jews and the Berber-speaking Muslims. These origin stories legitimize a minority community while at the same time accentuating the distinctive features of that community, which can in some situations define itself with reference to what it shares with the island's other inhabitants, and in others with reference to their differences. This combination of both shared and distinctive features reaffirms the rootedness of the Jews on the island as well as their religious identity. The affirmation of a Jewish legitimacy in Tunisia in general has, since the 1990s, been broadcast by both Tunisian Jews and Tunisian officialdom. This is somehow contradicted by recent fieldwork amongst the Muslim majority who often fail to see a distinction between Jews and the State of Israel.

Among Jerba's Jewish legends and traditions, the version that gives the earliest timing for a Jewish presence on the island tells us that at the time of Joshua, the Hebrew leader who succeeded Moses, an element of the tribes of Israel, discontented with the sharing of land, left with the defeated Canaanites and traveled to Egypt and thence to the Maghreb (Tmarzizet and Perez 1993: 75). Another legend places the arrival of Jews at the time of King David; one of David's generals pursued the Philistines as far as Jerba where he founded the first Jewish community (Valensi and Udovitch 1984: 8; Tmarzizet and Perez 1993: 74). A third version has Jews arriving by sea ("like the Phoenicians" [Valensi and Udovitch 1984: 8]) at the time of King Solomon (around the eleventh century BC [Tmarzizet and Perez 1993: 75]) to settle on the coast. Other versions present the settling of the Jewish community as a consequence of the first or second destruction of the Temple, either after 586 BC (Valensi and Udovitch 1984: 8; Tmarzizet and Perez 1993: 75) or after AD 70 (Sebag 1991: 10).

The first version is anchored in a religious past going back to the times of the tribes of Israel and the succession to Moses, presenting a Jewish community with roots in Jerba and detached of its own free will from its origins in the Holy Land. One legend insists on the rootedness of the Jews on the island, and tells of the Jews of Jerba refusing to follow Ezra the scribe to take part in the rebuilding of the Temple, predicting that the Temple would be destroyed a second time (Haddad De Paz 1977: 118). A variation on this links this refusal to a curse that kills the island's Levites (Tmarzizet and Perez 1993: 87; also in Corré 1978). The curse on the Levites is the price they pay for their rootedness in Jerba, and also the mark that they are not like other Jews. This version of the settlement of Jews in Jerba presents also a striking analogy with the history of the Ibadite Muslims who took refuge in Jerba in the tenth century and have marginal status within mainstream Islam.

The two versions which trace the Jewish presence to the times of King David and King Solomon indicate that the island's Jews have a place in a religious history—the establishment of monotheism—which their Muslim neighbors know and recognize.

The story comparing the Jews to the Phoenicians sets the Jewish community in the historical context of the foundation of Carthage, a reference point for all Tunisians, while presenting the Jews as descendants of traveling traders. Jerbians define themselves as a community of hard workers, travelers, and traders. Trade is one of the keys to the good relations between the different communities of Jerba, and people turn to the Jews for the buying and selling of gold and silver because *nass thiqa ou khaddama* (these people are trustworthy and hardworking)[4] (Valensi and Udovitch 1984: 121). Asked about this, a Muslim jeweler in Jerba told me that, amongst the Muslims in Jerba, dealing with silver and gold was once seen as taboo and associated with usury. The mixed connotations (usury and honesty) of the Jewish jeweler in Jerba exemplify a mixed and ambivalent representation of the Jewish community.

Legends of the Ghriba

The legends of the origin of the Ghriba synagogue and of the cult of the saint *Ghriba*[5] are many. One legend of the *Ghriba* presents her as a lone young woman who "accepted no family's hospitality and refrained from having any contacts with her close neighbours" (Tmarzizet and Perez 1993: 87). She was suspected of sorcery, and when her hut caught fire she was left to burn to death by the villagers; but, on seeing that the fire had left her beauty intact, they eventually realized she was a saint.[6] In this legend, recounted by a Muslim author, we note the justification for the villagers' failure in their duty of hospitality. Muslims are perplexed by the strict observance of kosher rules by Jerbian Jews; in Muslim terms, hospitality towards an outsider involves meal-sharing, which is precluded by these rules. This story also illustrates the link between the supernatural and sanctity: the miracle makes the saint. The same identifying mark of sanctity is found in a similar version told in the Jewish community.[7] However the particular point of the failure to help during the fire is ignored. The girl is simply shown as a hermit whose hut catches fire, and on its site they decide to build the Ghriba synagogue. In the synagogue, under the scrolls of the Torah is the crypt of the *Ghriba*, built on the site where her body was found. This spot is called the *maghara* and plays an important role in the ritual of the pilgrimage.

Other Jewish stories of the synagogue's origins mention a sanctuary built on a fragment of the First Temple of Jerusalem—in some versions stones from the Temple, in others a fragment of a door. Rabbis in Jerba hand on this story where there is no mention of a girl. Another legend of the Ghriba has a stone falling from heaven to show where the synagogue is to be built.[8] This version has a striking similarity to the story of the origin of the Kaaba, shrine of Abrahamic monotheism, although the events narrated are supposed to have occurred before the advent of the prophet Mohammed. In terms of discourse, this version has the characteristics of minority discourses that build their legitimacy on elements borrowed from majority discourses. Another discourse defining the Ghriba synagogue as the Jerusalem of Africa (Valensi and Udovitch 1984: 15–16), or as the second most holy place after Jerusalem, uses the same strategy and is a symbolic exchange with Muslims, for whom Jerusalem is the third holiest shrine after Mecca and Medina.

Most versions have the *Ghriba* as a mysterious girl, with no details of her belonging to the Jewish or Muslim community.[9] Two oral versions collected during fieldwork amongst the Muslim community, however, have the *Ghriba* as a woman, a clan chief "like the Kahena," a judaized Berber queen who fought and was killed by the Arabs in the Aurès at the time of the conquest. These versions show the Jewish communities as groups of diehards, and recall the presence of a converted Berber component among the Jewish population (Sebag 1991: 35–36). As Berbers were indigenous to the whole of North Africa before the Arab conquest, this indicates an ethnic element shared with the Muslim descendants of the Berbers who make up the majority of the Tunisian population. The Kahena, seen as Jewish by Arabs, is seen as a Berber by Jews. She probably practiced a Berber-Jewish syncretism. A Jewish folk song from Constantine, recalled by Chouraqui, makes her a murderous queen washing her feet in the blood of Jewish children (Chouraqui 1973: 36).

It is in the second version collected from the Muslim community that I came across a new element for which I could find no traces in written sources. I heard it from a Muslim islander in his forties. The Jews arriving on the island incurred a divine curse which left all the men of the clan dead, but to ensure offspring to the bereaved women God miraculously allowed them to reproduce by mating with their dead husbands. In this version the *Ghriba* is once again a tribal chief, "like the Kahina," and as a leader of the bereaved women she allows this transgression to take place. From these dead men was born the first generation of the island's Jews, and that is why the *Ghriba* has miraculous powers for barren women and girls seeking a husband. This version again represents the Jew/Other as ambivalent in connotation. This miracle granted to the Jews shows a recognition of a special relationship with God, but above all it expresses the misgivings felt by Muslims over this "special relationship," particularly as it pertains to Jewish religious certainties and their resistance to conversion. A proverb remembered by older generations says: *s hih kif din lihoud* (firm as the faith of the Jews).[10] This version of the *Ghriba* legend reflects an image of a people simultaneously blessed by miracle and perpetuating a dead lineage. Implicitly, the complementary vision of Muslims by themselves is of a vigorous people, proselytizing heirs of the last revealed, and therefore truest, religion.

The Ghriba, a Shared Shrine?

When I visited Jerba as a student in the summer of 1978, I was advised by a local, a fellow Muslim, to visit the shrine "to find a husband." To visit a *zawiya* "to find a husband" or "to have a son" is part of popular culture in Tunisia, and in this case the recommendation to visit the Jewish shrine underlined its strong reputation. I visited the shrine and found it familiar because of its similarity to other places of worship in Tunisia. This was outside the time of the pilgrimage and during the Bourguiba era when the site was not advertised as a symbol of tolerance. More recently, while researching data on the mixed status of the shrine, I found contradictions between information collected from the media, scholars, and officials and my own data collected during fieldwork. In 2008 a rabbi in his thirties with good insider knowledge of the synagogue was at first adamant that the shrine and the *ziyara*, the pilgrimage to the Ghriba, are for Jewish people only.

When I formulated the question differently and asked whether the Muslims too believed in the saint and visited her, he told me that it might have happened in the past but that it would have been rare. Interviews with Jerbian women in 2008 revealed no Muslim women claiming to have visited the *Ghriba*, although one rural woman, a domestic helper in her early sixties, laughed as she told me: "I visit all the saints whatever they are, Jews, Muslims, why not the *Ghriba* ..." before changing her story the day after when I was asking for more details: "I would never visit a Jewish saint." This testimony shows the persistent taboo status of the Jew amongst Tunisians as reflected in the common expression *Yihoudi hashak* (God preserve you from a Jew), but it also shows an admission of the holiness of the *Ghriba*—similar to that of other Muslim saints—in popular culture.

Indeed the holiness of the saint for both Jews and Muslims is mentioned in scholarly articles: "It is only in the second half of the 19th century that accounts proliferate on the prestige of this synagogue whose sacred character is recognized even by Muslims" (Valensi and Udovitch 1984: 130) and "the Jerba synagogue, sacred for Jews and Muslims"[11] (Fellous 2003: 11). Analysing Judeo-Muslim pilgrimages in Morocco, Ben-Ami (1990: 61) mentions that Jews would often offer mediation for a Muslim friend or neighbor in a Jewish shrine. For Ben-Ami this is an example of shrine sharing, and a similar example of shrine sharing in the Ghriba is to be found in a Jewish testimony describing the pilgrimage in 1956: "The Jerbian Arabs respected the pilgrims, they gave the rabbis sheep to be slaughtered for sacrifice, there was no animosity, they were proud and happy to welcome us and respected the holy places" (Hajkloufette: undated). Although it has been almost impossible to collect evidence of the sharing of the shrine today, I did find evidence of a practice of Jewish mediation; in response to my enquiry about Muslim belief in the miracles performed by the *Ghriba*, a Jerbian Muslim woman told me that, after her complaints to a Jewish jeweler a few weeks earlier about her swollen wrists, he offered to heal her with *ktiba* (literally "writing," in context, Jewish prayer). This last informant mentioned what can be described as cross-community intercession; intercession is widespread in the Ghriba where Jewish pilgrims pay for prayers intended for absent friends and family, and even get a receipt. This last example of an accepted practice of cross-community intercession gives credence to the reality of the Ghriba as a shared shrine, even if it has been difficult to observe directly any actual Muslim devotion in this Jewish space.

Nonetheless, many testimonies confirm the participation of Muslims during the pilgrimage. Reporting on the 1996 pilgrimage, Conord describes being introduced as a non-Jewish student and welcomed by the organizer: "But there's no problem, we accept everybody! There are even Arabs who sometimes come with us" (Conord 2001: 402). Valensi and Udovitch indicate the presence of Muslims inside the synagogue: "Behind the pilgrims, behind the curious, Jewish or not, who joined in the procession ... Men, women and children filled up the space, passed each other drinks, nuts and sunflower seeds. Jerbian Jews and pilgrims, tourists passing through or Muslim islanders rubbed shoulders and crowd together one last time" (Valensi and Udovitch 1999: 144).

In 2007, a Jewish couple living in Tunis showed me photos of their 1982 pilgrimage which they had attended with Muslim neighbors. A local Jewish man in his thirties and a regular at the pilgrimage ("I attended all my life"), when asked in 2006 whether Muslims attended the pilgrimage, replied: "No, the pilgrimage is for the Jews." When I persisted, commenting that others had spoken of their presence during the pilgrimage, he replied "the Arab (*el'Arbi*, i.e., the Muslim) likes to drink and there is *bukha* (the local fig spirit) so they come and they get drunk because they don't know how to drink and they misbehave. We don't want them." Here Muslim men and their drinking in the sanctuary is reluctantly accounted for and, by implication, reluctantly tolerated. This illustrates a topsy-turvy carnivalesque dimension of the pilgrimage, as does the fact that Jewish women, normally excluded from Jewish ceremonies in the synagogue, are not only allowed in during the pilgrimage but are also allowed to then violate the near taboo on their drinking (Conord 2001: 491). These exceptions would seem to suggest that Muslim shrine-sharing, like women's participation, is a marginal practice allowed only at exceptional times.

Nonetheless Tunisian official discourse in the French media and French media discourse have amplified the practice of shrine sharing from the marginal to the normal:

"The synagogue is revered by Muslims and Jews alike." (journalist commenting on *La source de vie*, Jewish religious program, France 2 "Les Juifs de Djerba: l'île des anciens," 22 April 2001).

"In Jerba the women have always brought offerings to the *Ghriba* whether they are Jews or Muslims … In the *foundouk* [inn] and the synagogue alike, Muslim neighbours and friends are around and join in … Here tolerance and mutual respect are part of tradition." (voiceover on French TV program *Matin Bonheur*, Antenne 2, 29 June 1992).

"There were never any problems with their neighbors (between Jerbian Jews and Muslims) back then? It's even said that this synagogue attracted Muslims."

"That's right, there has never been a problem here, Jerbians live together." (interview by journalist of Dr. Daniel Kalfon, Jewish doctor from Tunis in French TV program, *Matin Bonheur*, Antenne 2, 29 June 1992. Note that the point made by the journalist that Muslims are said to join in the worship is not commented on by the Jewish interviewee).

"We are a family, Muslims, Jews, we are first of all Tunisians." (speech by the Tunisian minister of tourism during the pilgrimage on the French TV program, *Matin Bonheur*, Antenne 2, 29 June 1992).

In the same television program, a Jewish pilgrim gives a more realistic idea of the presence of Muslims when he mentions a miracle at the shrine:

"The only miracle I've seen myself was two years ago when someone, a girl who wasn't married, she was divorced and she wanted to make a wish, she was a Muslim who believed, she made the wish here and the next year she was married and she made a good marriage, I've even seen her this time" (French TV program, *Matin Bonheur*, Antenne 2, 29 June 1992).

The convergence of French media discourse with Tunisian official discourse finds justification in the UNESCO agenda for the 1995 "Year for Tolerance" promoting cultural diversity with scheduled events in Tunisia. Interviewed by France 2 in a special program on "Tolerant Tunisia," the award winning director, Ferid Boughedir, expressed the wish that his forthcoming film *Un été à La Goulette* (1996) would teach "tolerance and respect for difference" ("Musiques au Coeur de la Tolérance," broadcast on 14 May 1995). The film is a charming and idealistic representation of a multifaith Tunisia brutally disrupted by the Six-Day War in 1967, and expresses a desire to recapture a lost innocence. Analysing recurrent representations of Tunisia as a "pluralistic historical mosaic," Bond underlines "the problem for Tunisian commentators 'rediscovering' a cosmopolitan past" and ending up becoming "minor hierophants in the official memory temple" (Bond and Melfa 2008).

The Evolution of the Pilgrimage, from Jewish to Multifaith, from Regional to International

According to a brief inscription in the synagogue—"586 before the common era"—the Ghriba is over two thousand years old. It is recognized as Africa's oldest synagogue. The synagogue was restored in 1920 and as a result its architecture today is in the Arabo-Moorish style. The fame of the Ghriba synagogue is based on numerous traditions and beliefs that emphasize its antiquity and importance among the local Jews, as well as the former Jewish communities of Tunisia and neighboring Libya.

Deshen, reporting on Jewish communities in the 1940s, notes that the Ghriba synagogue "was the scene of a great annual pilgrimage that brought considerable income to the Ghriba" (Deshen 1996: 140). The provenance of pilgrims from the Jewish communities in Tunisia and in Libya is mentioned by Zaoui (1950: 135): "Once a year people come on pilgrimage to the Griba [*sic*] synagogue from all over Tunisia and Libya." An old (undated) poem in praise of the Ghriba also mentions that pilgrims come from various places in Libya and southern Tunisia (Sfax, Medenine, Gabès, Ben-Gardane).[12] Valensi and Udovitch too note that, from the 1850s, the Ghriba attracted visitors from Libya and Tunisia (Valensi and Udovitch 1984: 130). In a travel book written in the late 1950s, an informant says of the Ghriba that "at the time of pilgrimage people come from all over the world … Sfax, Tripoli, as far away as Tunis" (Anthony 1961: 192), while in 2000, in a speech in front of state representatives commemorating the opening of the pilgrimage, Albert Simeoni, a representative of the Tunisian Jewish community and an active blogger on the Harissa.com website, recalled how difficult the pilgrimage was for visitors at the time of his childhood (he was born in 1945), and how important it was to the Jews: "Going up (*talya*) to the Ghriba at one time, not so long ago, was an ordeal ... there is no finer heritage for us Tunisian Jews than to go, once a year, with our means, on this pilgrimage."[13] He concludes by merging one of the assumed ages of the community with the age of the ritual, referring to the Ghriba pilgrimage (which dates back to 1828)[14] as "a two-thousand-year-old rite." Here the transformation of the age of the ritual shows the invention of a tradition in progress.

In the local and international media today, great emphasis is put on the pilgrimage's international appeal and on the participation of Jews from Israel (Thabet 2008; AP 2008). Comments from Tunisian Jewish bloggers on the Harissa.com website stress this international appeal: "I won't tell you about the crowds (see photos) of the Jews coming from all over the world, from France, America, India, Israel, etc ..." ("Jules": 2000). For Jews coming from abroad, the pilgrimage is organized by selected travel agencies[15] and hotels offering kosher deals.[16] As early as 1984, Valensi and Udovitch noted that: "Of all these synagogues (in Jerba), the Ghriba alone is known outside Jerba, frequented for the Lag Ba'omer pilgrimage and visited throughout the year by Jews who come there to recite prayers. For tourists, stopping off at the Ghriba is part of the obligatory tour programme" (Valensi and Udovitch 1984: 127).

Official and media discourses, however, also stress the interdenominational appeal of the Ghriba. The official website of the Tunisian government under Ben Ali (TunisiaOnlineNews.com) comments that "tourists from all faiths and nationalities ... come to discover this religious and cultural festival as well as to visit the island,"[17] while the Agence France-Presse, reporting in an article on the 2008 pilgrimage, noted the presence of a Tunisian Muslim woman pilgrim from Nabeul accompanying her childhood Jewish friend (AFP 2008b). The transformation of the *ziyara* from a local and largely Jewish event to one of international and intercommunal significance began in the early 1990s. The connection of this development with the Ben Ali era (starting in 1987) is clear, as is the desire of the Tunisian and Israeli regimes to promote the Ghriba as a symbol of peace between Jews and Muslims in the wake of the 1993 Oslo Declaration of Principles, when Israel and the PLO agreed to mutual recognition, and Arafat and Rabin historically shook hands in front of the White House (Barrouhi 2007). In an interview with French television, Dr. Gabriel Kabla, president of the Association of Tunisian Jews in France, traced this transformation to an initiative between Tunisian Jews living in France, tour operators interested in bringing religious tourists to Jerba, and the Ben Ali government's "openness policy":

> In 1992 there were 200 pilgrims organized by tour operators from France who came to make their pilgrimage to Jerba. Jewish associations from Tunisia in France, with the opening up by the Tunisian government and President Ben Ali at its head, said why not bring [more] people and that would bring peoples closer together and it got going and the 1993 pilgrimage had 1300 people and since then there's been a big rise. (*La source de vie*, Jewish religious program, France 2, "Les Juifs de Djerba: Ghriba la Sainte," 13 May 2001)

Other key dates in raising of the profile of the pilgrimage were the departure of the headquarters of the PLO from Tunis in 1994 (it had been based in Tunis after its 1982 expulsion from Beirut), and the 1990 move of the headquarters of the Arab League to Cairo after eleven years in Tunis. The departure of both the PLO and the Arab League allowed the Tunisian state to distance itself from Arab nationalism and to catch up with Morocco in building up an image of peace and tolerance:

> Recently, there has been a reunion between the States of Morocco and Tunisia and their former Jewish communities, this time with Morocco in the lead, having since the mid-1970s opened up its gates wide to its former Jewish inhabitants and their descendants. They have paid for it by sending back over the world media the image of a tolerant and peaceful Sharifian Kingdom, with everything needed to be an "honest broker" between Israel and its Arab neighbours. A role that, obviously, could not go to Tunisia which, for years, had sheltered Yasser Arafat and the infrastructure for its war against Israel on its territory. (Abitpol [1999] 2003: 190)

Other Tunisian initiatives confirm the Tunisian state's desire to be perceived as peaceful and tolerant, for instance its signing of the Charte de Carthage sur la Tolérance en Méditerranée in 1995,[18] and its creation at the Université de Tunis El Manar of "la Chaire universitaire pour le dialogue des civilisations et des religions"[19] in November 2001.

The Tunisian government has been promoting what can be described as "state tolerance," the promotion mechanisms and limitations of which are similar to those used in instituting "state feminism" (Lamloum and Toscane 1998). The official government discourse on state tolerance is indirectly disseminated by the French media, in particular Antenne 2—renamed "France 2" in September 1992—with which the Tunisian Government signed an agreement in 1989 allowing the broadcasting of the channel's programs over the national network. The French language—and consequently French media—are the preferred medium to convey a modernity broadly assimilated to Westernization (Carpenter-Latiri 2004). A clear example of the role taken by the French media in promoting Tunisia as a "land of tolerance" is the previously mentioned France 2 special "Musiques au coeur de la tolérance"; another is the France 2 Muslim program "L'organisation de la vie religieuse en Tunisie" broadcast on 25 May 1997 (30 minutes) on which a Tunisian official representative advertised peace, security, and tolerance as characteristics of the Tunisian regime. Although the Tunisian government unilaterally interrupted the broadcasting of France 2 in Tunisia in 1999 following news reports criticizing the regime (Ferjani 1999), French television is still widely watched in Tunisia via satellite, perhaps even more so since censorship by the regime. One hypothesis on the choice of the Ghriba as an al-Qaeda target in 2002 could be the 3-part France 2 television special on the Jews of Jerba, broadcast on 22 April 2001 (30 minutes), 13 May 2001 (45 minutes) and 27 May 2001 (42 minutes) in the Sunday morning Jewish program *La source de vie* produced by Rabbi Josy Eisenberg. The program insisted on the peaceful coexistence of Jews and Muslims on the island. This peaceful coexistence is still repeatedly advertised, directly and indirectly, by Tunisian officials, with the Ghriba being constructed as a metonym of Tunisia as a tolerant, open, mixed space. It is this very metonym that was targeted by al-Qaeda which announced in its wake that "[t]his operation was carried out by a young member of Al Qaida, who could not stand seeing his brothers in Palestine getting killed, while Jews move around, enjoy themselves and worship freely in Tunisia" (Gas 2002). The suicide attack was perpetrated by a young Tunisian living between Jerba and Lyon in France.

On the whole, under Ben Ali, the Tunisian regime was keen to advertise its religious tolerance internationally, especially after the 9/11 attacks and also after the al-Qaeda attack on the Ghriba in 2002.[20] Locally, after the Bourguiba era, which was characterized by a desire for modernity and a rejection of religion and superstitions, the Ben Ali era saw a revival of the cult of saints. Portraits of Ben Ali could be found in many *zawiya* and were everywhere during the Ghriba pilgrimage, where his name was chanted in processions. Despite this, there were reservations and contradictions. On the ground the perception of the protective and tolerant state was sometimes more down-to-earth: "'Ben Ali, a democrat? For us Jews, yes! For Tunisians, no!' a woman weakly dares to protest one day. But the feeling of being welcome in Tunisia and not being at risk—so great are the security measures—sweeps all other considerations aside" (Beaugé 2008).

During my fieldwork, it was obvious that security measures carried out for the protection of both the shrine and its international visitors were leading to the exclusion of local Muslims and an on-the-ground masking of intercommunal relations. Even I, as a non-Jewish academic visitor to the 2007 pilgrimage, had to seek official authorization and present a badge at several police checkpoints. When, in 2008, I asked Jerbian Muslims if they attended the pilgrimage or if they knew of Muslims who did, I was told that a lot of Muslims came from abroad to attend the pilgrimage but it was preferred that this not be known.

The Ghriba: Sabbath Visits and Pilgrimage

The Ghriba synagogue is a place of worship. Before the al-Qaeda attack of 2002 it was open at all times other than the Sabbath (i.e., closed Friday afternoons and Saturdays) to visitors from all backgrounds, including tourists curious about a Jewish place of worship and pilgrimage in an Islamic land. Today visitors must undergo police searches at the entrance, which are stepped up at the time of the pilgrimage.

On entering the Ghriba, one is struck by the syncretic convergence between Jewish and Muslim religious practices as well as between sacred and profane rituals. On entering, visitors take off their shoes as in a mosque, and cover their heads as in a synagogue. The benches are covered with woven mats typical of the Tunisian South. The synagogue is decorated with Stars of David and Hebrew calligraphy. In a small room there are cases with many silver ex-votos in the shape of traditional local protection symbols such as the hand of Fatima or the fish.

Many of these had been brought by emigrating Jews from other Jewish temples in the region: "the town communities, whose Jews had gone, could not take these treasures out of the country. They took them to Jerba, which had remained the last active refuge of Judaism" (Bar-Shay: undated).

Figure 7.1. Ghriba Lamp. Photo by D. Carpenter-Latiri.

In the same room, lamps burn in honor of Rabbi Shem'oun, Rabbi Meier, and the *Ghriba* herself, also known as the *sbiya*, "the girl/virgin." Below the *Ghriba*'s lamp is a small wooden door leading to the *maghara*, the crypt of the *Ghriba*. During the pilgrimage, and whenever a special favor is sought, people light candles or oil lamps in honor of the *Ghriba*. During the festival hundreds of eggs, candles, and lamps are placed inside the *maghara*; these are disposed of in the evening after the crowd has dispersed. Oral tradition holds that if a woman praying for a husband or a son eats one of these eggs she will have her prayer answered by the end of the year. Conord followed women pilgrims from Paris in the 1996 pilgrimage:

> According to tradition, pilgrims must come back to the crypt later on and take it [the egg] back to the girl [waiting] to be married. But none of the women I knew had done this: for one thing, being tired at the end of the day, they told me they did not want to face the crowd again at the crypt entrance; for another their wishes were not always about a wish for a girl to find a husband. (Conord 2001: 444)

As in Muslim *ziyaras*, traditional practice is to make a prayer with a promise to return to visit the saint when the prayer is answered. The features of the Ghriba ritual are strikingly Jerbian and at the same time Jewish; symbolically, and subconsciously, they display both a belonging and an affirmation of a differential local identity.[21]

Rabbi Shem'oun Bar Yohai and Rabbi Meier Ba'al Haness, the other patron saints of the pilgrimage, were two mystics who lived in Palestine in the second century and who are credited with many miracles. Their cult is so strong among Tunisian Jews that they are often taken for local saints. Four days before the procession, the pilgrimage begins with the celebration of Rabbi Meier. Then follows the commemoration of the death of Rabbi Shem'oun, to whom the book of the *Zohar* is attributed and whose *hilloula*, his mystical union with his creator in death, is celebrated. The symbolism of marriage is used to represent this union. The procession of the *Menara*—also known as the *aroussa*, the bride—leaves the *oukala*, the caravanserail for pilgrims opposite the synagogue, and moves through the nearby village of Hara Sghira, not unlike the way the bride in a traditional Jerbian wedding is taken on a palanquin from her family home to that of her husband. The *Menara* is a five-tiered hexagonal structure covered in traditional Jewish symbols, not to be confused with the seven-branched *menorah* candlestick. When covered with scarves it resembles a bride's palanquin. The procession ends with the *Menara* being brought to, and entering, the Ghriba synagogue.[22]

I was able to observe the celebrations at first hand in 2007. Women, traditionally excluded from the liturgy, are the majority inside the synagogue. They are also the majority in the *oukala* (turned during the festival into a souk with Tunisian kosher specialities and souvenirs) and around the *Menara* during the procession. Most of the pilgrims are Jewish Tunisian émigrés, especially from France and Israel. The languages heard in the *oukala* are Tunisian Arabic, French and Hebrew. The songs

Figure 7.2. Aroussa Procession. Photo D. Carpenter-Latiri.

during the celebrations come from the traditional Tunisian repertoire (to which many great Jewish singers have contributed), the pan-Arabic repertoire (Om Kalthoum) and the Israeli repertoire (nationalist songs, along with a song of Om Kalthoum sung in Hebrew by young Israeli singers). In the *oukala* before the *Menara* leaves, there is an auction to raise funds for the synagogue and the community; bids are made in Tunisian dinars and euros. The pilgrims display their allegiance to the Tunisian state and to Israel, and during the 2007 procession, the Tunisian national anthem (in standard Arabic) was sung three times.[23] The 2007 Ghriba pilgrimage took place shortly before the French presidential election, and the master of ceremonies urged people to vote for Sarkozy. The identity of the pilgrims seems complex, rooted in Tunisia, France, and Israel.

Excursions are organized on the following two days for those who wish to extend the pilgrimage by visiting the tomb of Rabbi Ishaq el Ma'rabi in El Hamma, near Gabès, and thus to take part in an expedition into the Tunisian interior. Explaining this second stage of the pilgrimage, a Jewish informant compared it to the visit to the tomb of the prophet Mohammed in Medina during the hajj: "Mecca then Medina, Jerba then El Hamma." I have heard some Muslim islanders call the Ghriba pilgrimage *Hajj lihoud* (the hajj of the Jews), despite the fact that in Tunisian Arabic the term *hajj* is normally used only for the pilgrimage to Mecca, while an annual ritual around a local saint is usually called a *ziyara*, the term Tunisian Jews use for the pilgrimage to the Ghriba. This use of the term *hajj* and the comparison between Medina and El Hamma in this context underlines a recognized religious similarity between Tunisian Jews and Tunisian Muslims, and gives a high and special status to the Jewish pilgrimage in Jerba.

Figure 7.3. Auction and Israeli choir in the Oukala with Tunisian flags and portraits of Ben Ali in 2007. Photo by D. Carpenter-Latiri.

The mirroring of Muslim practices and discourse expresses a quest for legitimacy. Among the Jewish pilgrims, the manifestations of joy and solidarity towards the Jewish community remaining in Jerba, and towards Tunisia and Tunisians, illustrate nostalgia and indicate how Jews from France or Israel still identify with Tunisia as their former home. As for the Muslims present (today most of them traders, cameramen, policemen, and other authorized observers and officials), they suddenly find themselves a minority. This inversion of the relation between communities introduces relativity to the respective status of majority or minority, and demonstrates that Jews and Muslims share common modes of religious celebration. Podselver, analysing a Tunisian Jewish pilgrimage in honor of Rabbi el Ma'rabi d'El Hamma transposed to Sarcelles in France, asks: "Is this a nostalgic group engaged in its auto-celebration, so much so that it may be asked if it is not precisely community presence which carries within itself a share of the sacred?" (Podselver 2001: n.p.). In the pilgrimage as I observed it, it does seem that this auto-celebration is present. Also celebrated is the brotherhood between Jews and Muslims. This is striking in accounts by pilgrims posted on the Jewish Tunisian website Harissa.com (see Tibi 2008, and Derai undated) where the enthusiasm is in some way proportional to the intensity of the Israeli-Palestinian conflict.

The pilgrimage has become a focus for exiled Tunisian Jews, providing an opportunity for them to return, reaffirm their roots and identity, and renew contact with the Muslim community. In 2000, there were 8,000[24] pilgrims, a figure which plummeted to 200 in 2002 after the attack on the World Trade Center and the attack on the synagogue itself. Since then the number of pilgrims has risen again, with 4,000 in 2005, mostly Jews now living in France, but 1,000 from Israel. In 2007, there were 5,000 pilgrims, including around 700 from Israel, mostly from families who once lived in Tunisia or North Africa. In 2008, the numbers exceeded 5,000 (Beaugé 2008), and the Ghriba committee (AFP 2008a) as well as Tunisian government sources (Info Tunisie 2008) claimed 6,000 pilgrims, with around 1,000 from Israel.

The Al-Qaeda Attack

The synagogue attracted international attention after the al-Qaeda attack in April 2002, a few months after 9/11. The Tunisian government at first claimed it was an accident, and only after pressure from Germany did the enquiry confirm the bombing as a terrorist attack. The Ghriba Committee publicly backed the Tunisian government's first announcement that it was an accident (Tuquoi 2002), whilst Allali (undated) recalls a reaction from the capital:

> Mr Gérard Berrebi, an influential member of the Tunis community thinks things should be kept in proportion. He told the press: "I want to make it perfectly clear that in Tunisia we live in safety and not in insecurity, even better than in a number of European countries." He added: "Even if it were an attack, what country can claim that acts like that happen only every 17 years?" He recalled the incident that happened in 1985 when a policeman opened fire on Jews in Jerba, killing two people.

The 1985 attack is barely mentioned in the media today, while the current high security is blamed on the 2002 attack. It is relevant to note that it was a policeman—supposedly in charge of security—who opened fire in 1985. Hauschild, Zillineer, and Kottman state that the "Al Qaida's attack hit not only this enclave-like local ecology but at the same time the German culture of commemoration of Nazi crimes and the resulting and lasting German interest in Jewish culture" (2007: 326).

On the ground, however, in Tunisia, there is almost no knowledge of the "German culture of commemoration of Nazi crime" although there is resentment towards the tourism industry in general (which attracts mainly German tourists in Jerba) and also towards the Ghriba pilgrimage. For example, I heard a Jerbian restaurant owner, his business disrupted by the 2007 festival, mutter to me: "7,000 policemen for 500 Jews, it it's a bit much," before correcting himself: "but of course security is important." The heavy security locks away businesses from tourists and pilgrims, and in 2008 the islanders complained that they did not really benefit from the festival, with only selected businesses being allowed in the hotels and in the *oukala* for shoppers. This heavy security as well as the meager redistribution of profit—from tourism or from other Tunisian sources of income— was characteristic of the Ben Ali regime, and will need to be reassessed in the wake of the revolution.

Tunisian Jews Today and After the Al-Qaeda Attack

The Jewish population of Tunisia has fallen from an estimated[25] 70,971 in 1946 (Attal and Sitbon 1979: 289) to 57,792 in 1956, to 10,000 in 1970 (Sebag 1991: 300), and to an estimated 1,500[26] today. In Jerba the population is currently estimated at around 1,000 (AFP 2008a). Historically, Tunisian Jews have emigrated mainly to Israel or to France (Sebag 1991: 300). The drop in the size of the Jewish population is linked to the birth of the State of Israel in 1948, to the independence of Tunisia in 1956, to the Bizerte crisis in 1961,[27] and to Arab-Israeli conflicts which have generated anxieties amongst Tunisian Jews, often suspected of conflicting loyalties. Passionate support for the Palestinians is widespread amongst the Tunisian population and freely expressed; Tunisian and Arab media frequently focus on the brutality of the State of Israel. In 2008, a Jerbian rabbi described to me his pain on reading regular anti-Jewish propaganda in Tunisian papers reporting on the Middle East. Faced with low-level racism based on what he feels is ignorance amongst uneducated Tunisians, he finds it more hurtful and more damaging when coming from the Tunisian media.

What appears is that Jewish and Muslim relations are complex, but even if contemporary tensions are linked to situations in the Middle East, there were tensions before the birth of the State of Israel. Sebag reminds us of the historical status of the *dhimmi* in Tunisia before the proclamation of the *Pacte fondamental* in 1857 (Sebag 1991: 118) which (under Western influence) marks the birth of the modern state in its guaranteeing of equal rights without distinction of origin or religion. The historical status of the *dhimmi* brought protection from the ruler to the Jewish minority in exchange for loyalty and payment of taxes. The current situation could be interpreted as a repetition of the historic episode of the *dhimmi*.

Since large-scale emigration to France and Israel began, the significance of the pilgrimage has inevitably altered for both the Jewish and Muslim communities. Tunisia has a very young population, and for the majority of Tunisians living on the mainland their image of Judaism is Israel, and even the memory of Jews as fellow Tunisians is lost. Nonetheless the Tunisian origin of the returning pilgrims is a fact, and in undertaking the pilgrimage they are affirming this fact both for themselves and for Muslims, who they still see as compatriots. The high proportion of pilgrims from Israel is striking: after centuries in which the Promised Land had been yearned for, we can see Jews traveling from Israel to Tunisia and seeing the journey as a return.

The *Ghriba*, the outsider woman saint, becomes a natural patron for a paradoxical pilgrimage which brings Jews back from a new diaspora. The saint with her suffering becomes a model for empathy with the marginal and the minority. Conord, describing women's ritual relations to the *Ghriba*, calls them a "quest for the miraculous, offering to a woman—the *Ghriba*—who suffered during her life and who can therefore understand them" (Conord 2001: 436).

There is a discourse among the Muslim majority which expresses regret and nostalgia for an idealized and historical multicultural Tunisia (Bond and Melfa 2008). This discourse expresses a need for otherness in a society with few identifiable minorities. My close analysis of Jerba and Tunisian Jews, through the questioning of the shared shrine status of the Ghriba, brings out an ambivalence in Tunisia between the expression of openness, tolerance, religious and cultural pluralism, and the affirmation of a strong Arab-Islamic identity, in which loyalty to the Palestinian cause extends to resentment towards Tunisian Jews. Whilst both Zaoui (1950: 136) and the Jewish informer interviewed by Anthony (1961: 192) predicted in the 1950s that all the Jerbian Jews would migrate to Israel, Valensi and Udovitch (1984, 1999) more recently demonstrated the rootedness of the Jerbian Jews in Jerba and their attachment to their traditional local religious practices.

Amongst Tunisian Muslims, current shrine sharing is marginal; the adoption of the shrine by Tunisian state officials with indirect endorsement by French media inflates the shrine-sharing dimension. During the Ghriba pilgrimage, the religious practices and discourses mirror the local Muslim practices and discourses to lay claim both to a rootedness in Jerba and a religious idiosyncrasy. The narrow interstice between similarity and assimilation allows the local Jerbian Jewish community to define itself and to survive, whilst their pragmatic consent to state interference demonstrates their status as latter-day *dhimmis*. In these early days after the ousting of the Ben Ali regime, one focus of the political debate that will lead to the writing of a new Tunisian Constitution is Tunisian political, cultural, and ethnic diversity, so as to promote the cause of a democratic and secular state in which the freedom to worship might be defined without the "dhimmification" of the Tunisian Jews. Since the 2011 revolution, some Tunisian Jews have expressed worries about the future, whilst others have expressed their relief at the end of a "state tolerance" that impeded a more genuine brotherhood among Muslim and Jewish Tunisians. The rituals and representations around the Ghriba shrine will remain a locus for observation of the state, the tourism industry, and interactions between the communities.

Notes

1. On the differences between the two Jewish communities, see Valensi and Udovitch 1984.
2. This renaming, especially the choice of Er-Riadh (like the Saudi capital), was perceived as insensitive by some members of the Jewish community.
3. To refer to themselves, Tunisian Muslims use the term "Muslims," whereas the Jews, when referring to their Muslim compatriots, would call them "Arabs."
4. For the original versions of French quotations translated into English in this article, see my University of Brighton research profile at http://artsresearch.brighton.ac.uk/research/academic/carpenter-latiri/portfolio/the-ghriba-in-the-island-of-jerba.
5. Here I italicize *Ghriba* to refer to the saint as distinct from the synagogue.
6. "they feared that this [the failure of the fire to destroy her] might be the result of this young unknown girl's practising of witchcraft, and being scared to be paralysed by her magic, no one among the villagers seemed to have enough courage to approach the fire ... Nobody ever knew by what miracle the victim's body had been spared by the flames ... After a long wondering, they came to the conclusion that the Stranger—*The Ghriba*—was a saintly and pure woman" (Tmarzizet and Perez 1993: 88). In this Tunisian work, the "Arab" Kamel Tmarzizet wrote the text, and the "Jew" Jacques Perez took the photographs.
7. Version told to the author in Jerba by Yaacoub B'chiri during the 2007 pilgrimage. It is also found in Valensi and Udovitch (1999: 143).
8. Sources for this story are oral, and I have only found written references to it on travel websites, e.g., Kjeilen 2007.
9. "Nobody ever knew if she was Jewish, Berber or Greek" (Tmarzizet and Perez 1993: 97).
10. *s hih* is polysemic and means both "firm" and "true/just." I have heard a similar saying among the Maltese: firm like the faith of the Maltese (against Muslim proselytism). A newer ironic use makes it mean "true like the religion of the Jews," i.e., false.
11. Here the discourse is similar to the discourse on Jerusalem—"sacred for Jews, Christians, Muslims"—and implicitly reaffirms the status of the Ghriba as the 'Jerusalem of Africa' as it is sometimes described today.
12. A translation of the poem in English is available at http://www.uwm.edu/~corre/arab/pilgrim.html, accessed July 2008.
13. See http://www.harissa.com/D_Communautes/Tunisie/discoursghriba.htm, accessed July 2009.
14. Date given by the president of the Ghriba Committee (Le Comité de la Ghriba) (AFP 2008a).
15. One travel agency based in Paris is owned by René Trabelsi, son of Pérez Trabelsi, president of the Jerba Jewish Community; Khartago airlines, which carries many pilgrims to Jerba, was co-owned by the brother-in-law of President Ben Ali.
16. See http://www.harissa.com/D_Annonces/voyages.htm.
17. "Jewish Pilgrimage Attracts Thousands to Island of Djerba," Tunis, 22 May 2008. http://www.tunisiaonlinenews.com/index.html, accessed 25 May 2008.
18. http://www.tunisieinfo.com/documents/choix/chapter8.html, accessed 18 July 2009.
19. http://www.chairebenali.tn/, accessed 18 July 2009.
20. The minister (of tourism) assured the faithful that "Tunisia will remain a welcoming and tolerant country." AP Tunisie: des milliers de pèlerins juifs font la fête à la Ghriba, 22 May 2008.

21. See Valensi and Udovitch (1984: 9) which shows how, in the Jewish narratives of the legends, there is an affirmation of their Maghrebi identity.
22. The procession is a ritual on the fringe of the *hilloula*. While the *hilloula* focuses on the saint, the procession symbolizes the mystical union of the Jewish people with their creator (Valensi and Udovitch 1984: 136). More specifically I interpret the coming and going between the non-religious area of the *oukala* and the sacred space of the synagogue as a symbolic interpenetration of the divine and the humane.
23. In her research on the Tunisian Jewish pilgrimage in Sarcelles (France), Benveniste (2004) describes similar displays of allegiance.
24. Figures are estimates drawn from various media sources.
25. After Tunisian independence, no distinction has been made in the census between the different ethnic groups. Statistics for the population are estimates, as no mention of religious practice or affiliation is requested. Indicators used in official data are gender, age, geographical origin, rural/urban (see www.ins.nat.tn).
26. La communauté juive de Tunisie, http://www.terredisrael.com/comm_juive_Tunisie.php.
27. In 1961 hostilities erupted over a French military base that had been maintained in the port.

References

Abitpol, Michel. (1999) 2003. "La modernité judéo-tunisienne vue du Maroc," in *Juifs et musulmans en Tunisie. Fraternité et déchirements. Actes du colloque international de Paris, Sorbonne, organisé par la Société d'Histoire des Juifs de Tunisie et l'université de Tunis 22–25 mars 1999*, ed. Sonia Fellous. Paris : Somogy éditions d'art, Société d'Histoire des Juifs de Tunisie, 181–90.

AFP (Agence France-Presse). 2008a. "Milliers de juifs au pèlerinage à la Ghriba sous haute protection." 22 May.

AFP. 2008b. "Pèlerinage de la Ghriba: vieux rites juifs perpétués dans la joie à Djerba." 23 May.

Allali, Bernard. n.d. "La communauté juive de Tunisie serait-elle en danger ? La vérité sur l'affaire de la Ghriba." http://www.harissa.com/D_Communautes/Tunisie/lacommunautedejerba.htm, accessed 21 March 2011.

Anthony, John. 1961. *About Tunisia*. London: Geoffrey Bles.

AP (Associated Press). 2007. "Tunisie: environ 5.000 fidèles au pèlerinage juif de la Ghriba." 6 May.

AP. 2008. "Tunisie: des milliers de pèlerins juifs font la fête à la Ghriba." 22 May.

Attal, Robert and Claude Sitbon. 1979. *Regards sur les Juifs de Tunisie*. Paris: Albin Michel.

Barrouhi, Abdelaziz. 2007. "Retour à la Ghriba." http://www.jeuneafrique.com/jeune_afrique/article_jeune_afrique.asp?art_cle=LIN13057retouabirhg0, accessed 21 March 2011.

Bar-Shay, Avraham. n.d. "Ma Djerba l'insolite." http://www.harissa.com/D_Communautes/Tunisie/madjerbalinsolite.htm, accessed 21 March 2011.

Beaugé, Florence. 2008. "L'an prochain à Djerba," *Le Monde*, 25 May 2008. http://www.lemonde.fr/cgi-bin/ACHATS/acheter.cgi?offre=ARCHIVES&type_item=ART_ARCH_30J&objet_id=1037379&clef=ARC-TRK-D_01, accessed 28 March 2011.

Ben-Ami, Issachar. 1990. *Culte des saints et pèlerinages judéo-musulmans au Maroc*. Paris: Maisonneuve et Larose.

Benveniste, Annie. 2004. "Nouvelle figure du pèlerinage. Sanctification périphérique dans le judaïsme tunisien," in *Fabrication des traditions. Invention de modernité*, ed. D. Dimitrijevic. Paris: Éditions de la Maison des Sciences de l'Homme, 189–97.

Boissevain, Katia. 2007. *Sainte parmi les saints, Sayyda Mannûbiya ou les recompositions culturelles dans la Tunisie contemporaine.* Paris: Maisonneuve et Larose.

Bond, David and Daniela Melfa. 2008. "Tunisia: Colonial Tensions and Contemporary Challenges." Conference paper at the *IX Convegno of Società per gli studi del Medio Oriente*, Turin, 16–18 October.

Camau, Michel. 1989. *La Tunisie (que sais-je?).* Paris: Presses Universitaires de France.

Carpenter-Latiri, Dora. 2004. "Langues, modernité et mondialisation en Tunisie," *Revue d'aménagement linguistique* [formerly "*Terminogramme*"]—*Office québécois de la langue française* (special issue on the Maghreb) 107, 185–204.

———. 2010. "The Jewish Pilgrimage of the Ghriba in the Island of Jerba and the Semantics of Otherness." *Pilgrimages Today (Scripta Instituti Donneriani Aboensis)* 22: 38–55.

———. 2011. "Harissa.com: Narrative(s), code-switching and nostalgia—a case study," in Code-Switching, Languages in Contact and *Electronic Writings*, ed F. Laroussi. Frankfurt am Main: Peter Lang.

Chouraqui, André. 1973. *Between East and West.* New York: Atheneum.

Cohen, David. 1964. *Le parler arabe des juifs de Tunis.* Paris: Editions EHSS.

Cohen, Victor, 1992. "Histoire de la Tunisie." http://www.harissa.com/D_Histoire/ histoirevictorcohen.htm, accessed 21 March 2011.

———. 2001. "Sidi Mahres." http://www.harissa.com/D_forum/Culture_Tune/ sidimahrez.htm, accessed 21 March 2011.

Conord, Sylvaine. 2001. *Fonctions et usages de la photographie en anthropologie. Des cafés bellevillois (Paris XXe) à l'île de Djerba (Tunisie): échanges entre des femmes juives d'origine tunisienne et une anthropologue-photographe* (Paris X, 2001). Thèse de doctorat en sociologie. Nanterre: Université de Paris X.

Corré, Alan. 1978. "A Visit with Rebbi Bouaz." http://www.uwm.edu/~corre/ occasionalw/jerba.html, accessed 21 March 2011.

Derai, Yves. n.d. "Ghriba Ghriba la douce, Ghriba l'infidèle." http://www.harissa. com/D_Communautes/Tunisie/ghriba.htm, accessed 21 March 2011.

Deshen, Shlomo. 1996. "Southern Tunisian Jewry in the Early Twentieth Century," in *Jews among Muslims Communities in the Precolonial Middle East*, eds. S. Deshen and W. Zenner. London: Macmillan, 133–43.

Fellous, Sonia (ed.). 2003. "Juifs et musulmans en Tunisie. Fraternité et déchirements." *Actes du colloque international de Paris, Sorbonne, organisé par la Société d'Histoire des Juifs de Tunisie et l'université de Tunis 22–25 mars 1999.* Paris: Somogy Éditions d'Art.

Ferjani, Riadh. 1999. "Antenne 2/France 2 comme enjeu social et politique en Tunisie. © Les Enjeux de l'information et de la communication." http://w3.u-grenoble3.fr/ les_enjeux/2001/Ferjani/index.php, accessed 21 March 2011.

Gas, Valérie. 2002. "Attentat de Djerba: la famille du kamikaze en garde à vue." http:// www.rfi.fr/actufr/articles/035/article_18055.asp, accessed 21 March 2011.

Haddad de Paz, Charles. 1977. *Juifs et Arabes au pays de Bourguiba.* Aix en Provence: Paul Roubaud.

Hajkloufette. n.d. "Souvenirs de la Ziara de Rebbi Chemaoune." http://www.harissa. com/D_Religion/ziararabbichemaoune.htm, accessed 21 March 2011.

Hauschild, Thomas, Martin Zillinger, and Sina Kottman. 2007. "Syncretism in the Mediterranean: Universalism, Cultural Relativism and the Issue of the Mediterranean as a Cultural Area." *History and Anthropology* 18(3): 309–32.

Info Tunisie. 2008. "Plus de 6 mille juifs effectuent le pèlerinage annuel à la Ghriba."
http://www.infotunisie.com, accessed 15 May 2008.

"Jules". 2000. "Pèlerinage à la Ghriba." http://www.harissa.com/D_Communautes/
Tunisie/pelerinageghribajules.htm, accessed 21 March 2011.

Kjeilen, Tore. 2007. "Jerba/Hara Sghira: The Synagogue." http://lexicorient.com/tunisia/
hara_sghira.htm, accessed 21 March 2011.

Lamloum, Olfa and Luiza Toscane. 1998. "The Two Faces of the Tunisian Regime.
Women's Rights, but Only for Some." *Le monde diplomatique.* http://mondediplo.
com/1998/07/12tunis, accessed 21 March 2011.

Mourali, Soufia and Evelyne Heyer. 2001. "La génétique des populations de l'île de Jerba
(Tunisie): une recherche en cours." http://www.harissa.com/D_Communautes/
Tunisie/lagenetique.htm, accessed 21 March 2011.

Podselver, Laurence. 2001. "Le pèlerinage tunisien de Sarcelles: De la tradition à
l'hédonisme contemporain," *Socio-Anthropologie*, N°10, *Religiosités contemporaines.*
http://socio-anthropologie.revues.org/index157.html, accessed 21 March 2011.

Sebag, Paul. 1991. *Histoire des juifs de Tunisie.* Paris: L'Harmattan.

Thabet, Fatah. 2008. "Pèlerinage de La Ghriba 2008: Ferveur et liesse." *Le Temps.* 25
May.

Tibi, Nadine. 2008. "Salam-Shalom de la Ghriba." http://www.harissa.com/
D_Communautes/Tunisie/salamshalomghriba2008.htm, accessed 21 March 2011.

Tmarzizet, Kamel and Jacques Perez. 1993. *Djerba, synagogue el Ghriba.* Tunis: Editions
Carthacom.

Tuquoi, Jean-Pierre. 2002. "Plusieurs touristes tués à la synagogue de la Ghriba, à
Djerba." *Le Monde.* 12 April. http://www.lemonde.fr/cgi-bin/ACHATS/acheter.
cgi?offre=ARCHIVES&type_item=ART_ARCH_30J&objet_id=750728, accessed 28
March 2011.

Valensi, Lucette and Abraham Udovitch. 1980. "Etre juif à Djerba," *Annales-Economies/
Sociétés/Civilisations* 3–4: 199–225.

———. 1984. *Juifs en terre d'Islam. Les communautés de Djerba.* Paris: Editions des
Archives Contemporaines.

———. 1999. "Les Juifs de Djerba." Tunis: SIMPACT Editions.

Zaoui, André. 1950. "Djerba ou l'une des plus anciennes Communautés juives de la
diaspora." *Revue.*

Chapter 8

"SACRED WEEK":
RE-EXPERIENCING JEWISH-MUSLIM COEXISTENCE
IN URBAN MOROCCAN SPACE

Aomar Boum

Introduction

> Essaouira is a new pre-Islamic Mecca. Just like Mecca thrived because
> of its annual fair, 'Ukaz,[1] Essaouira improved because of the *baraka*
> of its musical fairs.[2] Visitors arrive in thousands to its sanctuary
> without fear of being harmed. By the sanction of its custom of
> tolerance, tourists, national and foreign, Muslims and Jews, are
> protected by the blessings of its Jewish and Muslim shrines.
> Ahmed (a pseudonym), Essaouira. Personal communication, 2004.

Throughout Morocco, shrines are spaces where religious, folkloric, economic, cultural, and political beliefs and practices are socially highlighted, publicly celebrated, and communally enforced. Historically, Morocco provided a distinctive environment where Muslims venerated Jewish saints and Jews visited Muslim shrines (Westermarck [1926] 1968: 1; also see Voinot 1948; Ben-Ami 1998; Gitlitz and Davidson 2006; Kosansky 2002, 2003; Stillman 1996; and Lévy 2003). However, the Jewish migration between 1948 and 1982 to Israel and other Western countries, and the emergence of an orthodox Islamic fundamentalist interpretation in the late 1970s, led to a decrease in saint celebrations and shrine visits by Muslims and Jews.[3] In the wake of Moroccan independence in 1956, saint veneration gained new meanings (Reysoo 1991; Levy 1997). These celebrations were exploited to disseminate a national ideology and reinforce the spiritual legitimacy of the monarchy (Reysoo 1991: 178; Kosansky 2003; Boum 2007). In addition, some cities such as Fes, Essaouira, and Asilah were defined on the basis of cultural diversity and a presumed memory of Jewish-Muslim coexistence to create a neutral space of tolerance with the intent of improving national tourism (Elboudrari 1985; Reysoo 1991; Belghazi 2006; Eickelman 1976).

Focusing on the city of Essaouira (see Lapassade 1994), historically a vibrant Jewish urban space (Park 1983, 1988; Schroeter 1988; Lévy 1994), I argue that the annual Essaouira Gnawa and World Music Festival[4] exhibits all the signs of shrine festivities where Jews, Christians, and Muslims negotiate new social meanings in an officially publicized "culture of tolerance." At this time, the whole city of Essaouira, with its Jewish and Muslim shrines, becomes a sacred and neutral sanctuary. Westermarck wrote that "the holiest part of a sanctuary in which a saint is buried is of course the grave itself" ([1926] 1968, Vol. 1: 63). In the case of Essaouira, the local Jewish and Muslim shrines are never highlighted in the official discourse as the main focus of the celebration. Instead, the whole circumference of Essaouira is imagined as an urban sanctuary.

Based on a set of interviews conducted with residents of Essaouira and government officers during my ethnographic research in 2004, this article embarks on an understanding of both the symbols and rhetoric that surround the festivalization of the urban space of Essaouira, as well as of the meanings of cultural dialogue and religious toleration which take place therein (Turner 1982a).[5] Annually, the city hosts two major festivals sponsored by the Essaouira-Modagor Association—Essaouira Gnawa and World Music Festival and the Festival of Andalusias of the Atlantic. The urban fairs—which have replaced traditional *mawasim*[6] and *hillulot*[7]—are officially sponsored by the state and promote a discourse of Jewish-Muslim tolerance within the confines of the city. Wide segments of Jewish, Christian, and Muslim populations flock to the city for what some locals called a *ziyara* (pilgrimage) during these festivals. Essaouira festivals, as Abrahams and Bauman noted in their study of similar phenomena, are structured to "draw together opposing elements in [society] ... more closely and harmoniously than at any other time in the year ... [T]he two sets of elements, each clearly identifiable, participate together within a unified event productive of enjoyment and a sense of community. The picture is not one of hostility, but harmony" (Abrahams and Bauman 1978: 206–7).

It should be noted that the festival is not publicly advertised as a Jewish-Muslim context for tolerance. The focus of the developers is largely on Gnawa music.[8] Nonetheless, the urban space during the festivals becomes a space where an official national ideal of tolerance is disseminated in a state-imagined conflict-free space where Jews and Muslims interact economically and socially. Underlying this event is the official nostalgic reinvention of a Jewish-Muslim symbiosis blessed and protected by the monarchy.

Each year since 1998, the organizers of the Essaouira Gnawa and World Music Festival have capitalized on that Judeo-Islamic cultural heritage to market urban festivals which involve what I call "rituals of tolerance." Approaching one of the primary organizers, André Azoulay, I use Ernest Gellner's (1972) concept of the "effective *Igurramen*" (holy men; singular *aggurram*) to understand why many Souiris (natives of Essaouira) see him as someone who possesses a local, national, and global political and economic *baraka* (supernatural blessing). Azoulay, as economic advisor to the king of Morocco and a native of Essaouira, has, like other "effective *Igurramen*," the ability to build intratribal and intertribal alliances (Gellner 1981: 120) and to thereby turn the urban space into a *haram*, a sanctuary for Jews, Christians, and Muslims.

Theoretical and Ethnographic Contexts:
The Rhetoric of Symbolic Parallelism

Every June, the coastal city of Essaouira becomes a destination for local and foreign tourists attending the annual Gnawa World Music Festival. The festival draws upon Morocco's African cultural traditions by focusing on the artistic heritage of the Gnawa, descendants of black Africans. Thousands of tourists flock to the city, putting a strain on its limited infrastructural capacity. When I visited the festival in 2004, the city was so crowded that people slept in its narrow streets and along its beaches. Unlike the visitors of traditional fairs and shrines, Essaouira's visitors are largely foreign tourists and young Moroccans. This audience makes the festival different from other modern regional celebrations and traditional *mawasim*. Essaouira was conceived to be a populist gathering where people from different economic and social backgrounds could meet and socialize. In fact, the heavy presence of young Moroccan visitors to Essaouira compared to those of the cultural festival of Asilah and the World Sacred Music Festival of Fes is very noticeable. According to Taieb Belghazi (2006), the festivals of Asilah and Fes tend to draw only a small number of local visitors and international tourists. The festival of Essaouira on the other hand has successfully managed to bring large number of tourists from different areas of Morocco as well as international visitors.

Throughout 2004, I was in Morocco doing an ethnographic study of the rural Jewish communities south of Essaouira. I was staying in the southern rural settlement of Akka, which used to house a rural Jewish community that connected with Essaouira as a major coastal terminus for its trans-Saharan trade with the southern city of Timbuktu. On 30 September 2004, I visited Essaouira to attend the second Festival of Andalusias of the Atlantic. The Essaouira-Modagor Association and the Fondation Alizés organized the festival as part of the annual commemoration of Andalusian contributions to modern North African, Spanish, and Latin American culture and music. This festival "makes use of the images conjured up by medieval Andalusia as a place of tolerance and peace, and enjoys the support of the Moroccan State" (Belghazi 2006: 106).

In the morning I attended a colloquium on Haim Zafrani (1922–2004), a renowned scholar of Moroccan Jewish culture and history. Zafrani was a former emeritus professor at the Université Paris VIII where he headed the Department of Hebrew Language and Jewish Civilization. He influenced many researchers through his teaching and publications, and became known for his advocacy of a cultural pluralism rooted in profound intercultural linkages (Park and Boum 2006: 362). The symposium was organized to celebrate his contributions to the scholarship of the language, law, literature, poetry, religion, and culture of North

African Jews. Afterwards, I took a midday stroll along the beach and ended up in a coffee shop at Place Moulay Hassan—named after the Alawite sultan who had transformed the city into a major commercial port during the eighteenth and nineteenth centuries. I ordered a cup of coffee, and in a tight corner found space to fit my rusty chair next to an old man who seemed to be immersed in deep self-contemplation. For a moment, while I made notes in my notebook, the old man and I engaged in an exchange of glances, hoping that one of us would take the initiative and start a dialogue. When noise within the coffeehouse abated, the old man—I call him Ahmed—abruptly started commenting on the importance of Essaouira not only as a major annual tourist destination, but also as a sacred place where Judeo-Muslim cultural and religious dialogue could be revived at a time of growing Jewish-Muslim animosities in the Holy Land.

Ahmed talked about his job as a fisherman and the history of Essaouira as a city that had undergone major transformations since the mid-1990s. The religious and cultural dimensions of the city are akin—in his view—to the economic and spiritual significance of the Meccan *'Ukaz* fair. He told me:

> This historical city would not gain this worldwide attraction without the attention it received from its Jews since 1994, chiefly Azoulay. They made it a world destination and marketed its Jewish heritage. Azoulay has turned Essaouira into a *mahaj* (pilgrimage site) for all communities, Jews, Muslims and Christians, in the way that Sultan Sidi Muhammad Ben Abdallah transformed it into the most commercial coastal city of Africa and home to one of the largest Jewish communities of Morocco in 1764. Look around you, Jews are coming back to live where they did before Independence. Azoulay is trying to make it a destination for tourists throughout the year. He is launching musical festivals and *mawasim*. In June, Essaouira becomes *hurma* (sacred) during the week when the festival takes place. It becomes a *hurma usbu'iyya* (Sacred Week). You know during the times of the Prophet, Peace Be Upon Him, Allah ordained what is described in the Qur'an as the Sacred Months when Muslims and non-believers coexisted in the boundaries of Mecca. I believe that Azoulay is trying to do the same thing in the borders of Essaouira. Think about it, during the Festival of Gnawa, Essaouira becomes a destination for Jewish, Christian, and Muslim pilgrims in search of interfaith dialogue and communication. Last year, I remember even after the terrorist attacks of May 2003, Essaouira remained a *hurma makania* (sacred space) in the way Mecca was during the Sacred Months in the pre-Islamic period.

According to Ahmed, the city of Essaouira has become a sanctuary area within which visitors can be sure of personal safety and protection. This sacredness is partly derived from the religious shrines sheltering tombs of Jewish and Muslim saints located within the walls of the city. They are, Ahmed claimed, *damant Essaouira* (Essaouira's insurance). In addition, Ahmed noted that these holy men had come to the city from sacred lands, from Palestine and Mecca. In addition to their "invisible influence," the "visible power" of Sultan Sidi Muhammad ben Abdallah secured the outer boundaries of the city during the eighteenth century.[9] For Jews and Muslims to move around these weekly markets, the sultan's agents needed to ensure the sanctity of the place. This sanctity today is ensured by the Moroccan sultan and, by implication, by his economic advisor, André Azoulay.

Sanctuaries are often objects of pilgrimage (*hajj*) at which rituals are performed. In the past, fairs were held every year in Essaouira and the countryside after the barley and wheat harvesting and threshing to honor local saints. The festivals attracted a large number of local tribes as well people from other cities such as Marrakesh, Tiznit, and Goulmim. Participants would camp within and outside the walls of the city for a period of between two days and a week. Dancing and entertainment were organized by local religious brotherhoods, especially the Gnawa. Animals were slaughtered at the sanctuaries' tombs. Gifts and candles were left at shrines to be collected by their wardens (*mqadmin*). In addition, markets were held in the vicinity of sanctuaries, ensuring the peace of the markets, and special blessings and protection to them. Today, however, the religious dimension of the festivals of Essaouira is not highlighted as it used to be. The modern festivalization of urban space in Essaouira is instead effected through music and the consumption of local commodities.[10]

Ahmed connected the sacred places and the seasonal as well as weekly markets within and outside Essaouira with the markets that took place around Mecca during the early Islamic era. In those days, Arab Bedouins traded their commodities at the market of 'Ukaz and were protected by the holiness of the shrine of Ka'ba. Ahmed used the contemporary idea of the "sacred week" to connect with the "sacred months" of early Islam. These "forbidden months" were four months during which truce (*hudna*) was maintained between Muslims and non-believers.[11] These truces were not only occasions for conflict resolution, but also opportunities for the exchange of ideas and information. Ahmed linked Essaouira and its festivals to sacred space (*hurma makania*) and time (*hurma usbu'iyya*). He expressed his idea of the contemporary revivalism of interfaith dialogue within Essaouira as part of a modern Jewish-Christian-Muslim exchange in an urban space, and established interesting symbolic parallels between the modern urban festivals of Essaouira and early Islamic space and time. His view of the festivalization of Essaouira is based on his understanding of the history of Mecca during the pre-Islamic period:

> If you think seriously about it, our time is not different from the pre-Islamic Meccan context. Why? In those days the tribes of Mecca and Ta'if, the Jews of Madina, and the Arabs of Yemen were all in conflict. They battled and pillaged each other. The only moment of truce was during four months, described as the sacred months in the Qur'an, when nobody was allowed to kill and all tribes went on pilgrimage and gathered in 'Ukaz. This is not different from what goes on in Essaouira today! Don't you think so? Look around you, people from everywhere, Jews from all over the world dance with Muslims as if there is no such a thing as the Palestinian-Israeli conflict. That is the beauty of the annual festivals of Essaouira. They remind us that Jews and Muslims not only can talk to each other, but also can dance together.

Ahmed here not only echoes some of the official Moroccan statements about the significance of the festival, but also links those with a comparison between one of the most sacred places and times in Islam and a modern urban space that had historically been home to Jewish and Muslim communities. The hajj and the sanctuary of Mecca are sacred categories that one would assume should be differentiated from the urban space of Essaouira that, despite its inclusion of shrines, is effectively secular. Nevertheless, Ahmed's construction creates a symbolic parallel between the Essaouira festivals and the actual experience of hajj.

Essaouira: Geo-Ethnic Diversity and Cosmopolitanism

In 1764, Sultan Sidi Muhammad Ben Abdallah (1757–1790) founded the new town of Essaouira and established it as the main seaport for Moroccan trade with Europe. The sultan's objective was to ensure that all foreign trade was concentrated in one port closely administered by the palace. The new royal port also guaranteed a consolidation of the power of the central government in the south, and an increase in state revenues through customs duties (Schroeter 1988; Park 1988). In order to attract local Muslim and Jewish traders as well as European merchants to this new coastal city, the sultan lowered customs duties and built, and allowed traders to build, houses. This royal policy attracted powerful European and Moroccan Jewish merchants who became important components of the city. Jewish merchants of Agadir, Safi, Fes, and Marrakesh transferred their businesses to the new royal town. Prominent Jews from Algiers, Amsterdam, London, and Livorno arrived in Essaouira and established trading networks extending along the Moroccan inland trade routes. European merchants, protected by their respective consulates, were also encouraged to move from Rabat, Safi, Agadir, and other Moroccan ports, making Essaouira the only maritime port for foreign trade.

Despite an increase in the number of French, Dutch, Danish, Spanish, and Portuguese merchants, "it was the Jewish merchants who left their imprint on the town. As the official merchants of the Sultan (*tujjar as-Sultan*), they were accorded houses in the lavish *casbah* quarter where the government administration and foreigners resided" (Schroeter 1988: 19; see also Park 1988). Unlike the privileged Jewish elite, poor Jews occupied the northwestern corner of the city. These Jewish commoners lived as their Muslim neighbors until 1807 when they, as Schroeter argues, "were forced [in]to a Jewish quarter by ... Sultan Sulayman who, for certain reasons, decided to confine the Jews in a number of coastal towns to *mellahs*" (Schroeter 1988: 20).

The prosperity of the new port, in the midst of the frequent agrarian crises brought on by southern Moroccan droughts, attracted many non-Jewish immigrants from neighboring tribes as builders or settlers. Furthermore, as a defense mechanism against the enemies of Islam, in particular the Portuguese, Essaouira was built in the Islamic architectural tradition of the *ribat* (fortress). The city required the constant presence of military contingents which were largely formed by black soldiers, known as *abid al-Bukhari*, as well as tribes providing military service for the palace, known as the *guich* (Schroeter 1988; Ottmani 1997). Apart from these black soldiers, brought to Morocco during the Sa'dian dynasty after Sultan Ahmad al-Mansur's conquest of the Songhay Empire in 1591, enslaved blacks from Sub-Saharan Africa also became resident in Essaouira. These slaves and their descendants would later be known as the Gnawa. As Muslims, they claimed descent from Bilal, the only black companion of the Prophet. This ethnic construction is the result of their consciousness of themselves as a different group within the spectrum of the city and of their attitudes towards enslavement at the hands of Arabs and Berbers. The Gnawa would emerge as a *zawiyya* (Sufi religious brotherhood) with ties to communities in Meknes, Marrakesh, and Essaouira. Moroccan historian Chouki El Hamel notes:

> The Gnawa have constructed their Islamic identity by emphasizing a privileged status among Muslims—they converted to Islam even before Quraysh, the tribe to whom Muhammad belonged. Hence, it is not surprising to find the name of Bilal in many Gnawa songs. Additionally, to honor their spiritual and emotional link with Bilal and Islam, the Gnawa built a unique shrine in Essaouira dedicated to Bilal: the Zawiya Sidna Bilal, a place to celebrate their culture. Bilal is the symbol of the dialectic between Diaspora and homeland (El Hamel 2008).

From *Mawsim* to Festival: The Construction of a New Sanctity

In Morocco, tombs of religious figures are objects of veneration, particularly during the *mawsim*. *Mawasim* are communal festivals that coincide with periods of agricultural harvest (al-Susi 1966; Rosen 1979; Rabate and Oudaani 1976; Boum 1997) and which have traditionally taken place in areas of southwestern Morocco economically connected to Essaouira. Generally, Jews and Muslims attend these fairs.[12] Jews tend as well to celebrate their own festivals, known as *hillulot*, based on the veneration of a Jewish saint (*saddiq*). These Jewish festivals are not always celebrated at the same time as Muslim festivals are held. However, historically, Muslims and Jews were brought together around these festivals at least in relation to commercial transactions held alongside social and religious celebrations. These fairs, which combined market and pilgrimage at sites along the axes of the western trans-Saharan caravan route, structured the lives and habits of Souiri Muslim and Jewish residents.

The modern conception of urban festival inside the walls of Essaouira is partly influenced by this history of Jewish-Muslim relations. After independence most Jews left their neighborhoods within the city for political and economic reasons (Park 1983). Few remained in the city or kept their property. Some Jews began to return in the last decade.[13] Now, in the absence of the traditional market as a place of encounter between Jews and Muslims, post-independence Jewish-Muslim coexistence is officially marketed through cyclic music fairs. Unlike the traditional *mawasim* and *hillulot*, collective Muslim and Jewish celebration within Essaouira does not revolve around the *saddiq* or the *marabout*. Although Jews still celebrate the local *saddiq*, *Hillulot* are generally downplayed in the public discourse of festivity within Essaouira. Instead, festivalization is constructed around modern discourses of toleration, and takes meaning from Andalusian and Gnawa musical heritages.

"Effective *agurram*": The Azoulay Factor

André Azoulay is one of the most visible public figures of the Jewish community of Morocco. He was born in 1941 in Essaouira. A socialist and political dissident in the 1960s, he migrated to France after his participation in anti-Palace student demonstrations[14] (Laskier 2004: 260) where he served as director of the editorial board of the economic weekly, *Maroc-Informations* (Park and Boum 2006: 48). In Paris, he studied journalism, economics, and political science. After 1967, he emerged as a successful banker with high profile positions in Dutch and French banking institutions. From 1969 to 1991, André Azoulay was an executive vice president of the Paribas Bank. During this period of "exile," Azoulay turned his attention to seeking resolution to the Palestinian-Israeli conflict. He came to believe that the Moroccan monarchy is the only force that can guarantee not only the safety and protection of Moroccan Jews, but also initiate a Jewish-Muslim dialogue. In 1976, Azoulay, René Coriat, Jo Aflalo, André Illouz, René Ohana, Victor Malka, and Robert Assaraf founded an association called "Identité et Dialogue."

> Members of the *Identité et Dialogue* movement defined themselves as Arab Jews who not only searched for their patrimonial roots and Judeo-Muslim understanding but were uncompromisingly dedicated to the idea of promoting an Israeli-Palestinian dialogue. They regarded their natural allies to be the Moroccan king and the recently leftist Peace Now movement in Israel (Laskier 2004: 260).

According to Robert Assaraf (2005), the objective of *Identité et Dialogue* was to demonstrate to Israelis, using the testimony of Moroccan Jews, that Jews can coexist with Arab Muslims.

In 1991, Azoulay returned to Morocco to serve as economic and financial counselor to King Hassan II. His closeness to the late King Hassan II enabled him to implement ideas he had had about developing Essaouira when he lived in Paris. He surrounded himself with people who favored his marketing strategy for developing the city, but nonetheless faced opposition from certain sectors of the government. Azoulay "told the late King Hassan II of his frustrations" about some local administrators in Essaouira, and the king appointed as governor of the province Amin Belcadi, who emerged as "the second major 'motor' of the city's development, actively promoting the activities of NGOs, the Gnawa Festival, and windsurfing infrastructure among other things" (Ross et al. 2002: 32).

Azoulay managed to create not only a better bureaucratic environment for governance within the city, but also a new culture that would facilitate his conception of the city as a space for toleration between races and religions. Evidently, Azoulay, according to my informants, possesses *baraka siyasiya* (a supernatural blessing they qualified as political). Ahmed went as far as describing Azoulay as an *agurram* (saint) because of the positive changes he thought that he brought to Essaouira since he came back from France. He noted, "Just like we have shrines around the city for Muslim and Jewish holy men, we should build shrines for people who help others find jobs. Azoulay is a Jew but in mind he is better than any Muslim you see around you in this city. He is an *agurram.*" Azoulay's ascribed holiness is evidenced by the material prosperity he brought to Essaouira. Ernest Gellner defines *agurram* as someone who "possesses baraka, divine grace and approval, which manifests itself in further ways such as material prosperity and magical power" (Gellner 1972: 60). In normal circumstances, *agurram* is defined partly in terms of descent traced to the Prophet. Westermarck wrote, "No man has possessed more *baraka* than the prophet Muhammad. His *baraka* was transmitted to the *shereefs,* that is, the descendants in the male line of his daughter Fatimah" (Westermarck 1968 vol. 1: 36). Azoulay, a Jew, does not possess this genealogical characteristic. However, in the eyes of Ahmed, Azoulay fulfills what Gellner describes as "the criteria of *agurramhood,* notably prosperity, and the willingness to entertain generously" (Gellner 1972: 61). Again, although he is not a religious figure, "he is pacific. He does not fight, feud, or, by extension, litigate" (ibid.: 60). Gellner maintained that an "*agurram* is simply he who is held to be one. One attains *agurramhood* by being held to possess it. *Agurramhood* is in the eye of the beholder" (Gellner 1969: 74). In the eyes of the Souiri community, Ahmed argues, Azoulay's popular *agurramhood* is based upon his ability to market their city economically.

"Economic *Baraka*": A Jewish Attribute Too!

The idea of economic fecundity is also a distinctive feature of the traditional view of *baraka* (see de Foucauld [1888] 1939, Levi-Provençal 1922, Abun-Nasr 1965, and Eickelman 1976).[15] *Baraka* is associated with "productivity and abundance of the means of living" which are transmitted through saints (Eickelman 1976: 61). In *Reconnaissance au Maroc,* Charles de Foucauld noted that during his journey through Boujaad the special virtues of Sidi ben Dawd were seen to "fertilize the earth and make herds prosper" (de Foucauld 1939: 122). An unpolluted *baraka* leads to abundance in crops, to fertility of women and to the prosperity of the country. However, Westermarck noted "*baraka* is extremely sensitive to external influences and [could] be easily spoiled by them" (Westermarck [1926] 1968 vol. 1: 229). These external influences, Westermarck reported, are largely defined as women, blacks, and Jews. Westermarck listed many cases in which the *baraka* of a place or person was being negatively affected by the influence of Jews. He wrote that:

> [*Baraka*] is polluted by contact with infidels. One reason why the Sultan Muläi Abdl'aziz lost his *baraka* was the presence of Christians at court. The barbers of Andjra say that there is no *baraka* in the razors used by their colleagues in Tangier, because they are sharpened by Christians. A prayer said in a Christian's house or in the house or garden of a Jew is of no avail. If a Jew enters the house of a Moor, the angels will desert it for forty days. A scribe from the Rif told me that if a *hajj,* or person who has made the pilgrimage to Mecca, wants to retain his *baraka,* he must never go to the market and expose himself to the looks of the Jews who are gathered there. Nor are the latter allowed to come near the place at the market where the Moslems sell their grain, so as

not to spoil its *baraka*. A Jew must not tread on threshing-floor nor enter a granary … If the holy spring *Igzer*, which is frequented by the saints of *Demnat*, runs dry, it is a certain sign that some Jew has taken water from it. (Westermarck [1926] 1968 vol. 1: 229–30)

Here, Westermarck asserts that Jews are seen as anathema to *baraka* and are, like women, believed to be unclean (Westermarck [1926] 1968 vol. 1: 229–37). In his discussion of the *mawsim* of Sidi Hamd U Musa, Daniel Schroeter argues that "Jews were not allowed to reside in, or enter, the village of the shrine; they were consigned to an encampment on the outskirts of the village during the time of *mawsim*" (Scroeter 1988: 98).[16] Paul Pascon noted that the descendants of the Sharif told him that the Jews were allowed to open shops in the proximity of the *mawsim*, but were forbidden from entering the boundaries of the shrine (Pascon 1984).

Paradoxically, as Westermarck's statement also suggests, Jews were closely associated with markets, *loci* of exchange which, for a trade-based economy such as Morocco's, were clearly sites of economic productivity. The market is not a "clean" place, but at the same time it is a necessary space. Traditionally, then the Jewish-Muslim encounter in the market is acceptable as long as it does not impinge upon the sanctity of the *haram*.

During my ethnographic study in southern Morocco, many informants commented that the best solution to the communities' economy would be the return of its Jews. The Jew is now emerging in the general consciousness of these communities as somebody who has the magical skills to revive their economy. Thus in opposition to traditional attitudes which saw the Jew as endangering *baraka* and the market as a polluting place which had to be isolated from holy places, today Azoulay, a Jew, is seen as an *agourram* who embodies the *baraka* necessary for the economic revival of Essaouira, while stories circulate of past Jewish-Muslim interactions within Muslim shrines. In light of this shift and its opposition to historical formulations, we can argue that informants' new definition of *baraka* and their assertions of previous Jewish-Muslim encounters within the boundaries of the *haram* are new and invented claims which tie in with a national discourse and serve the political orientations of the Moroccan state.

"Rituals of Tolerance" in the Boundaries of an Urban Moroccan Space

In recent years, there has been an increase in the number of music festivals sponsored by the Moroccan ministries of Culture and Tourism (Belghazi 2006; Boum 1997, 2007; Park and Boum 2006).[17] The government has argued that these events attract internal and foreign tourists and provide occasions to improve and develop local infrastructure. Traditionally, the Moroccan Ministry of Tourism has marketed the country as a tolerant nation. André Azoulay emphasized this asset by highlighting the historical and cultural diversity of Morocco in general, and of Essaouira in particular. Recently, as a member of the United Nations Alliance of Civilizations, he claimed that Morocco would emphasize the sacred elements and historical particularities of Essaouira as an example of cultural and religious tolerance. He said:

> My dignity, the justice I want for myself, or the freedom I want to enjoy, means nothing if my neighbor does not enjoy the same. Today, as a Jewish person, my neighbor is Palestinian. My name is André Azoulay. I am one of the advisors of his Majesty the King of Morocco Mohammed VI. From Mauritania to Indonesia, unfortunately, you will not find another Muslim or Arab country with a Jewish person in such a position as mine. As a member of the high level group for Alliance of Civilisations, I have said many times that culture could help us a lot. You can change the mind of the people more easily and deeply through culture than through ideology ... I have created many music festivals, for instance, with people on the stage coming from all over the world from all origins or religions, and last year, 500,000 attended. It was so powerful! It was so beautiful! And it was a magical moment of union and of consensus and peace! It was peace and love! I feel like a hostage for those who are instrumentalising the name of God, or the message of God, just to preach hate or confrontation. We have to retake the message of God, the name of God, and, when I said we, I mean Muslims, Jews, and Christians—the believers. Being Jewish in a Muslim country is something that belongs to the art of the possible; and it is showing that there is an alternative to hate, to confrontation; and there is also the possibility of mutual understating, mutual respect, and the large potential of working together with the same values, with the same causes, and also understanding the Palestinian issue is a vital challenge. (Azoulay 2008a)

Azoulay constructs a discourse about tolerance in terms of a reinvented history of Essaouira which he and the government present as an arena of sacredness. Morocco is presented as a space where Jews and Muslims coexisted in the past and will be able to do so in the future. Given that one event would not foster this culture shift, the government has created many cultural festivities or fairs in different seasons (Boum 2007). On this ground, Essaouira has two festivals organized in two separate seasons.

It could be argued that the Essaouira festivals are part of a movement started in October 1994 with the Fes Festival of World Sacred Music which was sponsored by the Fes Sais association. Like Essaouira, Fes includes within its walls religious sanctuaries, not only of its founder but also of Jewish and Muslim saints.

As a sacred site, Fes exists as a conflict-free space marked by piety and tolerance. A neat fit is established between the place, the music played during the festival, and sacredness. Furthermore, the inscription of sacredness on Fes is effected through the rhetoric that is mobilized by the conference organizers and circulated in the literature of the festival and the media. The discursive strategy deployed by the Fes Festival organizers essentializes the city and turns it into a homogenized, undifferentiated entity that transcends the conflict-ridden global times (Belghazi 2006: 102–3).

For Azoulay, however, the cosmopolitan character of Essaouira devolves not from its holy sites but from its originary construction as an open, imperial port city:

> The fact is that Essaouira was from time immemorial a city open to the rest of the world and that its founder Sidi Mohamed Ben Abdallah had a profound and modern geopolitical vision which was reflected in this city. The Sultan developed his visionary

policy starting from Essaouira which he placed in the heart of the world. This was not completely random. He made it the first offshore city in the world on the commercial and financial level. What a modernity! Today, we speak of commercial and financial free zones as if it is a new invention. He did that in the 18th century. Who were *Tujjar al-Sultan*[18] after all? It was about the process, then revolutionary, of giving to this city a certain number of characteristics and privileges to make of it a centre of economic, cultural, political and strategic radiation. It was from Essaouira that one left towards the rest of the world. It was in Essaouira that one was in connection with the merchants of Manchester and Denmark. We were bound to Europe, the Mediterranean, the Atlantic and the rest of the world.[19] (Azoulay 2008b)

In addition to this history of open borders, the Andalusian memory of tolerance is also evoked as an integral component of the spirit of Essaouira. Every year, during the festival, Jewish or Muslim artists are remembered. André Azoulay described Essaouira as the incarnation of a city that remained true to "its past of peace." Unlike other parts of the world, Essaouira maintained a culture of tolerance evocative of pre-*Reconquista* Andalusia.

The city developers led by André Azoulay have publicly announced that the cathartic effect of this urban ritual of tolerance vivifies the city not only socially but also economically. Essaouira festivals offer some structural and thematic similarities with Kapchan's concept of marketplace. Kapchan argues that "the marketplace represents a symbolic locus of contact with the foreign, whether the connection be physical or abstract, in goods, tongues, or ideas. At such moments old hierarchies are put into question, supplanted, or reinstated anew" (Kapchan 1993: 309).

Here the city becomes a Turnerian liminal space that other communities are invited to enter (Turner 1969, 1982b); the foreign is not a stranger within the sanctuary of Essaouira. Azoulay announced in a mode that was almost utopian that:

> In Essaouira, one is elsewhere. One is elsewhere because the other is seldom foreign. The other is seldom suspect. Any of my fellow-citizens whether Moslem, Christian or Jewish, would reiterate what I said. This gives the city a unique identity. It is true that today when we speak of tolerance we could be seen as demagogue. Perhaps I exaggerate, but it is true that on our premises the concern of the other is a way of being and a way of life (Azoulay 2008b).

Conclusions

> *You can change the mind of the people more easily and deeply through culture than through ideology ... I have created many music festivals, for instance, with people on the stage coming from all over the world from all origins and religions.*
> André Azoulay, 2007 (Azoulay 2008b)

Visiting Essaouira during its festivals has been likened by Souris to journeys to Mecca's market during the sacred months in the pre-Islamic periods. My informants postulated that Essaouira as a secular space can be converted into a sacred space that commands reverence. Jewish as well as Muslim subjects idealized this urban "sanctuary" as a space of economic exchange, cultural relations, and religious tolerance. They claimed that Essaouira is an example of tolerance that everybody wishing to achieve a global coexistence should learn. Belghazi's study postulated that the Fes Festival is an "event that serves the interests of the Fes urban elite in perpetuating the status quo" (Belghazi 2006). During my ethnographic study, I discovered that Essaouira festival moves away from "the elitist" nature of Fes festival. Azoulay and other developers promoted the city by using the cultural symbols and religious tones of the urban space to highlight populist shared sacred elements.

During one of his interviews on the historical relations between Muslims and Jews in Essaouira, Azoulay noted,

> A memory marked my life. In my family, my father had a very dear friend. We called him the imam. Each year, this man went for pilgrimage to Mecca and al-Quds before 1967. This man influenced me because whenever he returned from Mecca, he came to see my father. He gave a bag of soil to my father and said "I return from a place which is sacred to me and to you." He placed the bag on my father's desk, kissed it, and left. (Azoulay 2008b)

This personal belief in the possibilities of cultural and social dialogue between Jews and Muslims is one of the driving forces behind the festivalization of this urban space. These festivals present many economic opportunities for the city and its disenfranchised inhabitants and decaying infrastructure, but they present risks as well. Azoulay is trying through these festivals to reverse the social order of things in which a natural Jewish-Muslim enmity is assumed. Such cultural celebration might, as Turner argues with reference to ceremonies in general, "bring about a temporary reconciliation between conflicting members of single community. Conflict is held in abeyance during the period of ritualized action" (Turner 1982a: 21). In the eyes of many Islamists, this effort amounts to a call for the normalization of relations with Israel. These rituals of tolerance remain an ideal and are still far from being a *habitus* of toleration. There is no indication that this elitist discourse of tolerance manifests itself during these festivals in the form of dialogue between Jews and Muslims. Despite this, during the only occasion where hundreds of Jews gather annually to celebrate the *hiloula* of Rabbi Nessim Ben Nessim, a few Muslims can be seen participating.

Therefore, despite the *agurramhood* of Azoulay and its general impact on Essaouira, the future of these rituals of tolerance may be connected to the future of the Palestinian-Israeli conflict. Azoulay has been aware of this connection, and every year the image of the "Palestinian neighbor" has been an important component of the festival. In the eyes of the organizers, the festival of Essaouira provides an opportunity for movement towards Israeli-Palestinian agreement. By demonstrating Jewish-Muslim coexistence in the borderlands of one sacred urban space, a Jewish-Muslim encounter within another—the Holy Land—is shown as something that could happen. In many interviews, Azoulay goes as far as to argue that Essaouira not only provides an instance of coexistence between different faiths and cultures, but becomes a example for Israelis and Palestinians to follow as they negotiate a future peace agreement.

Notes

1. A fair held on the high plateau east of Mecca during the pre-Islamic era. See 'Uqayli 1984.
2. The most extensive discussion of the concept of *baraka* was carried out by Westermarck 1968; also see Sabour 1993, and Jamus 1981.
3. Many Islamic modernists and traditionalists have challenged the visitation of shrines. For more discussion, see Nakash 1995.
4. For a discussion of Gnawa music groups, see Kapchan 2007 and Pâques 1991.
5. For more discussion on the concept of "festivalization" as it relates to modern urban space, see Falassi 1967; Schuster 2001, 1995; Belghazi 2006; and Turner 1982.
6. The annual fairs and festivals held in commemoration of saints (sing. *Mawsim*; French *moussem*; in Tashelhit, *amuggar*). Literally, *mawsim* stands for "season."
7. Jewish festivals organized to celebrate the anniversary of a saint's death (sing. *hillulah*).
8. For a discussion of the dynamics of the festival, its features, and manifestations, see Kapchan 2007 and Ross et al. 2002.
9. For a discussion of "visible power" and "invisible influence", see Fogg 1938: 428–58.
10. The 2004 national census cited the total population of Essaouira as 452,979. For more information on the historical development of Essaouira's population, see Schroeter 1988: 219–221.
11. See for instance, Qur'an 2: 217, which says "They ask you of war in the holy month. Tell them: 'To fight in that month is a great sin.'" (Trans. Ahmed 1990: 38).
12. Kosansky (2003) and Schroeter (1988) have noted that we have to be careful about reproducing the trope of Jewish-Muslim presence in the *mawsim*. Although I have heard this claim from many of my Muslim informants, Kosansky and Schroeter argue that many of their older informants, especially Jews, never talked about this. I would argue that Muslims and Jews had some form of contact during these festivals and that some forms of regulations conditioned their relationships. Jews were probably never allowed within the religious sanctuary of the *mawsim* and kept largely outside its borders.
13. This notion of return is largely constructed within Morocco as part of a country which is tolerant, compared to other Arab nations, of its Jewish population. We should be careful not to romanticize this return, given the fact that very few Moroccan Jews have actually come back and settled in Essaouira.
14. A sharp increase in the price of sugar triggered riots and civil unrest in Casablanca in 1965. These riots were led by students' and workers' unions, and led to the suspension of parliament and the declaration of a state of emergency.
15. See de Foucauld (1888) 1939, Levi-Provençal 1922, Abun-Nasr 1965, and Eickelman 1967.
16. This conflicts with Oskar Lenz's report on Sharif Houssein of Iligh who gave permission to Jews to enter the boundaries of the saint's sanctuary (Lenz 1886 vol. 1: 364). In *La Maison d'Iligh et l'histoire sociale du Tazerwalt*, Paul Pascon (1984) questioned Lenz's claim.
17. Islamists have criticized this festivalization of urban spaces as a waste of public funds and a violation of Islamic moral principles (see www.attajdid.ma, accessed 25 November 2008). Many critical articles on Essaouira festivals have been written by journalists affiliated with *Attajdid*, an Islamic newspaper with close ties to the Islamic Justice and Development Party (PJD).
18. Jewish merchants who enjoyed intimate relationship with the sultans of Morocco. They were recognized as the sultan's merchants.
19. "Interview with André Azoulay." http://www.7-dragons.com/maroc/actualites/azoulay2.php, accessed 25 November 2008 (my translation from the French).

References

Abrahams, Roger and Richard Bauman. 1978. "Ranges of Festival Behavior," in *The Reversible World: Symbolic Inversion in Art and Society*, ed. B. Babcock. Ithaca and London: Cornell University Press, 193–208.

Abun-Nasr, Jamil M. 1965. *The Tijaniyya: A Sufi Order in the Modern World*. London: Oxford University Press.

Al-Susi, Muhammad al-Mukhtar. 1966. *Iligh qadiman wa-hadithan*. Rabat: al-matba'a al-malakiyya.

Assaraf, Robert. 2005. *Une certaine histoire des juifs du maroc 1860–1999*. Paris: Jean-Claude Gawsewitch.

Azoulay, André. 2008a. Interview on the United Nations Alliance of Civilizations. *http://www.youtube.com/watch?v=4nLzF8bN2Gk&feature=related*, accessed 25 November 2008.

———. 2008b. Interview with André Azoulay. *http://www.7-dragons.com/maroc/actualites/azoulay2.php*, accessed 25 November 2008.

Belghazi, Taieb. 2006. "Festivalization of Urban Space in Morocco." *Critique: Critical Middle Eastern Studies* 15(1): 97–107.

Ben-Ami, Issachar. 1998. *Saint Veneration among the Jews in Morocco*. Detroit: Wayne State University Press.

Boum, Aomar. 2007. "Dancing for the Moroccan State: Ethnic Folk Dances and the Production of National Hybridity," in *North African Mosaic: A Cultural Reappraisal of Ethnic and Religious Minorities*, eds. N. Boudraa and J. Krause. Newcastle: Cambridge Scholars Publishing, 214–37.

———. 1997. *Folk Dance between Reality and Ideology: Ahwash as a Case Study*. Unpublished Master's thesis. Ifrane: Al Akhawayn University.

———. 2006. *Muslims Remember Jews in Southwestern Morocco: Social Memories, Dialogic Narratives and the Collective Imagination of Jewishness*. Unpublished PhD dissertation. Tucson: University of Arizona.

Eickelman, Dale E. 1981. *The Middle East: An Anthropological Approach*. Englewood Cliffs: Prentice Hall.

———. 1976. *Moroccan Islam: Tradition and Society in a Pilgrimage Center*. Austin: University of Texas Press.

Elboudrari, Hassan. 1985. "Quant les saints font les villes. Lecture anthropologique de la pratique sociale d'un saint marocain du XVIIe siècle." *Annales: Economies, Sociétés, Civilisations* 40(3): 489–508.

El Hamel, Chouki. 2008. "The Gnawa Music of Morocco." *http://www.afropop.org/multi/feature/ID/618*, accessed 25 November 2008.

Falassi, A. 1967. "Festival: Definition and Morphology," in *Time Out of Time Essays on the Festival*, ed. A. Falassi. Albuquerque: University of New Mexico Press, 1–10.

Fogg, Walter. 1938. "A Tribal Market in the Spanish Zone of Morocco." *Africa: Journal of the International African Institute* 11(4): 428–58.

Foucauld, Charles de. (1888) 1939. *Reconnaissance au Maroc*. Paris: Imprimerie Nationale.

Gellner, E. 1981. *Muslim Society*. Cambridge: Cambridge University Press.

———. 1972. "Political and Religious Organization of the Berbers of the Central High Atlas," in *Arabs and Berbers: From Tribe to Nation in North Africa*, eds. E. Gellner and C. Micaud. London: Lexington Books, 59–66.

————. 1969. *Saints of the Atlas*. Chicago: University of Chicago Press.

Gitlitz, David M., and Linda Kay Davidson. 2006. *Pilgrimage and the Jews*. Westport, CT: Praeger Publishers.

Jamus, Raymond. 1981. *Honneur et baraka: les structures sociales traditionnelles dans le Rif*. Paris: Éditions de la Maison des Sciences de l'Homme.

Kapchan, Deborah. 1993. "Hybridization and the Marketplace: Emerging Paradigms in Folkloristics." *Western Folklore* 52(2/4): 303–26.

————. 2007. *Traveling Spirit Masters: Moroccan Gnawa Trance and Music in the Global Marketplace*. Middletown, CT: Wesleyan University Press.

Kosansky, Oren. 2003. *All Dear unto God: Saints, Pilgrimage and Textual Practice in Jewish Morocco*. Unpublished dissertation. Michigan: Department of Anthropology, University of Michigan.

————. 2002. "Tourism, Charity, and Profit: The Movement of Money in Moroccan Jewish Pilgrimage." *Cultural Anthropology* 17(3): 359–400.

Lapassade, Georges. 1994. "Ethnographies d'Essaouira," in *Essaouira: mémoire et empreintes du présent* (Actes des journées d'études, 26–28 October 1990, Agadir). Casablanca: Najah al-Jadida, 45–50.

Laskier, Michael M. 2004. *Israel and the Maghreb from Statehood to Oslo*. Gainesville: University Press of Florida.

Lenz, Oskar. 1886. *Timbouctou, voyage au Maroc, au Sahara et au Soudan*. Paris: Hachette.

Levi-Provençal, E. 1922. Les *historiens des Chorfa*. Paris: Librairie Orientaliste Paul Geuthner.

Levy, André. 2003. "Notes on Jewish-Muslim Relationships: Revisiting the Vanishing Moroccan Jewish Community." *Cultural Anthropology* 18(3): 365–97.

————. 1997. "To Morocco and Back: Tourism and Pilgrimage among Moroccan-Born Israelis," in *Grasping Land: Space and Place in Contemporary Israeli Discourse and Experience*, eds. E. Ben-Ari and Y. Bilu. Albany: SUNY Press, 25–46.

Lévy, Simon. 1994. "Le peuplement juif d'Essaouira et son parler," in *Essaouira: mémoire et empreintes du présent* (Actes des journées d'études, 26–28 October 1990, Agadir). Casablanca: Najah al-Jadida, 51–59.

Nakash, Yitzhak. 1995. The Visitation of the Shrines of the Imams and the Shi'i Mujtahids in the Early Twentieth Century." *Studia Islamica* 1(81): 153–64.

Ottmani, Hamza Ben Driss. 1997. *Mogador: une cite sous les alizés, des origins à 1939*. Rabat: La Porte.

Pâques, Viviana. 1991. *La religion des esclaves: recherches sur la confrérie marocaine des Gnawa*. Bergamo: Moretti & Vitali.

Park, Thomas. 1983. *Administration and the Economy: Morocco 1880 to 1980: The Case of Essaouira*. Unpublished Ph.D. dissertation. Wisconsin: University of Wisconsin-Madison.

————. 1988. "Essaouira: Formation of a New Elite 1940–1980." *African Studies Review* 31(3): 111–32.

Park, Thomas, and Aomar Boum. 2006. *Historical Dictionary of Morocco*. Lanham, MD: Scarecrow Press.

Pascon, Paul. 1984. *La Maison d'Iligh et l'histoire sociale du Tazerwalt*. Rabat: Société Marocaine des Editeurs Reunis.

Rabate, M.R., and A. Oudaani. 1976. "Le moussem de Sidi Merri: Festivités du Mouloud dans un village du Maroc présaharien central." *Objects et mondes: la revue du Musée de l'homme* 16(1): 27–40.

Reysoo, Fenneke. 1991. *Pèlerinages au maroc féte, politique et échange dans l'islam populaire*. Paris: Éditions de la Maison des Sciences de l'Homme.

Rosen, Lawrence. 1979. "Social Identity and Points of Attachment: Approaches to Social Organization," in *Meaning and Order in Moroccan Society: Three Essays in Cultural Analysis*, eds. C. Geertz, H. Geertz, and L. Rosen. Cambridge: Cambridge University Press, 19–122.

Ross, Eric, et al. 2002. *Assessing Tourism in Essaouira*. Casablanca: Imprimerie Najah El Jadida.

Sabour, M'hammed. 1993. "La baraka: capital et pouvoir symbolique," in *Westermarck et la société marocaine*, eds. R. Bourqia and M. al-Harras. Rabat: Faculté des Letters et des Sciences Humaines.

Schroeter, Daniel. 1988. *Merchants of Essaouira*. Cambridge: Cambridge University Press.

Schuster, Mark. 2001. "Ephemera, Temporary Urbanism, and Imaging," in *Imaging the City: Continuing Struggles and New Directions*, eds. L. Vale and S. Warner Jr. New Brunswick, NJ: Center for Urban Policy Research, 361–96.

———. 1995. "Two Urban Festivals: La Merce and First Night," *Planning Practice and Research* 10(2): 173–88.

Stillman, Norman A. 1996. "Saddiq and Marabout in Morocco," in *Jews Among Muslims: Communities in the Pre-colonial Middle East*, eds. S. Deshen and W. Zenner. Basingstoke: Macmillan Press, 121–30.

Turner, Victor. 1969. *The Ritual Process: Structure and Anti-Structure*. Hawthorne, NY: Aldine de Gruyter.

———.1982a. *Celebration: Studies of Festivity and Ritual*. Washington, DC: Smithsonian Institution Press.

———. 1982b. *From Ritual to Theatre: The Human Seriousness of Play*. Village Station, New York: PAJ Publications.

'Uqayli, Muhammad Ahmad. 1984. *Suq 'Ukaz fi al-Tarikh*. Abha: Nadi Abha al-Adabi.

Voinot, Louis. 1948. *Pèlerinages Judéo-Musulmans au Maroc*. Paris: Éditions Larose.

Westermarck, Edward. (1926) 1968. *Ritual and Belief in Morocco*. London: Macmillan.

Chapter 9

NEW ANCESTRAL SHRINES AFTER THE COLD WAR

Heonik Kwon

In a classic study of dual religious symbolism in representations of death, Robert Hertz explored how society constructs a conceptual moral hierarchy on the basis of differentially polarized but identical symbols. He questioned why in European and other languages, the right side or right hand represented positive moral values of strength, law, and purity whereas the left was opposed, standing for negative values and sinister meanings. His more specific question was why, in the historical and ethnological material he drew upon, a 'good death' is ritually and metaphorically associated with the right hand while the left hand indicates the 'bad death' of those 'unquiet and spiteful souls' which society must exclude (Hertz 1960 [1907]: 78, 86). Hertz understood the symbolic contrast of the left and right as a biopolitical phenomenon by which society inscribes on the human body "the opposition of values and the violent contrasts of the world of morality" (Hertz 1973 [1909]: 21).

Hertz believed that the antithesis of left and right was both a complementary bipolarity and an asymmetrical relationship, with the former being the natural condition of *homo duplex* (the double human) and the latter resulting from the imposition of collective, hierarchical norms on the individual body. Moreover, he observed that this symbolic bipolarity was reversible in archaic or egalitarian societies, suggesting that these societies did not postulate a fixed moral hierarchy in the life of the dead as they lacked such a conception in their own life. Based on this observation, Hertz argued that "the evolution of society replaces this reversible dualism with a rigid hierarchical structure" (Hertz 1973: 8) and proceeded to express his vision of a progressive social order with a new biopolitical language referring to what I call the ambidextrous human body (see below).

The bipolarity of left and right has also been an important subject in modern political theory, although within a different frame of thought from that of the tradition of anthropological research. Hannah Arendt once said, when asked what her position was on the politics of right and left:

> I really don't know and I've never known. And I suppose I never had any such position. You know the left think that I am conservative, and the conservatives sometimes think

that I am left or I am a maverick or God knows what. And I must say that I couldn't care less. I don't think the real questions of this century will get any kind of illumination by this kind of thing. (Arendt 1979: 334)

If there was one political thinker who radically rejected the terms of the Cold War, it was Arendt, author of *The Human Condition*, who believed in the power of human creativity to move beyond "a monologic politics that is incapable of projecting beyond the subject, a polarizing politics in which the Other becomes simply a projection of one's own obsessions and fears … epitomized by the mutual balance of terror and conformity" (Isaac 1998: 284). For Arendt, politics was above all about difference and dissonance. She was concerned with the presence in the political arena of actors with alternative understandings and competing projects as well as with the existence of "others from whom one cannot escape and with whom one must share the world" (ibid.: 283). She believed that recognizing and respecting this otherness is central to genuine politics and free political life.

These two separate discourses about right and left—one about moral symbolic polarity in traditional societies and the other about ideological bifurcation in modern politics—forge a critical association in the history of mass death in the Cold War. If we consider the history of the Cold War in the light of the Western doctrine of deterrence, which is in effect imagining war in order to prevent war, it appears that political history and the morality of death have no meaningful relationship. If we extend the scope of the history and include in it the experience of violent ideological confrontations and containment politics within national and local communities, which is what the Cold War actually meant in much of the non-Western postcolonial world, the political bifurcation of the human community and a moral polarization of good and bad death become closely interrelated phenomena. In the history of global conflict in the latter sense, communities were driven to select politically good death from the mass of other war deaths and to extract an ideologically cohesive genealogy out of an enmeshed history of violence stretching across ideological borders. If the left and the right are both historically and genealogically constitutive of the social self, how can this identity be reconciled with citizenship in state societies based on the renunciation of one's relatedness to what the political community defines as the "wrong side"?

This chapter will consider that last question in the context of contemporary Vietnam and against the historical background of the country's long civil war (1961–1975). In southern and central regions of Vietnam, kinship rarely constitutes a politically homogenous entity. In many families and communities of these regions, genealogical histories are crowded with episodes of radical political disunity, relating to wartime mobilization by opposed political and military forces. This chapter will examine how this chaotic historical reality is manifested in today's domestic and communal ritual spaces, partly focusing on recent changes taking place in domestic ancestral shrines. Notable among these changes is the incorporation of diverse traces of war death into the ancestral ritual space in explicit and demonstrative forms, and the related transformation of the domestic or communal ancestral shrine into a politically mixed shrine, inclusive of both memories of heroic revolutionary war death and those of politically troubled death. Before we proceed to the details of these mixed shrines, however, it is necessary briefly to outline the controversial status of the Vietnam War in the history of the global Cold War.

The Vietnam-American War

The Vietnam War, in the dominant view of the outside world at the time of the conflict, was one of the major "limited wars" of the Cold War era, fought between the Soviet- (and Chinese-) backed northern communist forces and the US-supported southern regime. In Vietnam, however, the war is referred to as "the American War" (literally, "the war against America") and, as such, is officially considered to be an extension of the collective struggle against colonial domination ("the French War") and part of the long march towards achieving a fully sovereign and united nation-state.

Many distinguished scholars of modern history have delved into the contradiction between these two perspectives. Marilyn Young begins her seminal history of the Vietnam War with the troubled episode of the US Merchant Marines in 1945. While they were in charge of bringing home American troops from the Pacific, the Marines were ordered to ferry thirteen thousand French combat troops to Saigon and thus, against the protests of many sailors, to assist France's attempt to reoccupy Vietnam in the name of protecting its old colony from the threat of communism (Young 1991: 1–2). Odd Arne Westad foregrounds the dynamics of decolonization in the history of the global Cold War (Westad 2005). In his account, the anticolonial, postcolonial political movements of Africa, Asia, and Latin America, and the superpower competitions, appear to have shaped each other in a myriad of interpenetrative ways.

Bruce Cumings approaches the bipolar/postcolonial contradiction as a parallax effect embedded in modern geopolitics (Cumings 1999). The parallax vision is a key concept in early astronomical sciences, and it addresses "the apparent shift in an object's position when viewed alternatively from different vantage points" (Hirshfeld 2001: xii). Cumings extends this principle, originally applied to gauging the distance to stars, to an understanding of mid-century American foreign politics. In particular, he looks into the question that has puzzled many other historians of early Cold War, namely, how it was possible, in the words of Kuznick and Gilbert, that, after 1945, "the United States had repudiated the values underlying the liberal construction of World War II as the democratic war against racism, fascism, and colonialism" (Kuznick and Gilbert 2001: 4). From the American perspective, radical political movements in Asia changed after the end of World War II from being positive forces working towards the prospect of a postwar world of free nations to being negative, menacing forces serving the expansion of Soviet power. Cumings explains that this shift of identity was a parallax effect arising from the changing position of the geopolitical center rather than an actual change in the peripheral regions. According to him, American power, moving from membership of the anti-Axis alliance to pre-eminent leadership of a global anticommunist crusade, imposed on the Asian political movements an illusory translocation to the Soviet side.

Cumings discusses the geopolitical parallax within the broad context of postwar United States policies towards East and Southeast Asia, including the occupation of Japan, that of the southern half of the Korean peninsula, and the intervention in Vietnam. Mark Bradley explores early Vietnam-American diplomatic history through extensive archival research in Vietnam, the United States and Europe, confirming that Vietnamese revolutionary leaders, following the surrender of Japan in August 1945, eagerly anticipated that their demands for national independence would be endorsed by the United States, whose attitude to the non-Western world they saw as differing from that of the European imperial powers (Bradley 2000). The Vietnamese revolutionaries were encouraged by Franklin Roosevelt's denunciations of French colonialism, and when Ho Chi Minh declared Vietnam's independence in September 1945 he quoted Thomas Jefferson (Bradley 2000: 4; see also Luong 1992: 129–31). Bradley shows how this apparent convergence in diplomatic vision between Vietnam and America concealed the respective leaders' radically divergent expectations which were to become manifest in the violent clashes of the following decades. He proposes that the origin of the Vietnam War is unintelligible without relating the horizon of bipolar geopolitics to the field of postcolonial visions and "the visions and assumptions of the imagined Vietnam and America of Vietnamese revolutionaries and U.S. policy makers in a mutually constitutive fashion" (Bradley 2000: 178). The Vietnam-American war, he concludes, was the pursuit of a postcolonial future in the era of the Cold War.

Bradley's persuasive study inherits, and tries to go beyond, a "revisionist" tradition in Cold War international history. This tradition, sparked by disillusion with the "orthodox" interpretation of the origin of the Cold War that puts the blame for the escalation of hostility on the Soviet side, turned to the active role played by the US side in heightening tensions. The tradition has developed into the currently dominant "post-revisionist" approach, partly thanks to the accessibility of archival material held in the Eastern Bloc countries, and attempts to reassess East-West relations as a mutually constitutive, reciprocal "joint venture" (see Hunter 1998: 8–16) deeply implicated within the historical context of decolonization. Following the visual metaphor of Cumings, we may say that the revisionist school analytically refused the positional shift that resulted in the geopolitical parallax by placing the origins of the Cold War firmly within the US response to decolonizing traditional societies.

Although I fully endorse this approach and in fact spent part of my youth trying to digest some of the explosive ideas in Cumings' early seminal work on the origins of the Korean War (Cumings 1981), I also feel obliged to point out the limits of this perspective in comprehending bipolar modernity in a multidimensional, multifocal way, from inside out as well as from outside in, and from above as well as from below. The very strength of this approach in taking into account the views of peripheral actors (we can say that the revisionist tradition is more effective in representing "the native point of view" than the orthodox tradition) turns out to be its main weakness in that it renders this view unrealistically homogenous. In order to understand the political process in the bipolarized postcolonial periphery, our attention may have to shift, taking in a perspective opposed to that the revisionist historians have called for; we may have to consider postcolonial visions within the field of bipolarized historical experience. The Cold War's parallax was not merely geopolitical or diplomatic but furthermore created a parallax between state and society. When a revolutionary movement turned into a revolutionary state, its postcolonial vision could also turn into a doctrine imposed on the diversity of communal experience.

The Revival of Ancestor Worship

In the communities of southern and central Vietnam (what was South Vietnam before 1975), kinship rarely constitutes a politically homogenous entity. Genealogical unity is crowded with the remains of wartime political bifurcation. In the customary practices of *ve chau to* (literally, to gather to serve the ancestors), people face not only the memories of meritorious ancestors who contributed to the nation's revolutionary march to independence but also the stigmatizing genealogical background of those who worked against that state-defined "forward" march. As in Sophocles' epic tragedy of *Antigone*, which inspired Hegel in his philosophy of the modern state, many individuals and families were torn between familial obligation to attend to the memory of the war dead and the political obligation to forget those who fought against the revolutionary state. It is very common in this region, when a family has revolutionary martyrs from the American War to commemorate, that they also have to account for the siblings and other close relations of these martyrs, killed in action on the opposite side of the war's ideological frontier. The commemoration of the former group is legitimate and encouraged by the state hierarchy of the unified Vietnam while that of the latter group is the opposite. The dead in the ancestor worship of this region are, at once, united in kinship memory and bipolarized in political history.

Since the early 1990s, following general initiatives for socioeconomic reforms later known as *doi moi* (renovation) legislated by the Sixth National Congress of the Vietnamese Communist Party of December 1986, the above disparity in genealogical memory has become a critical social issue in the communities of the southern and central region. The report from that party congress focused on economic issues, including changing the organizational basis of agricultural production from collective to private units, opening the border to foreign capital investments, and raising the managerial skills of the state's political and administrative apparatus. On cultural matters, it highlighted investment in education to prepare the younger generation to be a skilled industrial workforce, and focused on the continued need to oppose "vestiges of feudal, colonialist, and bourgeois cultures [and] superstitions and other backward customs and practices" (Duiker 1995: 189). Despite this official caution, the reform sparked off, in local communities, a forceful revival of ancestor worship and other ritual activities which had previously belonged to that category of "feudal vestiges" and "backward customs and practices" (see Luong 1993; Tan 2000; Taylor 2004).

Throughout the 1990s, Vietnamese communities were seized by intense, sometimes competitive, mobilizations of human and financial resources to rebuild family and lineage ancestral temples (*nha tho toc*) and village communal houses (*dinh*). The largely voluntary popular activity of *viec ho* (the work of family ancestor worship) was less of a return to the old "backward customs" than the rise of a distinctive way to demonstrate economic development (Tai 2001; also Malarney 2003).

In the villages near Danang in the central region that I am familiar with, a large number of former partisan fighters of the American War took an active part in the ancestral ritual revival. Their participation contributed to the state administration's toleration of this communal initiative. In his letter to the district Communist Party office requesting permission for the construction of his lineage ancestral temple, a prominent war veteran and senior member of the lineage argued: "It is according to the principle of our revolution to share wealth and happiness with the generations of war dead who knew nothing but poverty and suffering. The nation's prosperity should benefit all the generations of Vietnam, not merely those who are alive" (Kwon 2006: 114).

Ordinary Vietnamese villagers might not be able to state so eloquently their concern with family affairs, but those I knew were nevertheless cognizant of the particular idea of human rights or justice embedded in the former partisan leader's statement; just as the living have rights to subsistence and rights to pursue economic prosperity, so too do dead people. In popular Vietnamese conception, subsistence means, for the dead, ritual commemoration which guarantees their inalienable right to social existence. The notion of justice in this moral economy is founded on general social intimacy with cultural traditions of remembering the dead on the one hand, and in engagement with the militant secularism and coercive enlightenment drive of revolutionary state politics on the other. The statement of the former partisan leader offers good dialectical reasoning to these two forces—tradition and revolution—and creatively grafts traditional norms to the tree of revolutionary morality using the new, reform-era language of national economic prosperity. The art of grafting (of old and new, foreign and native) has, as Neil Jamieson shows, been a principal metaphor in the historical imagination of modern Vietnamese intellectual history since the very early colonial era (Jamieson 1993).

The revival of ancestral rituals was a generalized phenomenon throughout Vietnam, but there were substantial differences between its operation in the north and in southern and central communities. Patricia Pelley highlights the importance of ritual politics in modern Vietnamese history and argues that the revolutionary

Vietnamese state, after taking power in 1945 in the northern half of the country, sought to divert ancestral ritual from the family and community to the state (Pelley 2002: 168). Describing the same process, Shaun Malarney explains how the state has penetrated into domestic and communal lives and turned their ritual space into an instrument of social integration and political control (Malarney 2002: 56–72). Whether the state has moved into family ritual life or ritual has moved to the hands of the state, the focus of these scholars is commonly on the politics of war heroes—a central, familiar element in the process of modern nation-building (Anderson 1991; Gillis 1994; Winter and Sivan 1999). The Vietnamese state has put great emphasis on the civic moral duty to remember the sacrifice of revolutionary patriots in the wars of liberation, and has invested enormous administrative resources into instituting the national memory of war. The result, at the local level, has been the establishment of war cemeteries and monuments at the center of village public spaces and the substitution of hero worship for traditional ancestor worship. In this new organization, Vietnamese villagers were to relate to the memory of young volunteer soldiers and eminent party activists in the same way as they had previously related to the founding ancestors of the community or the lineage. In domestic life, people were to replace family ancestral memorabilia with state-issued death certificates of revolutionary martyrs and mass-produced portraits of national leaders. Beyond the formal similarity, however, was a considerable semantic difference between the old and new forms of "ancestor worship." Worship practices strengthened the solidary relations of the local in the old form, whereas they were meant to integrate parochial local relations into the sacred community of the nation in the new.

Following reunification of the country in 1975, the institution of hero worship was extended to the southern half (see Malarney 2001). It served as a principal means of integrating this ideologically confused region into moral and political unity with revolutionary northern Vietnam. The imposition of the ritual political institution has, however, created formidable social problems in the south. The problems are related to the political complexity of genealogical memory, mentioned earlier, and ultimately to the question of what George Mosse has called "the myth of national experience" (Mosse 1990: 7) in war memory. Jay Winter and Jean-Louis Robert, extending Mosse's insights, show how World War I was experienced differently by Paris and London, and even by the various residential districts of Paris. They suggest that the history of the war should be approached in terms of multiple "convergences and divergences" (Winter and Robert 1997: 20–24) rather than according to a unifying, mystifying scheme of national or European experience. The same is true of the history of the American War.

The institution of hero worship made sense, relatively speaking, in the context of northern Vietnam, where the memory of the war dead was predominantly of the "voluntary" soldiers who had left their homes to fight in distant battlefields. Here it could be felt that the communities these soldiers had belonged to had handed over their precious offspring to the state, which subsequently brought their bodies back to the community and honored their memory. It is not easy to extend this classic relationship between civil society and the nation-state to the postwar situation in the southern regions. The war efforts in these regions had not constituted a clear division between the home front of war economic production and the distant horizon of actual battlefields, but functioned instead as a *xoi dau* (a popular idiom for "village war"), turning communal life inside out and producing a vicious, confused battleground (see Trullinger 1994).

Xoi dau is the name of a Vietnamese ceremonial delicacy made of rice flour and black beans. As a metaphor, it refers to wartime village life seized by and oscillating between two contending sides as regularly as the change of day to night. When people savor *xoi dau*, they need to eat both the white and the black part of the pastry. Likewise, survival in the village "Cold War" means to accept both sides of that dual world. I heard of many painful episodes of living in "harmony" with thundering bipolarity, and many creative stories about subverting the zero-sum logic of the situation. One very common episode concerns brotherly disunity: how one brother joined "this side" (*ben ta*, the revolutionary side) and another brother (usually the younger one) was dragged to "that side" (*ben kia*, the American side). The situation is tragic, and the result often painful; neither returns home alive and the younger has a problem returning home even in memory. Yet *xoi dau* can also generate creative strategies. For instance, families whose children fought on different sides of the battlefield hoped that at least one would survive the war or, should it happen that all returned home alive, that the brother on the winner's side would be able to help rebuild the life of the brother on the loser's side.

South of Danang, the family's ancestral altar in the home of a stonemason displayed two framed pictures of young men. One man wore a military uniform and his name was inscribed on the state-issued death certificate hanging above the altar. The other man, dressed in his high-school uniform, had also fought and died in the war, but his death certificate, issued by the former South Vietnamese authority, was carefully hidden in the closet. In 1996, the matron of this family decided to put the photographs of the two soldiers together. Other mason families were to follow in her footsteps over the next couple of years, but hers was one of the first initiatives among members of the stonemasons' guild. She took the Hero Death Certificate down from the wall and placed it on the newly refurbished ancestral altar. She placed the picture of her older "hero" son on the right-hand side of the altar, the place usually reserved for seniors. She enlarged a small picture of her younger son that she had kept in her bedroom. She invited some friends, her surviving children and their children for a meal. Before the meal, she held a modest ceremony in which she said she had dreamed many times about moving the schoolboy from her room to a place next to his elder brother. Placing the younger son's picture next to that of his elder brother she addressed her children and grandchildren:

> Uncle Kan admired Uncle Tan. Uncle Tan adored the Little Kan. And the two were sick of the thought that they might meet in a battle. I prayed to the spirits of Marble Mountains that my two boys should never meet. The goddess listened. The boys never met. The goddess carried them away to different directions so that they could not meet.

The gracious goddess carried them too far. She took my prayer and was worried. To be absolutely sure that the boys don't meet in this world, the goddess took them to her world, both of them. We can't blame the goddess. So, here we are. My two children met finally. I won't be around, breathing, for much longer. You, my children, should look after your uncles. They don't have children, but they have many nephews and nieces. Remember this, my children. Respect your uncles.

In her speech, the brothers are seen as being able to help each other overcome the bipolar structure of enmity even though they are dead, and the opening of this imaginative reciprocity has been one of the prominent aspects of the recent ritual revival in the southern regions.

Figure 9.1. Patriotic memorial at a village communal house. Photo H. Kwon.

Just as the initiatives of revolutionary war veterans, such as the one cited above, helped to legitimize communal initiatives to reconstitute traditional communal ancestral rituals, so too did the presence of revolutionary death certificates on those shrines assist in assimilating stigmatized genealogical memories into the domestic ritual space. In the greater Danang area where, in the second half of the 1990s, I conducted research on the local history of war, it was clear that residents were holding regular ancestral rites more publicly than before and hoping to hold death commemoration rites within a more open circle of relatives than previously permitted. The latter rites involved the identities of war dead from "that side" who would, previously, have been labeled "counterrevolutionary" (*phan dong* in Vietnamese). In the places I observed, this regionally specific aspect of the ritual revival was first brought into action by families with a meritorious revolutionary credential (and there were many of them in the area). It was apparent to me, in studying the domestic space, that the presence of certificates testifying to revolutionary death facilitated the bringing home of the memory of the "un-revolutionary" dead. The positive moral value of the former contributed to neutralizing the negative political value of the latter.

This political economy of ancestral worship particular to southern and central Vietnam has not yet been properly addressed in existing studies on Vietnamese social development, but it has, in my opinion, far-reaching implications not only for Vietnam's future but also for comparative studies of Cold War history and culture. Here we will confine our discussion to the second question.

Figure 9.2. Burning votive offerings to the dead. Photo H. Kwon.

New Ancestral Shrines

The Vietnamese politics of heroic war death are largely based on a prevailing postcolonial vision. Their commemorative art, including the monumental forms found in any village or district, clearly renders the sacrifices in the American War as elements of a continuum taking in not only earlier struggles against colonial occupation but also ancient battles against Chinese intrusions. In Cold War historiography, the change of perspective from the dominant, singular Cold War framework to the alternative framework of disjunctive parallax effects between decolonization and bipolarization has proved an important, constructive paradigm shift. While the postcolonial paradigm better represents "the native's point of view," it is weak when analysis turns from the domain of international history to that of local history. Whereas the postcolonial perspective is attentive to the intentions and historical particularities of the peripheral other, unlike the geopolitical perspective that tends to be oblivious to them, it itself has the tendency to be analytically oblivious to the fact that the peripheral national other in Cold War conflicts has itself already assimilated the bipolar geopolitical worldview and is therefore not reducible to a homogenous, unified identity.

We must cautiously approach the idea of a "global experience" (see Borneman 1998: 3) of the Cold War just as we must hesitate to make assumptions about a "national experience" of the conflict. Any such assumptions are particularly problematic where the conflict involved radical and violent bifurcation of social forces. The postcolonial historical perspective has not yet come to terms with an ironic progression of bipolar history in which the very "native point of view" it tried to represent has turned into a locally hegemonic force, thereby stamping out divergent experiences and memories.

The revival of ancestral and death-commemorative ritual in southern and central Vietnam should be considered as a creative local response to the place of the postcolonial vision in the changing global structure of power. The practice of reuniting brothers away from their bifurcated history of death is primarily a family affair, but it is simultaneously an initiative to change the prevailing political hierarchy of war death to a more historically accountable, socially democratic form. This voluntary cultural movement is in line with a growing intellectual movement in Vietnam, among writers in particular, which attempts to use for the most part fiction and poetry to rework the history of the American War, so that it is less a coherent, unified historical narrative of self-determination than a less coherent, diverging set of stories of the experience of a "domestic conflict" (see Bradley 2000: 189–92; Duiker 1995: 191; Jamieson 1993: 321–22). This emergent "civil war" perspective on the history of the war is not, as Young indicates, a negation of the foreign and international dimensions of the conflict (Young 1995: 516) but is instead an expression of civil society in the process of self-empowerment. If the war was a communal conflict as well as an international one, then the community should play as active a part in bringing the conflict to an end as state and international organizations (Kwon 2006: 174–75).

In the southern Vietnamese context, I have located the cultural sphere of death commemoration as a site of major communal initiatives for the resolution of bipolar conflicts, and the milieu of what Hertz would have called morally "ambidextrous" (1960: 113) social practices. It is partly thanks to this scholar, whose promising intellectual life was cut short in the fields of World War I's mass mechanical slaughter, that anthropological research has been analyzing the close relations between social attitudes to death and the structure of political power. Hertz was interested in how societies biopolitically construct hierarchies, and he explored the question through his investigation of diverse sources, including studies on Maori cosmological concepts and those on traditional mortuary customs in an Indonesian society, the latter expressing the moral hierarchy of "good death" versus "bad death" through their symbolic association with the "right hand" and the "left hand" (Hertz 1960; see also Parkin 1996: 59–65). The notion of symbolic ambidexterity that Hertz (1960: 113) coined at the end of his classic *Death and the Right Hand* was an alternative to the prevailing moral and hierarchical bipolarity between the symbolic properties of the right and of the left. Hertz saw that that the pre-eminence of the right hand is the inscription of principles of social hierarchy (including "good death" versus "bad death") on the human body, and he expressed his alternative political vision using the same symbolic language:

> The distinction of good and evil, which for long was solidary with the antithesis of right and left, will not vanish from our conscience … If the constraint of a mystical ideal has for centuries been able to make man into a unilateral being, physiologically mutilated, a liberated and foresighted society will strive to develop the energies dormant in our left side and in our right cerebral hemisphere, and to assure by an appropriate training a more harmonious development of the organism. (Hertz 1960: 22)

The new "ambidextrous" commemorative practice in central Vietnam has a further dimension relating to ritual organization (Kwon 2008). Traditionally gods and ancestors are commemorated inside the house while ghosts are commemorated outside. The typical ritual action in this concentric-dualist structure consists of kowtowing to the respectable placed identities, and turning in the opposite direction to repeat the action towards the placeless beings imagined to wander about in the exterior environment. This organization rendered the identities unassimilated to the interior ritual space, including those of deceased kin who fought on the "wrong" side, categoric ghosts. The interiorization of the politically engendered ghosts of the "counterrevolutionary" dead by their assimilation into the space of the ancestral shrine challenges that moral opposition at the same time as it reworks a political dualism.

The new ancestral shrines in Vietnam are inseparable from the country's deep-rooted cultural tradition of death remembrance, on the one hand, and, on the other, from the history of mass death Vietnam suffered in the transition from colonial to postcolonial rule. Their morally ambidextrous social practices rise from this particular background of culture and history. If the question of "which Cold

War?" is central to thinking about the origins and end of the Cold War as the historian Walter LaFeber (1992: 13–19) says, historical enquiry should recognize the fact that clashes between "this side" and "that side" took place in the past century not merely between political communities but also within the moral community of kinship. Arendt wrote that the hidden forces of modern politics may be unraveled within the rich and manifold conditions of intimate domestic interaction that the political order strives to reduce to privacy (Arendt 1998: 71–73). Ancestral shrines in Vietnam tell a story of global bipolar history; the new ones show a way to rework how we habitually tell that history.

References

Anderson, Benedict. 1991. *Imagined Communities*. London: Verso.

Arendt, Hannah. 1979. "Hannah Arendt on Hannah Arendt," in *Hannah Arendt: The Recovery of the Public World*, ed. M. Hill. New York: St. Martin's, 301–39.

———. (1958) 1998. *The Human Condition*, 2nd edn. Chicago: University of Chicago Press.

Borneman, John. 1998. *Subversions of International Order: Studies in the Political Anthropology of Culture*. Albany: SUNY Press.

Bradley, Mark P. 2000. *Imagining Vietnam and America: The Making of Postcolonial Vietnam, 1919–1950*. Chapel Hill, NC: University of North Carolina Press.

Cumings, Bruce. 1981. *The Origins of the Korean War: Liberation and the Emergence of Separate Regimes, 1945–47*. Princeton: Princeton University Press.

———. 1999. *Parallax Visions: Making Sense of American-East Asian Relations at the End of the Century*. Durham, NC: Duke University Press.

Duiker, William. 1995. *Vietnam: Revolution in Transition*. Boulder, CO: Westview.

Gillis, John, ed. 1994. *Commemorations: The Politics of National Identity*. Princeton: Princeton University Press.

Hertz, Robert. (1907) 1960. *Death and the Right Hand*. Aberdeen: Cohen and West.

———. (1909) 1973. "The Pre-eminence of the Right Hand: A Study in Religious Polarity," in *Right and Left: Essays on Dual Symbolic Classification*, ed. R. Needham. Chicago: University of Chicago Press, 3–31.

Hirshfeld, Alan W. 2001. *Parallax: The Race to Measure the Cosmos*. New York: W.H. Freeman.

Hunter, Allen, ed. 1998. *Rethinking the Cold War*. Philadelphia: Temple University Press.

Jamieson, Neil. 1993. *Understanding Vietnam*. Berkeley: University of California Press.

Isaac, Jeffrey. 1998. "Hannah Arendt as Dissenting Intellectual," in *Rethinking the Cold War*, ed. A. Hunter. Philadelphia: Temple University Press, 271–88.

Kuznick, Peter, and James Gilbert, eds. 2001. *Rethinking Cold War Culture*. Washington DC: Smithsonian Institution Press.

Kwon, Heonik. 2006. *After the Massacre: Commemoration and Consolation in Ha My and My Lai*. Berkeley: University of California Press.

———. 2008. *Ghosts of War in Vietnam*. Cambridge: Cambridge University Press.

LaFeber, Walter. 1992. "An End to Which Cold War?" in *The End of the Cold War: Its Meaning and Implications*, ed. M. Hogan. Cambridge: Cambridge University Press.

Luong, Hy Van. 1992. *Revolution in the Village: Tradition and Transformation in North Vietnam, 1925–1988.* Honolulu: University of Hawaii Press.

———. 1993. "Economic Reform and the Intensification of Rituals in Two North Vietnamese Villages, 1980–90," in *The Challenge of Reform in Indochina*, ed. B. Ljinggren. Cambridge, MA: Harvard Institute for International Development, 259–91.

Malarney, Shaun K. 2001. "The Fatherland Remembers Your Sacrifice: Commemorating War Dead in North Vietnam," in *The Country of Memory: Remaking the Past in Late Socialist Vietnam*, ed. H. Tai. Berkeley: University of California Press, 46–76.

———. 2002. *Culture, Ritual, and Revolution in Vietnam.* Surrey: Routledge Curzon.

———. 2003. "Return to the Past? The Dynamics of Contemporary Religious and Ritual Transformation," in *Postwar Vietnam: Dynamics of a Transforming Society*, ed. Hy Van Luong. New York: Rowman and Littlefield, 225–56.

Mosse, George. 1990. *Fallen Soldiers: Reshaping the Memory of the World Wars.* Oxford: Oxford University Press.

Parkin, Robert. 1996. *The Dark Side of Humanity: The Work of Robert Hertz and its Legacy.* London: Routledge.

Pelley, Patricia. 2002. *Postcolonial Vietnam: New Histories of the National Past.* Durham, NC: Duke University Press.

Tai, Hue-Tam Ho, ed. 2001. *The Country of Memory: Remaking the Past in Late Socialist Vietnam.* Berkeley: University of California Press.

Tan, Viet. 2000. *Viec ho* (The work of family ancestor worship). Hanoi: Nha xuat ban van hoa dan toc.

Taylor, Philip. 2004. *Goddess on the Rise: Pilgrimage and Popular Religion in Vietnam.* Honolulu: University of Hawai'i Press.

Trullinger, James W. 1994. *Village at War: Account of Conflict in Vietnam.* Stanford: Stanford University Press.

Westad, Odd A. 2005. *The Global Cold War.* Cambridge: Cambridge University Press.

Winter, Jay, and Jean-Louis Robert. 1997. *Capital Cities at War: Paris, London, Berlin, 1914–1919.* Cambridge: Cambridge University Press.

Winter, Jay, and Emmanuel Sivan (eds.). 1999. *War and Remembrance in the Twentieth Century.* Cambridge: Cambridge University Press.

Young, Marilyn. 1991. *The Vietnam Wars, 1945–1991.* New York: Harper Perennial.

———. 1995. "Epilogue: The Vietnam War in American Memory," in *Vietnam and America: A Documented History*, eds. M. Gettleman, E. Marvin, J. Franklin, M. Young, and B. Franklin. New York: Grove. 515–22.

Notes on Contributors

Dionigi Albera is a senior researcher at the CNRS (France) and director of the Institut d'Ethnologie Méditerranéenne, Européenne et Comparative (CNRS-Université de Provence). He is the author of several anthropological works on kinship, migration, and religion in Europe and the Mediterranean. He has recently edited (with Maria Couroucli) a book on shared sanctuaries in the Mediterranean area (*Religions traversées. Lieux saints partagés entre chrétiens, musulmans et juifs en Méditerranée*, Actes Sud, 2009).

Rohan Bastin teaches anthropology at Deakin University, Australia. He has conducted research on religious interaction and ethnic conflict in Sri Lanka since 1984, analysing Tamil Hindu-Sinhala Buddhist relations as well as urban processes within the Sinhala Catholic population. He is the author of *The Domain of Constant Excess: Plural Worship at the Munneśvaram Temples in Sri Lanka* (2002) and co-editor with Barry Morris of *Expert Knowledge: First World Peoples, Consultancy, and Anthropology* (2004).

Anna Bigelow is Associate Professor of Religious Studies at North Carolina State University. Her book, *Sharing the Sacred: Practicing Pluralism in Muslim North India* (Oxford University Press, 2010) is a study of a Muslim majority community in Indian Punjab and the shared sacred and civic spaces in that community. Bigelow's current research, funded by the Scholars Program of the Carnegie Corporation of New York, involves further study of contested and cooperatively patronized multi-religious sacred sites in South Asia and the Middle East, focusing on the inter-religious dynamics that complicate or ameliorate these relations in plural communities around the globe.

Aomar Boum is an assistant professor at the School of Middle Eastern and North African Studies and Religious Studies Program, University of Arizona, Tucson. He received his PhD in Socio-Cultural Anthropology from the University of Arizona in 2006. He studies the history and historiography of the Jewish communities of Morocco and anthropological issues of ethnic and religious minorities in the Islamic world.

Glenn Bowman is Reader in Social Anthropology in the School of Anthropology and Conservation at the University of Kent, where he convenes the postgraduate programme in the Anthropology of Ethnicity, Nationalism, and Identity. He has done extensive field research on Jerusalem pilgrimage, as well as on intercommunal shrine practices in the Middle East and the Balkans. He has worked for over twenty years in Jerusalem and West Bank Palestine on issues of nationalism and resistance, and has also carried out work in Former Yugoslavia on contemporary art and political mobilization.

Dora Carpenter-Latiri is a Senior Lecturer at the School of Humanities at the University of Brighton. She was born in Tunisia, and studied at the University of Sorbonne (Paris IV) where she did her doctorate on the application of linguistic methodology to literary work. She moved into the academic world after a first career in publishing and lexicography in France (Le Robert) and in the UK (Oxford University Press, Cambridge University Press). Her publications deal with language and intercultural issues, migration, and representations of minorities, and they follow a multidisciplinary approach.

Adam Yuet Chau is University Lecturer in the Anthropology of Modern China in the Department of East Asian Studies at the University of Cambridge. He received his PhD in anthropology from Stanford University in 2001. He has researched on the politics of religious revival in contemporary rural China and is interested in the larger issues of better conceptualizing religious practices, both in today's China and historically. He is the author of *Miraculous Response: Doing Popular Religion in Contemporary China* (Stanford University Press, 2006) and editor of *Religion in Contemporary China: Revitalization and Innovation* (Routledge, 2011).

Maria Couroucli is Senior Researcher at the CNRS. A member of the Laboratoire d'Ethnologie et Sociologie Comparative at Université Paris Ouest Nanterre, she teaches at the graduate program of the department of Ethnologie et Sociologie Comparative. Her research is on the historical anthropology of Modern Greece, combining fieldwork methods andwork on archives and documents. She published on kinship and family, identity and nationalism, before turning to religious practices in the post-Ottoman world and, more recently, on questions of memory and identity in relation to the Greek civil war (1944–49).

Heonik Kwon is a professorial senior research fellow of social anthropology at Trinity College, University of Cambridge. Author of several prizewinning books including *Ghosts of War in Vietnam* (2008) and *The Other Cold War* (2010), he is currently directing an international project that explores the history and memory of the early Cold War in global and local contexts with a focus on the Korean War. His new book is *North Korea Beyond Charismatic Politics* (2012).

Will Tuladhar-Douglas teaches anthropology of religions and the environment in the Religious Studies group at the University of Aberdeen. He is the director of the Scottish Centre for Himalayan Research, and was the Tung Lin Kok Yuen Distinguished Visiting Professor of Buddhist Studies at the University of Toronto for 2010.

INDEX

Lightning Source UK Ltd.
Milton Keynes UK
UKOW06f0816241015

261300UK00006B/56/P

9 781782 387442